SMACK DAB

LIVING IN THE CENTER OF GOD'S WILL

COLLEEN MYERS

HangaR
33
Publishing

CONTENTS

© 2019 by Colleen Myers

Published by Hangar 33 Publishing, a division of PLUR Life Ministries

Post Office Box 953

Lake Arrowhead, California 92352

www.RaveOutreach.com

Ebook ISBN: 978-0-9995357-8-3

Print ISBN: 978-0-9995357-9-0

Library of Congress Control Number: 2019913955

Verses marked NIV are THE HOLY BIBLE, NEW INTERNATIONAL VERSION®, NIV® Copyright © 1973, 1978, 1984, 2011 by Biblica, Inc.® Used by permission. All rights reserved worldwide.

Verses marked NLT are Holy Bible, New Living Translation, copyright © 1996, 2004, 2015 by Tyndale House Foundation. Used by permission of Tyndale House Publishers, Inc., Carol Stream, Illinois 60188. All rights reserved.

Verses marked ESV are the Holy Bible, English Standard Version. ESV® Text Edition: 2016. Copyright © 2001 by Crossway Bibles, a publishing ministry of Good News Publishers.

Scripture quotations marked NKJV are taken from the New King James Version®. Copyright © 1982 by Thomas Nelson. Used by permission. All rights reserved.

The Cry of the Kalahari (Mariner Books, 2014) by Mark and Delia Owens.

Cover photo and author photo by Nicki Erber. Cover and interior design by Tandem Services Press. www.TandemServicesInk.com

Sketches by Colleen Myers

***To Savannah, Brooklyn, and Malachi - the three
little loves of my life:***

*I believe your generation may be the one to finally take the
gospel to the ends of the earth and I believe you will grow up to
spread the love of Jesus like a wave across the entire globe. God
will give you everything you need to do this.*

*May the passion to fulfill the Great Commission burn in your
sweet hearts like a fire that never goes out, and may you sense it
while you are still young. Enjoy your childhood. Play and
imagine and wonder. Don't grow up too fast. Your adult years
will require strong foundations to withstand the holy battle that
lies before you.*

*Savannah and Brooklyn, you are survivors; you are precious
fighters for a purpose; and you've got your mommy's sense of
humor. What an amazing combination! Malachi, you are very
strong and adventurous and kind; the best type of courageous.
Already, you three have blessed so many! I am on my knees in
prayer for you every single day.*

You've got this.

Grammy loves you very, very much.

INTRODUCTION

I added up my score, sitting at the table in shock, and a bit disgusted. I was an evangelist. I had taken a spiritual gifts assessment test. My results glared back at me. I instantly had visions of becoming someone I would never ever want to be... with big, platinum-blonde hair, tons of mascara would trickle down my face in black streaks from my tear-filled eyes as I looked into the television camera pleading for more money so I could go save the lost. This was my stereotype of an evangelist...and if I had been a guy, it would have included shiny, white-patent-leather dress shoes and a tad less makeup. Evangelist was not the label this girl wanted.

But I did, undeniably, have a heart for the lost. And in the years since then, I have embraced the title of my God-given gift.

I have discovered that my stereotype of an evangelist was not God's idea. It was man's way of messing it up. In fact, the ability to effectively evangelize is a gift that God gives freely, and it's one that He wants to give to those who follow His word and obey His Great Commission: To go therefore and make disciples of all nations.

The evangelist in my mind was not a true evangelist. It was someone who had perhaps once had this gift but had squandered it; or maybe someone who'd never had it at all. I believe now that the enemy used this to turn me off to evangelism. He's crafty like that.

J.I. Packer defined evangelism in his book, *Evangelism and the Sovereignty of God*. He wrote, "Evangelism is presenting Jesus Christ in the power of the Holy Spirit to sinful people, in order that they may come to put their trust in God through Him, to receive Him as their Savior, and to serve Him as their King in the fellowship of His church."

Yup, evangelism has nothing to do with mascara, big hair, or white shoes.

Studies conducted by Barna Research Group in 2018 show that millennials (those born 1981 to 1996) are unsure about the practice of evangelism. Forty-seven percent of millennials say that it's wrong to share one's personal beliefs with someone of a different faith in hopes that they will one day share the same faith, and sixty-five percent of millennials believe that people today are more likely than in the past to take offense if they share their faith. Like he tried to do with me, the enemy is trying to shut the mouths of the Christians of this generation and the next.

I can't help but wonder if the way that the church in North America has gone about evangelism, and not gone about discipleship, has both hurt the unsaved of this generation and caused the saved of this generation to not want to have any part of it. Evangelism has a bad reputation with almost everyone nowadays. And I totally get it. On the other hand, discipleship is practically unheard of.

Years ago, I began to research my gift. I sought out Spirit-led evangelists and disciple makers who were doing things God's way, and I asked God to teach me how to be a Spirit-led evangelist/discipler in my own ministry. This book is the result of that search. Please share it with those you know who, like the former me, don't want to be associated with evangelism and have no clue how to disciple people. This process changed my mind. Maybe it will change theirs. This is imperative, because this generation could quite possibly hold the key to finally getting the gospel to the ends of the earth, to all tribes and tongues.

For a long time now, I've kept a list of the qualities, core values, and beliefs of Spirit-led evangelists/disciple makers; tweaking it and adding to it for years. It's by no means exhaustive, but it's what I imagine would be inside a great evangelist's toolbox. One who disciples people would have a similar box. Since Jesus used the analogy of a fisherman for an evangelist, I picture this toolbox as a tackle box like any good fisherman would have.

I see this fisherman decked out in hip waders, standing in waist-high water in the middle of his favorite fishing hole in a cove of his favorite lake, pole in hand, snapping his line back and forth, and dreaming of the catch of his life. I want to be him. On the shore is that tackle box. It was a gift from his father, the best fisherman he's ever known. Legendary, actually. Come with me to that lake, and let's look at what's in that box.

One thing you need to know before we head down to the water. My favorite fishing hole is massive rave parties. Giant music festivals that feature DJs and electronic dance music. Yup! This evangelist is a recovering judgmental church lady, and I go to raves with teams of older moms and dads, grandmas and grandpas, to crash those parties with God's love.

We are called PLUR Life Ministries because of the ravers' motto: PLUR. It's not our term. It's an acronym that stands for Peace, Love, Unity, and Respect. That's what ravers are looking for, and they find a temporary form of it at raves as they party and dance together and "love" on each other. They may tattoo it on their bodies or you may see it scrawled on the windows of their car as they head to a rave. PLUR is a big deal.

The kids we minister to call us "rave moms" and "rave dads." These days, ravers are typically between eighteen to twenty-four years old. Since our rave moms and dads are typically forty to seventy years old, we call them kids. We attract attention as we old people walk through those events and the surrounding neighborhoods looking for young adults who are searching for love and acceptance.

Even though they don't realize it, we know they are searching for Jesus. And so, we go. We share the gospel. And since there is massive drug use at these events, we help kids in trouble, and rescue those in danger. We could write a whole book just about how God has used our teams and how my co-laborers in this mission field, the older moms and grandmas, who I lovingly call the "Menopostles," are making such a difference in this generation as they show God's love and partner with Jesus in seeking to save the lost, not condemn them.

Ravers handmake plastic beaded bracelets they call "kandi" to trade with each other as a sign of PLUR at raves. When we first heard about rave culture, it felt like God had handed us a mission field on a platter! They were looking for PLUR, and their bead bracelets reminded us of the ones we used to make in Sunday School with the "gospel colors" on them (black is for sin, red is for the blood of Jesus, blue is for faith, white is for forgiveness, green is for growth, gold is for heaven). It was perfect. We had God's PLUR to offer, and we could give them gospel bracelets that they'd want instead of gospel tracts that would end up all over the ground!

Since then, our rave moms have handed out hundreds of thousands of our rave-style bracelets made by Christians who pray over each one and the raver who will receive it. Our website, plurway.com, that shares the gospel, is spelled out in alphabet beads on the bracelets. Through that website, we share the way to true and lasting PLUR through Jesus, instead of the temporary and fake PLUR that is found through the use of popular rave drugs like Ecstasy.

Not all kids who go to raves do drugs. Some just go for the music. While they are only looking for a good time, our teams go looking for trouble. And we find it. Inexperienced party goers don't realize that they could possibly be in danger, especially outside the venues as they make their way to their cars or to their Uber rides. The vast majority of young adults who go to raves make it home safe, but some do not. We are trying to change that. It is our privilege to help them live another day. Another day to turn to Jesus and find true PLUR in Him.

Our message is clear. We love Jesus. We aren't against music and dancing. We are against drugs, predators, dosing, rape, human trafficking, and overdose deaths.

For one night, these young people become our kids, and we do whatever it takes to keep them safe. Our team sets up an RV in the parking lot or right outside of the rave venue. The dads hang there and make the moms coffee and meals as needed through the night. If we run into trouble or need a dad to intervene, they are right there and available to help. The rave moms head to the kids inside the party and search for those who need help outside the venue.

The ravers have welcomed us to their parties. They are intrigued that we are there. Our favorite questions are, "Why are you here?" and "Why do you do this?" Questions like these become invitations to share the gospel.

When their friends are overdosing, we hold them until paramedics arrive. When they get sick, we hold their hair back, wipe the vomit from their faces, and give them sips of water in Jesus's name. We tell them the bad choices they made on this night don't have to define them for the rest of their lives. We feel the enemy's presence as he swoops in to mock and shame them in their darkest hour, giving them names like worthless, loser, and fool. We counteract his lies with truth from God's Word and tell them they are precious and valuable, and the Creator of the heavens and earth wants to save them and call them friend.

It is our great privilege as moms to stand between predators and young women. To date, the predators have always backed down. You just don't mess with a mama bear. A mom is a wild card!

Because this generation is vastly unparented, these kids flock to us once they find out we aren't there to pass judgement on them. They crave love and attention from parents and grandparents, and we have plenty to give. When the parties let out, we are outside the venues with our FREE MOM HUGS sign. The ravers line up. The things they say to us as we embrace them can break your heart. "I haven't seen my mom since she took off with her boyfriend five years ago." "My mom lives across the country; I haven't had a mom hug since I left for college." "If you were my mom, I wouldn't be here."

God has used our teams to make good on the promise He has made to seek out and save these ravers. He's sending out an army to find them. He'll never stop searching and seeking to rescue them. And so, He takes us to raves to seek and save the lost. It's God's search and rescue mission.

Sometimes the rave venues offer camping. When they do,

we set up a family-style campsite and the dads make pancakes and tell ridiculous dad jokes, while the moms invite the ravers to eat breakfast with them at long tables covered in red-and-white-checked cloths. Hanging in the middle of our campsite is a sign that says, BECAUSE JESUS LOVES YOU. These camping raves allow us an amazing opportunity to listen to this generation and meet them where they are. God's love is thick at our breakfast table.

They hear the gospel as they eat, but they see it in action first. Similarly, those who we help on the streets hear the gospel, but they see it in action first.

We follow up by giving them an opportunity to join us for a free, no-cost "spiritual adventure weekend" at Camp 33. Moms and dads take them on a trip they will never forget, where they will experience PLUR that only comes from Jesus. For two and a half days, they take a journey from the mountains to the desert. They travel in Jeeps, ride on a boat, explore an abandoned gold mine, take dirt trails, eat in homes with the best food ever, and spend the night at a five-acre camp in the desert. And all along the way, they are introduced to PLUR from God as the Bible comes to life, and they are reading about Him and learning about who He is, taught by loving moms and dads and grandmas and grandpas. It's a family weekend at its best, and it's very effective.

Ravers can also continue contact with us through the website on the bracelets we give them to request personal discipleship or find Bible study tools on our discipleship website, hangar33.org. Sometimes they just reach out to us to get mom or dad advice. They remember us in times of crisis because they saw that we were there for them out on the street.

I share all of this as background, because I will be using examples from this, my favorite fishing hole, as I share how God has taught us to evangelize and disciple ravers for the last 10 years. They are lessons that can be applied to evangelizing and discipling all people from all walks of life. After all, these tools were given to us in a beautiful tackle box, by a legendary fisherman.

> *Jesus called out to them, "Come follow me, and I*
> *will show you how to fish for people!"*
> *Mark 1:17 (NLT)*

Jesus called the disciples to go on the adventure of their lives! I love how they just dropped everything and went.

And then further down the page it says, "Jesus and His COMPANIONS (emphasis mine) went to the town of Capernaum."

I had read this story lots of times. But when I read it after a time in my life when my heart had been broken with some of the things that break God's heart, it was like I was reading it for the very first time. Oh, how I wanted to be one of His companions! I wanted to hang out with Jesus. And I began to ask Him a whole lot of questions. Will you teach me how to fish? Where should I go? What bait should I use? Once I started doing that, He gave me a fishing hole.

Oh, how this has changed my life! In fact, that is my whole purpose for writing this book so that many, many others will experience the change that I have. When your purpose in life aligns with your Creator's purpose for you, everything aligns. Life is incredible. Will you still face challenges? Oh yes! Trials? Yes! Probably even more! But you will never want to turn back to your old way of living. Because there is nothing like holding the Creator's hand as He runs to the lost and uses you to speak for Him. It's the adventure of a lifetime, and you were created for it. You will never find total fulfillment in anything else you do. You may marry well, have great kids, have a beautiful home, and live an orderly life. But you will never experience real satisfaction in your lifetime until you are doing what God created you to do.

Would you like to have a fishing hole? Is God calling you to partner with Him in the search of a lifetime for the lost? You can bet your life on it!

Let's head on down to the water.

PART 1

THE INSTRUCTION MANUAL

CHAPTER 1

THE GREAT COMMISSION IS
NOT THE GREAT SUGGESTION

We have arrived at the lake, and the first thing we see when we flip up the latches and open the good fisherman's tackle box is an instruction manual. In this case, it's a Bible, and it contains all we need to know about the One who loves us so much that He would ultimately become the object of His own wrath in order to redeem us from it. The thread of His plan for redemption is woven throughout every chapter in the Bible. The good news of this redemptive plan is clearly laid out, and those who have discovered it and gratefully accepted it are tasked with sharing it with the rest of the world. This is what is commonly referred to as the Great Commission:

> Go therefore and make disciples of all nations,
>   baptizing them in the name of the Father
>   and of the Son and of the Holy Spirit,
>   teaching them to observe all that I have
>   commanded you. And behold, I am with you
>   always, to the end of the age.

Matthew 28:19-20 (ESV)

And he said to them, "Go into all the world and
proclaim the gospel to the whole creation."
Mark 16:15 (ESV)

... repentance for the forgiveness of sins should
be proclaimed in his name to all nations,
beginning from Jerusalem.
Luke 24:47 (ESV)

Jesus said to them again, "Peace be with you. As
the Father has sent me, even so I am sending
you."
John 20:21 (ESV)

But you will receive power when the Holy Spirit
has come upon you, and you will be my
witnesses in Jerusalem and in all Judea and
Samaria, and to the end of the earth.
Acts 1:8 (ESV)

For years, I acted like the Great Commission was the Great Suggestion. Maybe some of you know what I mean. Missionary work was reserved for someone else. Someone with a Master of Divinity degree or at least those who had been to seminary. *Go* was a scary word for a gal like me whose main goal in life was to live the American dream. I craved security. The Great Commission was anything but that! I was happy in my pretty house writing a check every once in a while to support those brave souls who took the commission seriously.

I don't think the phrase "Go, Send, or Disobey" had been coined yet, but I would've loved that. I was content to send, and that meant I was obeying, right? I could count on less than my perfectly manicured fingers the number of people who I'd shared my faith with. In fact, I mostly stayed away from non-believers and really preferred to be around well-behaved people.

And I'd never discipled anyone. Oh, I'd taught them a lot in my Bible classes at the private school where I worked in exchange for my children's tuition. But I had never walked beside a new believer day in and day out to show them the way.

To me, evangelism and discipleship meant inviting people to my church and relying on the pastor to do all of that. It wasn't my job. I stayed nice and snug within the four walls of my church, and I could rationalize with the best of them that decorating for a women's luncheon was evangelistic and was my way of helping to reach the lost. After all, lost people came to the luncheons where they'd hear someone else talk about Jesus and certainly the décor would make them want to come back for more, right?

I was not living my life in the center of God's will.

Have you noticed how often people wonder what God's will is for their lives? It's the subject of many books and is a question that comes up in every Bible study. Occasionally, I, too, would wonder if I was living in God's will, and I hoped that I was, at least some of the time. I remember being afraid to pray that God's will would be done in certain situations. I was afraid of what that would mean. I preferred to pray with my own agenda, giving God a to-do list that I felt would solve the problems I faced.

But that was many years, and a broken heart ago. And I've found the answer to what God's will for my life is in Matthew 28. God's heart is for the lost. He wrote a whole book about it. To partner with Him in the Great Commission is to live smack dab in the very center of God's will. He wants us to be His companions on His great search for the lost! And when He finds them, He wants us to walk beside them, teaching them what we've learned.

The Great Commission is not the Great Suggestion. It's a command, not an option.

It is so important to God that He gave us detailed instructions on how He wants us to do it. Not only is God's redemptive plan displayed throughout Scripture, but the way to share this good news is as well. Jesus likened it to fishing for men, and He told His disciples that He would teach them how. He is the master fisherman...the legend.

You may notice that I use the words *evangelism* and *discipleship* together a lot. They are both important parts of the Great Commission. Some people think that discipleship only happens after someone becomes a believer, but during our years of ministry, we have found discipleship sometimes starts way before a sinner prays for salvation. Discipleship often starts when someone begins to turn toward Jesus. Evangelism and discipleship are all wrapped up around each other. Like the chicken and the egg, it's hard to know which one comes first!

Here's how I land on all of this: Evangelism happens for the first time somewhere before the beginning of a new believer's life in Christ. Discipleship continues and lasts a lifetime. But evangelism should never really stop either. One definition of evangelism is, "The spreading of the Christian gospel by public preaching or personal witness." If that's the case, we should never stop evangelizing people and hopefully they will never stop evangelizing us. We need to gaze into the gospel again and again and again. We need to preach it to each other over and over. It's a story that must be told consistently. We humans are a forgetful lot. We must never ever forget that Christ died for us.

When Jesus called us to be fishers of men, He was calling us to evangelize and disciple them. All of us are called to do both, but some of us will be more gifted as evangelists—sort of the strike team—and some of us will be more gifted at discipleship, those who stay next to others for the long haul. Natural evangelists need to sharpen their discipleship skills, and natural disciple makers should sharpen their evangelism skills. Because it's all about being great fishers of men.

If we have the gift of evangelism, or we are experienced at making disciples, we are to share what God has taught us with other believers. If this is you, train others, teaching them what you've learned. It's called equipping the body of Christ. Oh, how that will please your Heavenly Father! If you don't feel you have these gifts, hang out with people who do. It will rub off!

> *And he gave the apostles, the prophets, the*
> *evangelists, the shepherds and teachers, to*
> *equip the saints for the work of ministry, for*
> *building up the body of Christ...*
> Ephesians 4:11-12 (ESV)

The way I see it, the church in America is in an emergency situation because we have not been about the business of fulfilling the Great Commission: evangelizing and making disciples. We have been a disobedient church. There are probably many reasons for this, and none of them are legitimate excuses.

Check this out. In 2001, Barna Research Group released

the results of a study they did, revealing a growing number of adult Christians believe that God has not given them any spiritual gifts. The study showed that only six percent of Christians believe that God has given them one of the gifts listed in Ephesians 4:11. Perhaps the most disturbing trend was that in 1996, a similar study conducted by Barna revealed that only four percent of Christians claimed to have the gift of evangelism, but by 2001, that number was a measly one percent. I hate to think what a current study would reveal!

God wants to give you gifts. First Corinthians 14 tells us to earnestly desire them! And when God gives you those gifts, He wants you to use them! Equip others! Pass those gifts on! I have a sneaking suspicion that way more than one percent of you have the gift of evangelism. Own up to it and use it. I finally did, and I can tell you from personal experience that you will never regret it.

Over the years, expert anglers have written "how to" books on fishing. I picked up a few of these to see what they had to say. In the introduction of Cliff Hauptman's book, *How to Fly-Fish*, he says, "For every aspect of the sport, there are nearly endless layers of intricacy, nuance, and discovery. That is what allows fly fishing to become an intense, lifelong calling, rather than just a pastime."

How much more of a lifelong calling is fishing for men! Our how-to book is the Bible, where we also find endless layers of intricacy, nuance, and discovery. In the pages of this amazing book, God Himself reveals His plan of redemption and invites us on the adventure of a lifetime, not a pastime, as He calls us to participate with Him in revealing His plan of redemption to others. He shows us how to fish for men. In the next few chapters, we will explore some things that we can learn from Jesus's example and some concepts that He teaches us in His how-to book.

PERSONAL REFLECTION AND GROUP DISCUSSION

- Have you lived your life as if the Great Commission is a suggestion or as if it is a command?
- Read Romans 12:6-8, 1 Corinthians 12:4-11, 1 Corinthians 12:28, and Ephesians 4:11. What do you believe are the spiritual gifts God has given you?
- Suggested verses to memorize: Matthew 28:19-20

CHAPTER 2

LOVE GOD AND LOVE OTHERS AS YOU SPEAK THE TRUTH

L ove God and love others. This is the highest command. All the rules given in Scripture are summed up in that one sentence.

> *One of them, an expert in religious law, tried to trap Him with this question: "Teacher, which is the most important commandment in the law of Moses?" Jesus replied, "'You must love the Lord your God with all your heart, all your soul, and all your mind.' This is the first and greatest commandment. A second is equally important: 'Love your neighbor as yourself.' The entire law and all the demands of the prophets are based on these two commandments."*
> *Matthew 22:35-40 (NLT)*

Have you ever met people who seem to be great at loving God but not so great at loving others? They appear to be uber holy, toeing the line, and following all the rules. But when it comes to people, their holier-than-thou attitude pushes others away.

Or have you met people who are great at loving others and making people feel all warm and fuzzy inside, but their lack of speaking and living out the truth compromises their love for God and His Word? For me, I must constantly pray that God keeps me balanced in both loving Him and others. It's easy to swing one way or the other. But when I'm off balance, I'm neither loving God nor others well.

Jude 1:23 should be a key verse for evangelists and disciple makers, so this is not the only time I will be referring to it. It's a guideline. It talks about being balanced: showing mercy and at the same time being cautious about showing mercy. It's a great illustration of how to live out this principle of loving God and loving others.

> *And you must show mercy to those whose faith*
> *is wavering. Rescue others by snatching*
> *them from the flames of judgment. Show*
> *mercy to still others, but do so with great*
> *caution, hating the sins that contaminate*
> *their lives.*
> Jude 1:22-23 (NLT)

We need to be cautious in our mercy! We must not be *loving* to others in such a way that it makes them feel okay about their sin. That is not true love. We are to hate the sin that separates them from God. It is toxic to them.

I have loved my friend through her whole journey through breast cancer, but I wanted her to go through the pain of cutting it out of her life. Was that not loving? Surgery and recovery were painful for her, but I rejoiced that she was going through it because it meant she would live. Can you imagine if I had stood by in the name of mercy and not encouraged her to do what it took to cut the cancer out?

SPEAK THE TRUTH IN LOVE

Jesus was nice, but He wasn't a pushover! It's because He spoke the TRUTH in LOVE. Many were attracted to Him and wanted to be around Him, but not everybody! He was offensive and off-putting to the arrogant and self-sufficient, those who really thought they had it all together. But, He was attractive to the broken and hurting, those who knew they couldn't do it on their own, who had gotten to the end of their rope, who hoped against hope that there was someone or something bigger than themselves who could fix their mess. Or those who had since stopped hoping.

Have you ever played the game Whack-A-Mole? These cute little moles pop up through holes on the game board. With a mallet, you're supposed to whack each one back down into their hole as fast as you can. That's what a Christian speaking the truth without love does to people. It's a devastating game of Whack-A-Soul. Just when someone pops up to hear words of life and hope, they are whacked back down into their miserable existence by a well-meaning Christian who was trying to give them truth but didn't do it in love.

Jesus is the way, the truth, and the life. No one comes to the Father except through Him. Whoever does not love does not know God, because God is love. Do you see what I did there? I combined two verses, John 14:6 and 1 John 4:8. God is love and truth. You leave out one of those, you leave out God. It's not godly to only speak truth without love, and it's not godly to only speak love without truth. We must do both. Telling someone they are on the path to hell is the kind and loving thing to do.

As long as we tell them they can turn and take a different path to heaven.

Don't call what you're preaching "the gospel" if you're only pointing out sin and not pointing to the way out.

Ministering to the arrogant starts with truth. They need to see their sin. They need to understand that they've broken God's laws. Only then will they see their need for a savior.

Ministering to the broken starts with love. They are very aware of their condition. They know they are sinners; they just haven't heard that there's a savior.

Arrogant or broken, the Bible tells us that God's law is written on our hearts. Because of that, we have all experienced shame.

Shame is the result of the enemy pointing out our sin, without the solution of a savior.

Because of this, at one point or another, all will be ready to hear the gospel. Don't you want to be the one who is there and ready to share when that happens?

The vast majority of kids we see at raves fall under the broken category. However, we have come across the defiant, arrogant ones. We have spoken the truth in love, and we've watched hearts change.

Consequently, we have a motto for our outreach teams to live by: the law for the arrogant and grace for the broken. And to discern who is arrogant and who is broken, you must be listening to people and the Holy Spirit. This is especially important. How many people have you met who come off as extremely arrogant at first, only to find out that their outward appearance of arrogance is really a protective defense they use to hide their hurt and broken heart?

A few years ago, as I was speaking to a women's group, I noticed a thirty-something crying. She continued to cry throughout my presentation. Afterward, she came up to talk to me and seemed angry. But I quickly realized that the anger was just a mask for regret. She asked, "Where were you when I was raving? Why weren't you there? You could've saved me from so many mistakes!" She calmed down as she wept and then she quietly shared, "You need to know that if you had approached me at a rave saying all the loving things you do and sharing the gospel, I would've gotten in your face to try to scare you off. I would've cussed you up one side and down the other. But inside, I would've been saying, 'Please stay. Please stay. Please stay.'"

Yes, we must be sensitive to the Holy Spirit who knows each heart and will reveal to us what each one needs to hear and how they need to hear it.

One night at the entrance to a rave in San Diego, California, it was surreal to be able to share the gospel with a gay couple as religious men with megaphones stood nearby shouting at the crowd that they were all going to hell. This couple had met some of our rave moms before at a rave in Miami and had observed them helping some kids who were sick from the drugs they had taken. Seeing us again in this setting prompted a conversation. They really wanted to know what made us want to go to raves and help kids. Their curiosity resulted in an opportunity for amazing dialogue that night.

Their mouths dropped open when we told them we were Christians. They hadn't visited our website on the rave bracelets we had given them in Miami, and they had assumed we were some sort of community activist group. They never imagined Jesus could be our motivation for being out there with them.

One of them said, "Wait! What?" They both winced as they pointed to the shouters and asked, "Are you associated with them?" After I assured them that we were not, one of them began to share that he had honestly never met a Christian before who showed him love. Ever. He pointed to the screamers again and said, "That has been my opinion of Christians. But now you're changing all that."

So right there, as the men blared half-truths with no love, prompting a very negative response from the crowd, I stood on the opposite corner and got to gently share the gospel with the couple. About the time I was sharing John 3:16 and 17 with them, one of the angry men actually shouted, "I AM JUDGING YOU!" It's hard to describe the feeling I had at that moment when I was quoting Scripture describing how Jesus didn't come to condemn the world, while completely opposite statements made in Jesus' name were blaring from megaphones.

You see, hell is real, but so is God's love. The shouters weren't telling the whole truth because they were only talking about the wrath of God without talking about the love of God. They were missing Jesus. They weren't being led by the Spirit. They assumed that the whole crowd was arrogant, and so they were feeding them the law. How did they know the hearts of their audience? How did they know who was arrogant and who was broken? Was there anyone there whose faith was wavering? Because if so, they were supposed to show them mercy! Here's that verse again.

> *And you must show mercy to those whose faith*
> *is wavering.*
> Jude 1:22 (NLT)

I just don't know of any other way to determine who is broken, who is arrogant, and who is wavering, except by listening to people. And the shouters were not doing any listening at all. They were decimating the broken, and quite possibly trampling down fields that were ripe for harvest by turning them against the very One they were shouting about. Oh, how God's own heart must have been breaking.

If these men had just stopped to listen, if they had just asked the Holy Spirit to give discernment and wisdom, they would've realized that many walking by already knew they were sinners. They didn't need someone shouting it at them to realize it. And if they had been speaking the truth in love, they would've been able to have amazing conversations like the one I was having just across the street.

You see, as I listened, I found out that one of the young men knew he was a sinner. And what an honor it was to tell him about a savior who could save him from his sins. While the shouters continued to turn people away from Jesus, here was this homosexual couple turning to see Jesus, quite possibly for the very first time.

In their arrogance and disobedience of God's Word, the shouters refused to see that showing love gives us the opportunity to speak truth. I was actually able to say some of the same things about hell and other consequences of sin that the shouters were saying, but what I said was being received and was causing a softening of hearts, while some of those same words, shouted in anger, were causing hardening of hearts.

*Spouting off before listening to the facts is both
shameful and foolish.*
Proverbs 18:13 (NLT)

About an hour later, a girl overcome by the drugs she had

ingested, happened to pass out on the curb directly in front of the megaphone men. Instead of rushing to her aid as our team of moms did, they continued their crusade and used her as an example of sin as they pointed to her limp body laid out in front of them. They said, "Look at her! This is what we are talking about. She's on her way to hell!" It was a disgusting picture of the depths to which the sin of religiosity can take us. Oh, how the church needs to back up that train! Oh, how we need to do what Scripture pleads with us to do:

> *...if my people, who are called by my name, will humble themselves and pray and seek my face and turn from their wicked ways, then I will hear from heaven, and I will forgive their sin and will heal their land.*
> 2 *Chronicles* 7:14 (NIV)

If we want to see healing in our culture today, the church must turn from our wicked ways and take seriously the command to speak the truth in love. God has some pretty serious things to say to the church who doesn't take care of His sheep. He holds us responsible when we do things that send the sheep running.

> *You eat the fat, you clothe yourselves with the wool, you slaughter the fat ones, but you do not feed the sheep. The weak you have not strengthened, the sick you have not healed, the injured you have not bound up, the strayed you have not brought back, the lost you have not sought, and with force and harshness you have ruled them. ... therefore, you shepherds, hear the word of the Lord:*

Thus says the Lord God, Behold, I am
against the shepherds, and I will require my
sheep at their hand and put a stop to their
feeding the sheep. No longer shall the
shepherds feed themselves. I will rescue my
sheep from their mouths, that they may not
be food for them. For thus says the Lord God:
Behold I, I myself will search for my sheep
and will seek them out. As a shepherd seeks
out his flock when he is among his sheep
that have been scattered, so will I seek out
my sheep, and I will rescue them from all
places where they have been scattered on a
day of clouds and thick darkness.
Ezekiel 34: 3-4, 9-12 (ESV)

If we believe that God is the same, yesterday, today, and forever, then we will take this passage seriously. It's from the Old Testament, but it still applies to us today. God help us to take care of your lost sheep.

PERSONAL REFLECTION AND GROUP DISCUSSION

- What does it mean to truly love people?
- How can we tell if we truly love God?
- Have you ever met someone who appeared to be arrogant, but then after you listened to them, you realized they were just trying to hide brokenness? Share your experience.
- Is there religion in your life that needs to be replaced with a relationship with God? Take a few minutes to silently reflect on this, then take a few

19

minutes to talk to God about it. Share any insight you would like to with the group.

- Just how important is it to speak the truth in love?
- What are some ways we can be careful not to scatter God's sheep?
- What are some ways we can partner with God to search for and rescue the lost?
- Suggested verses to memorize: Matthew 22:35-40

CHAPTER 3

PRACTICE BIBLICAL TOLERANCE

Have you noticed how the first two concepts—love God and love others, and speak the truth in love—sort of segued into each other? Well, these concepts continue to segue right on into a third concept found in Scripture: practicing biblical tolerance.

Tolerance is a very scary word for many conservative Christians. But the Bible tells us that perfect love casts out fear. So, if you are one of those that fears tolerance, let God's love help you not to be afraid of it.

The world's definition of tolerance says that "everything goes," and we should be okay with all of it. The world seems to be tolerant of everyone except Christians because the world believes everyone should be able to decide what is right and wrong for themselves. They aren't tolerant of people who believe in absolute truth, that God alone decides what is right and wrong. They aren't tolerant of us because we believe in the law of God.

Now let's look at biblical tolerance. If we are practicing godly tolerance, we won't expect non-believers to behave. We will expect them to break God's laws. Because we see them as lost, we will respond to them with compassion and the gospel, not condemnation. God Himself was tolerant. He didn't wipe out the entire world because of its sin. Instead, He came to the world. Not to condemn us, but to save us. To be tolerant, means we share this good news with gentleness and respect.

For me, tolerance looks like not focusing on the symptoms of sin but focusing on the fact that sin causes separation from God. When I am being tolerant, I can stand in front of a young man at a rave who is wearing a T-shirt with a pornographic image on it and still look into his eyes with love and compassion and share the gospel. If I can't get over what I see on his T-shirt, if I can't be tolerant of that, then it will shut down my opportunity to share really good news with him.

That T-shirt is just a symptom of what's going on in his soul. His soul is what I need to focus on, not the outward sign that his soul is not well. Focusing on the outward stuff will take my attention off the true problem, the core issue, that needs to be addressed.

The same goes for homosexuality. I know it's a hot topic today. But I just don't focus on what non-believers do in their bedrooms. I focus on their need for a savior. The one and only unforgivable sin is unbelief. Lying, gossiping, selfishness, heterosexual activity before marriage, or homosexuality are not unforgivable sins. All those behaviors are symptoms of a heart that is not surrendered to Jesus. That's the core problem. That's what needs to be addressed.

So, in this sense, I am tolerant of unbelievers' gossip and lying and selfishness and homosexuality and on and on. Is it all sin? Oh yes! Are these sins an indication that people need to repent and turn from their sin and surrender more and more to Jesus? Yes! Is my sin an indication of the same? Yes!

Once people are saved, the process of surrender will begin.

It doesn't begin beforehand because it can't apart from faith. The Bible says:

> And without faith it is impossible to please him,
>   for whoever would draw near to God must
>   believe that he exists and that he rewards
>   those who seek him.
> Hebrews 11:6 (ESV)

> But God showed his great love for us by sending
>   Christ to die for us while we were still
>   sinners.
> Romans 5:8 (NLT)

You don't have to clean up first. Getting yourself cleaned up has absolutely nothing to do with salvation. It's completely the work of God Himself, and not by anything we do or quit doing. So why would we focus on someone's sinful behavior before they even believe?

> God saved you by his grace when you believed.
>   And you can't take credit for this; it is a gift
>   from God. Salvation is not a reward for the
>   good things we have done, so none of us can
>   boast about it.
> Ephesians 2:8-9 (NLT)

At the moment of our repentance and salvation, we are justified before God...by faith in Jesus alone. We instantly become children of God. If we were to die right then and there, we would go to heaven and live eternally with Him. But if we aren't that blessed and have to live here for a few more years, the sanctification process begins.

I am experiencing this process in my own life. I lie less than I used to. I gossip less than I used to. But I lie more now than I will someday. I gossip more now than I will someday. After we are saved, we journey from more sin to less sin. That's why I don't focus on where people are right now. I focus on encouraging them to move closer to Jesus. It's called progressive sanctification. And it's a process that won't be complete until we are absent from our physical bodies and present with Jesus.

> But whenever someone turns to the Lord, the
> veil is taken away. For the Lord is the Spirit,
> and wherever the Spirit of the Lord is, there
> is freedom. So all of us who have had that
> veil removed can see and reflect the glory of
> the Lord. And the Lord—who is the Spirit—
> makes us more and more like him as we are
> changed into his glorious image.
> 2 Corinthians 3:16-18 (NLT)

Are the sins of those around us an indication that they are either not saved yet, or not fully surrendered to Jesus? Yes! Is my own sin an indication that I need to surrender more and more to Jesus, living up to my new position as a child of God? Yes!

Every. Single. Day.

Jesus taught us to deal with the sins in our own lives before pointing out others' sins.

> "And why worry about a speck in your friend's
> eye when you have a log in your own? How
> can you think of saying to your friend, 'Let
> me help you get rid of that speck in your
> eye,' when you can't see past the log in your

*own eye? Hypocrite! First get rid of the log
in your own eye; then you will see well
enough to deal with the speck in your
friend's eye."*
Matthew 7:3-5 (NLT)

This is biblical tolerance. And when we practice it, focusing on our own sin instead of others', we just may set an example that will encourage them to do the same. After we've gotten rid of that log in our own eye, by surrendering it to Jesus, the change they see in us might just make them ask us how it happened. And our answer will be really, really good news!

**Love the sinner but hate their sin? Nope!
Love the sinner and hate my own sin.**

PERSONAL REFLECTION AND GROUP DISCUSSION

- What does it mean to take the log out of your own eye first?
- Is it easier to tolerate your own sin than to tolerate the sins of others? Why or why not?
- Has the word *tolerance* scared you? Do you feel differently now about biblical tolerance?
- Share something you've learned lately on your sanctification journey.
- Suggested verses to memorize: Ephesians 2:8-9

CHAPTER 4

GREAT FISHERS OF MEN ABIDE

The Bible tells us to abide in Jesus. If we want to be great fishers of men, it is imperative to abide in Him.

> *Abide in me, and I in you. As the branch cannot bear fruit by itself, unless it abides in the vine, neither can you, unless you abide in me. I am the vine; you are the branches. Whoever abides in me and I in him, he it is that bears much fruit, for apart from me you can do nothing.*
> John 15:4-5 (ESV)

When we are abiding in Him, we will hear clearly the call that God places on our lives. I look at abiding like staying on the road to the fishing hole where God is sending us. He puts us in positions to hear that call; in the correct lane, if you will. Sometimes it's an offramp or an onramp. Maybe it's a U-turn. We know we are on the right road, abiding in Christ, when we are keeping His commandments.

> *"If you keep my commandments, you will abide*
> *in my love, just as I have kept my Father's*
> *commandments and abide in His love."*
> John 15:10 (ESV)

When we keep His commandments, when we abide/remain in His love, we stay on the road.

Jesus simplifies all those commandments into two categories. As we saw in chapter 2, they are categorized into loving others and loving God.

> *"This is my commandment, that you love one*
> *another as I have loved you. Greater love*
> *has no one than this, that someone lay down*
> *his life for his friends. You are my friends if*
> *you do what I command you."*
> John 15:12-14 (ESV)

Did you get what Jesus just said? He wants us to be His friends by giving up our whole lives in order to love others like He loved us. This is what it means to abide in Him. This should be our very purpose on earth. And if we are truly going to love others like Jesus loved them, we may end up losing our lives over it. All but one of the twelve disciples did. Why should we should have it better than any of them? That makes sharing the gospel at our place of work or at our local coffee shop seem easy, doesn't it?

Because the Bible uses the grapevine and branches to illustrate abiding—staying on the road—I decided to spend some time in a vineyard to meditate on abiding. What I learned there changed my life.

God showed me that in my early years as a Christian adult, I had wanted to look like a healthy vine and have all the beautiful fruit to show off to the world, without all the sacrificing and dying to myself that is required to abide. I had never really shared my faith or discipled anyone. Yet those are signs of someone that is abiding. You see, I was not totally attached to the vine.

The "fruit" I was producing (looking good, having well-behaved kids, working like crazy at church) was not the fruit God was looking for from my life. I was emotionally exhausted by trying to keep up with the Christian Joneses! I was never satisfied and was constantly comparing myself to others and what I wanted my fruit to look like.

Back to the road analogy, it was like I was trying to take a shortcut that wasn't there. But I kept trying to find it, and so I was focusing on the map instead of on the mapmaker. And when that happened on my road trip to nowhere, the loudest words I heard in my head were not words from the mapmaker. They were words from my childhood: You're not good enough. You will never amount to anything. You're worthless.

Because I wasn't abiding in Him, I couldn't hear His still, small voice, and I couldn't see His attempts to bring restoration and redemption to me. I wriggled away from His training and pruning in my life. I avoided the work of my vinedresser.

Along with spending time in a vineyard, I also spent some time at a local library and found some books on fruit and grapevines. In one of them, called *The World Encyclopedia of Fruit*, I read this interesting statement regarding the branches on a grapevine: "Left to themselves, they often produce rank growth and nearly exhaust themselves with over cropping. For ornamental purposes, that is no problem. However, for fruit, they are best hard pruned and trained on wires. The main framework is formed in the first years, covering the vines with stems that are furnished with fruiting spurs."

I about got kicked out of the library when I laughed out

loud at what was written on the bottom of that page: "Grapevine prunings make great kindling and attractive wreaths!"

WOW! I had been ornamental. I had wanted to be beautiful, but I was just an exhausted 1980s-looking grapevine wreath with plastic fruit hanging on it! And every time God tried to make me a beautiful fruit-bearer, I'd jumped off the training wires!

> For the moment all discipline seems painful
> rather than pleasant, but later it yields the
> peaceful fruit of righteousness to those who
> have been trained by it.
> Hebrews 12:11 (ESV)

Back to John chapter 15. Jesus says that I am like a branch on this grapevine. He is the vine, and God the Father is the gardener, or vinedresser. I continued to read my fruit encyclopedia. I was pretty sure that my job as a branch was to abide on the vine and submit to the training of the vinedresser. So what was His job?

As I read, I realized that the grape gardener seems almost obsessed with caring for his plants! Paragraph after paragraph described his job. I decided to make a list of the verbs that describe what he does.

In the first four years, at specific times, these are all the actions that a vinedresser takes, in order, with the branches on his vines: examine, prune, examine, cut, select, choose, cut, tie, examine, cut, let develop, examine, carefully break, remove, examine, select, tie, examine, rub off, examine, cut, examine, remove, examine, make cuts, tie, examine, rub off, examine, cut back. Year after year, on and on.

At the very end, the last precious verb listed in this whole long explanation was: KEEP.

Close your eyes for a moment and let that sink in.

It's not an accident that Jesus used the analogy of the grapevine to describe our relationship with Him. All that cutting and tying and rubbing and breaking is hard stuff! It sounds like one trial after another to me, but it's all necessary to becoming a fruit bearer; a great fisher of men. Let it happen. Stay. Abide. And be willing to be examined and pruned by the Gardener constantly! Because in the end it will be wonderful to hear God say, "She's a keeper!"

> *Search me, O God, and know my heart; test me*
> *and know my anxious thoughts. Point out*
> *anything in me that offends you, and lead*
> *me along the path of everlasting life.*
> *Psalm 139:23-24 (NLT)*

PERSONAL REFLECTION AND GROUP DISCUSSION

- Share about a time when you felt you were being broken, pruned, or cut. How did God use that in your life?
- Has God been pointing out something in your life that is offensive to Him? What are you going to do about it?
- Have you ever felt exhausted by trying to look like a "good Christian?" What can you do when you feel that pressure to perform welling up in you?
- Suggested verse to memorize: Hebrews 12:11

CHAPTER 5

WHEN HE CALLS YOU TO GO, DROP EVERYTHING AND GO!

*And immediately they left their nets and
followed him.*
Mark 1:18 (ESV)

Here were these fishermen, fishing for fish, and they leave their boats and nets and follow Jesus to learn how to fish for men instead. That day on the beach, they embarked on the adventure of their lives! And God asks us to do the same.

When will He call you? If you're a Christian, He already has. The Great Commission is the general calling that every single believer has on their lives.

All followers of Christ are to be His disciples, making disciples, who make disciples.

Some Bible scholars think a more accurate translation of Jesus' command to go and make disciples of all nations would be, "...*as you go*, make disciples of all nations." This reminds me of the instruction God gives in Deuteronomy 6: We are to love the Lord our God with all our heart and soul and might so that His words are constantly on our hearts. We are to teach those words to others diligently, talking about those words when we are sitting around at home, when we're out and about in town, when we are drifting off to sleep, and when we wake up. The gospel should be at our very core. It must be what we live and breathe and what takes up most of our thought life.

We are to get up and go out each day with His call and His words on our minds and hearts because He has called us to fulfill the Great Commission every single day of our lives. When you walk out your front door, you are walking into your mission field. But as for if, or when, God will call you to go to a specific place or people group? That's up to Him.

However, I do know that when God called me, I was ready to drop everything and go after Him. He had already made my heart ready. I was in a "here I am, send me" position. But I didn't get myself in that position. He did. And that process wasn't at all pretty, but it was very, very necessary.

Here's how He did it, in three easy steps (NOT):

FIRST, HE BROKE MY HEART WITH THE THINGS THAT BREAK HIS

And seeing my own sinful behavior was one of those things that eventually broke my heart into repentance as well. This took a long time. It was a process. Here are just a couple of the stories from that journey.

For years, I looked like a Christian, I talked like a Christian, but I was not living and walking by the Spirit. I had prayed for salvation as a child at Vacation Bible School, and I did my best to be a good little girl. Today, I truly believe that God in His great mercy saved me, and that if I had died young, I would have spent eternity in heaven. But as I got older, the truth was that my heart had not changed very much, and those closest to me knew it.

I was popular at my church. I led women's ministries for a while and then children's ministries. I was a leader at my local MOPS group. I had volunteered at an orphanage in Mexico. I graduated from Bible college. I had been licensed as a Minister of the Gospel. I was a church secretary. I managed a Christian bookstore. I could go on and on listing all the Christian "stuff" I did and accomplished. On the outside, I looked like a pillar of Christianity. But one day, when our two oldest children were still little and our family was on our way to church, that pillar came crashing down, and the truth came out.

My husband, Rob, and I led worship at a church that was about twenty minutes from our home. As up-front leaders, it was important to me that our little family looked good on Sundays. The kids' clothes had to be clean and pressed and coordinated. The hair bows had to be just so, perched atop perfectly curled hair, and the little jacket had to match the shoes. You know what I mean. My husband would wait patiently while I ran around like a crazed woman every Sunday morning doing things that he thought completely unnecessary.

We were late. A lot. Every single week, in fact. But so were many others who served at the church each Sunday. So, I wasn't too worried about it.

Then came the fateful elder's meeting where the staff was told that the tardiness must stop. They explained that it was not a sign of good leadership for all of us to be consistently late. Good leaders get there on time. Punctuality was stressed as a quality of utmost importance. I grasped what they were saying and wholeheartedly agreed.

For the next couple of weeks, I was amazing! I laid out the kids' outfits the night before and got up extra early on Sunday mornings to be sure everything went smoothly. We could have it all, and we could shine! My family could still look great, and we could also be great spiritual leaders at our church. I was proud that we had changed, but not only that, we were now the *first* people to arrive, ready to serve. If the elders weren't there to see it, I made sure they knew that we were doing the right thing. I saw to it that they knew we had been on time, early in fact. It felt really, really good.

Then a few Sundays into this new way of life, something happened that threatened to ruin my newly acquired on-time reputation. About a year before, I had heard that an old friend of ours had made a whole lot of mistakes, started hanging with the wrong crowd, left his wife, and slipped back into old habits from his addiction years. A mutual friend had shared with us that Louis was using heroin again. It didn't look good. No one had heard from him, and no one knew where he was.

Well, once again, on that fateful Sunday morning, I proudly got everybody out the door and into the car on time. But then there was a little glitch that cost us a couple of minutes. *NOOO!* We raced off to church, stressed but hopeful that we might still be able to make it, even though we might not be the first ones there. And then we saw Louis, standing on a corner, as we stopped for a red light.

My husband saw him first and pointed him out. "Oh my gosh, Colleen! Look! It's Louis. I think we should stop and talk to him. Maybe we can help."

My stomach immediately knotted up. Louis looked awful. He was half slumped over, and it appeared he hadn't had a change of clothes or a decent meal for days. It was a project that would take us hours to fix. We'd be late to church. And just when we'd fixed our reputation! We were leaders after all. Good leaders. That had to come first didn't it?

I voiced all of this with passion to my husband. When the light turned green, he reluctantly drove the car through the intersection and onto the freeway. The next week we got a call from our mutual friend. "Did you hear the news? They found Louis's body. He died of an overdose."

BUSTED! On the outside I looked like a God pleaser, but I was more interested in pleasing people. I was religion led. I was people led. I was not Spirit led. God help me.

I have received forgiveness for what I did to Louis. I am trusting that the Father who loves us so much took Louis into His arms that day, and he was finally free of addiction. I know for sure that Louis's salvation didn't depend on whether I stopped to help him that morning. Even so, I wish I could forget that day, but I never will. Louis was finally free, but that day also marked the beginning of the road to freedom for me. Because on that day, my recovery from an addiction to religion began as well.

Unfortunately, the road ahead of me was long. Religion is a hard thing to shake.

Years later, after our third child was born, we were taking stock of our lives and realized that things were pretty amazing. Our kids were well-behaved and beautiful. I was a very content stay-at-home mom. Rob owned his own plumbing company and made good money. I was homeschooling the oldest two, and we were all loving it. We really had this parenting thing down. I took most of the credit for our success. After all, I was home way more than Rob was.

One day, I heard about a ten-year-old orphan, living in another country, who was up for adoption. It was a long, sad story. I just knew that I could be the answer to that little guy's problems. He needed rescuing, and I was just the one to do it. Our family had so much extra love to share.

One year and $27,000 later, that little boy was ours. And all hell broke loose. We didn't know until we got him home that he had a severe case of Reactive Attachment Disorder (RAD). We learned over the next year and a half what that meant. We learned it the hard way. No amount of counseling or trauma therapy seemed to work. It was a nightmare.

Our little family was turned upside down. So was our once happy and orderly home. Furniture would go flying when the little guy wasn't happy. He'd make his nose bleed on purpose during his epic tantrums. Blood would spray on the walls and rugs and anything else within a foot or two.

One night I went into his room after he had fallen asleep. I knelt on the floor by his bed and earnestly prayed that God would change his heart. As I prayed, I heard God's voice say, "What about your heart, Colleen?"

I about had a fit! "Talk to the kid! He's the one causing all the problems here. I'm doing the best I can!" God seemed silent, so I said, "What?! You want me to be like Jesus or something?"

God responded simply with an, "Uh huh!" I was really ticked off.

The chaos in our home continued, and we continued to be the brunt of our adopted son's abusive behavior. Then came the awful day when he seriously hurt our three-year-old. Child Protective Services came to our home to investigate and make sure my husband and I weren't the ones initiating the abuse. They discovered it really was this little boy, and the need to "fix" him got real serious real fast.

We were told that if he hurt one of our children again, they would leave him with us and place our other three children in foster care where they would be kept safe from their new brother. The social worker who told me this was so kind. She had tears in her eyes as she delivered their decision. My voice trembled as I thanked her for being honest. This was certainly a wakeup call. I was numb.

What had happened to our sweet little family? I thought we had it so all together! I was the perfect mom. How could this be happening?

But when I set out to rescue that little boy, God set out to rescue me. I didn't have it all together. I could fool some of the people around me, but I couldn't fool Him. Once again, heartbreak was just what this girl needed.

We tried everything. In a last-ditch effort, we paid $8,000 for therapy specifically for RAD children. It was a failure. They said they had never seen a worse case. They sent us home and told us we must find other living arrangements for our little boy. He just couldn't assimilate into our family. Our three original kids were showing signs of Post-Traumatic Stress Disorder (PTSD) from the last year and a half, and they couldn't take much more.

The therapists sent us home with a safety plan and instructions they hoped would minimize his abusive behavior until we could find another placement for him. One of the things they said might help was for me to hold him in my arms and rock him like a baby once a day. They gave specific instructions. I was to wait for the right moment when he was calm. I would invite him to the rocking chair and pull him up onto my lap. Then I'd turn his face toward me and gently look at him in his eyes. I would offer him a Sugar Daddy sucker and feed it to him as if it were a bottle while I rocked him.

I was horrified. This boy had hurt my baby. How in the world was I supposed to do this? Over the first two attempts, I discovered that the only way I could get through these sessions was to sing worship songs.

Here was this worship leader, finally really learning how to worship. As those songs left my lips, it was like I was hearing them for the very first time. The words about the love of God sunk deep.

Here I was, Miss Perfect Christian, Miss Perfect Mom, and I couldn't even love an orphan because he had hurt my child. Yet God loved me even though my sin had crucified His child.

God loved me. And God loved the little boy I rocked in my arms. For the first time, I understood who I was: a sinner who needed a savior. And for the first time, I really saw who God was: that Savior who I desperately needed.

Without those days, and without others that came after, where God used circumstances to break my religious heart, I would not be living out the call that God has placed on my life. Because He doesn't call religious people who don't think they need a savior. He calls brokenhearted people who know what they've been saved from.

NEXT, HE USED VERY UNPLEASANT CIRCUMSTANCES AND FAILURE TO GET ME IN THE RIGHT PLACE

When the economy crashed in 2008, it devastated our plumbing company. We were just getting back on our feet after the challenges and heartbreak of our family trauma. And then this happened!

For the first time since we'd had kids, I had to go find a "real job" with benefits because we could no longer afford to pay for health insurance. I filled out resumes and went to interviews, kicking and screaming on the inside. I doggedly did not want to go back to work.

With absolutely NO drug background, I "somehow" landed a job in drug prevention under a county contract on the mountain where we lived. My new job required me to begin a five-year internship to become an addictions treatment counselor.

FINALLY, HE OPENED MY EYES TO A SPECIFIC NEED

About a year later, when our local high school reported a series of incidents involving the drug, Ecstasy, I was tasked with exploring where our community's kids were accessing the drug. My colleagues at the Department of Behavioral Health suggested that the teens might be getting Ecstasy at a nearby rave party held once a month, just thirty minutes down the mountain. Looking back on it now, I have to laugh. I had no idea what they were talking about and had to Google the word *rave*.

I was completely out of my element the night I donned my business outfit, grabbed a clipboard, and headed to that rave to conduct a "risk assessment." It was held at a nearly defunct water park that was losing money like crazy. The manager decided that hosting rave parties would help with the finances. So here I was, walking into this place that was called—get this! —Pharaoh's Lost Kingdom! I soon found out that the name was perfect for what was going on there.

The community at the bottom of our mountain was up in arms about the rave parties because of all the problems that resulted. Two months before my visit, two fourteen-year-old girls had gone missing. When they showed up a couple of days later, the girls had no recollection of where they had been.

It was common the morning after a rave for nearby business owners to find baggies of drugs in their parking lots, as well as used condoms, stray underwear, and piles of vomit. But these people just saw the aftermath of what went on during the party.

What I beheld there that night broke my heart. I couldn't

believe what I saw young adults doing, let alone what I saw twelve to seventeen-year-olds doing. I completed my task with a heavy heart, checking off boxes and filling in the blanks on my risk assessment paperwork. Without a doubt, this was where our mountain kids were accessing Ecstasy. At two a.m., I left for home and cried all the way up the hill. I woke my husband up because I was so shaken, and what I shared with him broke his heart as well.

The next day, we looked online. We found no ministry reaching out to kids at raves. It was then that we knew God was calling us to do it. Frankly, we weren't real happy about it. We were just hoping we could write a check to help a rave ministry, but God clearly spoke to us. Saying no wasn't an option.

We began to get a team together to go to raves. Less than ten years later, PLUR Life Ministries would be in multiple states ministering to young people at raves across the country and sharing the gospel with ravers from eighty other countries who fly in for our American rave parties.

And it all started because of an economic disaster that about ruined us. Trust me, I never ever would have heard of raves otherwise.

So, just four years after we had gone through the painful experience of giving our adopted son up to another couple, PLUR Life Ministries was born. And five years after that, the ministry had grown to the point that I needed to be there full time. I had to quit my job.

We made our little boy's old room into an office for me. We bought some basic office furniture. But it wasn't until I was sitting at my new desk for the first time, that it dawned on me that where I was sitting was over the exact spot where I had kneeled that fateful night, where God told me I needed to be more like Jesus.

I am the cofounder and coleader of a successful ministry,

but I will never forget where I sit and what happened there, and what I know to be true about my sinful heart, and what I know to be true about my Savior.

These days, when I introduce myself, I always start by saying, "My name is Colleen, and I'm a recovering judgmental church lady."

Remember my friend Louis? If you had been able to follow me around on that Sunday morning before I saw Louis for the last time on this earth, and you'd had a minute to have a conversation with me as I rushed to get my kids ready for church, and if you had told me during that conversation that someday I'd adopt and give up a child for adoption, have to be in therapy with my kids, be in full-time ministry to the lost and hurting of this generation, a certified addictions treatment counselor, and a chaplain who goes into prisons and emergency rooms to minister to young adults, I think I may have stopped curling my daughter's hair long enough to tell you that you were crazy and that I would never want anything to do with those kind of people!

But God!

So, here's what I've learned from all of this:

Don't ever underestimate failure in your life. Don't quickly assign all unpleasant circumstances to the enemy at work. Pain often precedes victory. For me, pain and failure were part of the construction process that God used in my life to build me into the evangelist/disciple maker that He had made me to be before I was even born. Through these situations in my life, He equipped me to fulfill the Great Commission.

Failures quite often prepare us for successes in the things that really matter in life.

43

Good things start with a broken heart. Embrace those times of brokenness. Let the breaking do what God wants it to do in your life. Your ministry will be found in the places where you have been broken. Your testimony will come when you look back and see how God has healed and restored you.

When will you find your fishing hole? When you are following Jesus. And when He calls you, you can be confident that He has prepared you and you can drop everything and follow Him!

What does that look like?

Have you ever run into someone who knows a "best-kept secret'? They know where to find the patch of delicious wild berries that no one else knows about, or where to get the best biscuits and gravy at the cutest little hole-in-the-wall restaurant. They don't want to tell too many people, or it will ruin it for the few who know about it.

Well, it's like that with people who fish too. Great fishing holes become well-kept secrets. If someone decides to let you in on the location, you go! You feel honored to be privy to the information. Let's say that you overhear someone talking about this special fishing hole at the local diner early one morning. They don't give enough information for you to get there yourself, but as you eavesdrop, you've gathered enough to know that as soon as they take their final swig of coffee, they are on their way there. They pay their bill and hop in their car. What would you do? If I loved to fish, I'd jump in my car and follow them!

Follow God like that! The Great Commission is God's mission! Get to know Him, dig deep into His word, let Him teach you all His secrets. Drop everything and stalk Him! When you do, He will show you some of the best places to fish!

PERSONAL REFLECTION AND GROUP DISCUSSION

- Read Deuteronomy 6:4-9. If we took this passage seriously and acted on it, what would that look like?
- How has God broken your heart with the things that break His?
- Share about a time that God used unpleasant circumstances in your life to get you in the right place.
- Have you heard a specific call of God on your life to meet a specific need? What have you done or what will you do about it?
- Suggested verses to memorize: Deuteronomy 6:5-7

CHAPTER 6

GO WHERE THE FISH ARE AND GET MESSY 'CAUSE JESUS DID!

GO WHERE THE FISH ARE

S o, does living in the center of God's will require that we all have a passport? Nope. Not all Australian Christians have to go share the gospel in the United States, and not all committed American Christians need take off for China. When God told us to go, He didn't mean that we all must go to the other side of the world. Check this out.

The last thing you say before you leave is usually the most important thing, right? *Drive safe! I love you!*

So, what was the last thing Jesus said before He left?

> "But you will receive power when the Holy
> Spirit comes upon you. And you will be my
> witnesses, telling people about me
> everywhere—in Jerusalem, throughout
> Judea, in Samaria, and to the ends of the
> earth." After saying this, he was taken up

> *into a cloud while they were watching, and*
> *they could no longer see him.*
> Acts 1:8-9 (NLT)

I just love this so much! He told us to share the gospel wherever we are and wherever we go! Since it was the last thing He said before He left, we can assume it was important to Him! It's not just the pastor's job! It belongs to all of us. And we don't need a degree, because the power and the ability to do this will come from the Holy Spirit. We will discuss this in depth later.

If we are listening to Him, He will tell us where to go. Going may actually mean staying at our home base and going up the street to our Jerusalem (our own hometown). It may mean boarding a plane or taking a road trip into our Judea or Samaria (our own country). For some of us, we may need that passport to follow the call God places on our life to take the gospel to the other side of the world (the ends of the earth).

Does the passage in Acts 1:8-9 give people like me, who didn't want to go far, an excuse to stay home and evangelize and disciple from there? Maybe some of us will start out that way. But I'll let you in on a little secret. Once you begin to partner with the Creator of the universe to fulfill the Great Commission, you will be blown away. You will see God working live, in real time. There is nothing else like it. What a rush! It won't be long before you will be willing to go whenever and wherever Jesus calls you. It's just that exciting! That's why the disciples dropped everything. They saw Jesus.

Whether you go, or whether you stay, OBEY!

Jesus was the first one to GO. He came to us; and He came right to where we were. That is why one of His names is Emmanuel. It means God with us. When He left this earth, He told us to be like Him. Part of that is going, going like He did to where the fish are. I love 2 Corinthians 5:18-20. If you've already got this underlined in your Bible, you may already have the gift of evangelism. To the spirit-led evangelist, this verse says it all:

> *"And all of this is a gift from God, who brought us back to himself through Christ. And God has given us this task of reconciling people to him. For God was in Christ, reconciling the world to himself, no longer counting people's sins against them. And he gave us this wonderful message of reconciliation. So we are Christ's ambassadors; God is making his appeal through us. We speak for Christ when we plead, "Come back to God!"*
> 2 Corinthians 5:18-20 (NLT)

Did you read that? WE SPEAK FOR CHRIST!

Well, not all the time! But when we are pleading with people to come back to Him? Yes! We are.

When Jesus described evangelism as fishing for men, He was very intentional. He wanted us to have that picture of a fisherman, and all that entails, in our mind's eye. Like a good fisherman—like the BEST fisherman of all—we are to go where the fish are.

The enemy of all men's souls will do everything to stop us from this mission. He's got strategies to do this. One of his greatest, most successful strategies in the United States, I believe, has been to get the church to think that they don't have to GO outside their four walls to effectively fish. They can stay on their comfy pews.

The American church in our current culture has largely become an organization that attempts to attract, in place of going. We have developed all kinds of programs and strategies to be seeker friendly. This would be okay if the congregation was going to the lost for the most part, and then using the church and its programs as a place to plug in the fish they'd caught. But instead, evangelism in the United States has been more like this: I find the coolest church possible, with the most attractive worship music, comfortable seating, best coffee bar, best kids' programs, and I hang out there on Sunday mornings. Occasionally, I invite people to come. The pastor needs to do the evangelistic work and share the gospel with my guests, mostly because I have no idea how to share my faith on my own. And then he needs to disciple them. It's the pastor's job. He's the one that gets paid to read the Bible every day.

Inviting people to come to church as a way of evangelizing them may have worked in the past. Most people in the United States had a basic knowledge of Jesus and at least had heard about Christianity's claims that He died on a cross and rose from the dead three days later. Most kids in America were dragged to Sunday School or sent to Vacation Bible School. It was a common family tradition to go to church. People would often claim to be Christians simply because they were Americans. But all this has changed in recent years.

Because people tend to stay within their own subculture and hang around only like-minded people, they often don't keep up on what's happening "out there." Consequently, they don't know that what used to work, may not work any longer. Just because church is attractive to us doesn't mean it's attractive to the world. In fact, from what I hear from this generation, the church in general has worked hard not to be attractive to them. So why don't we start doing things differently?

I believe the enemy of this generation is duping us into thinking our old ways of attracting people to come to church will still work today because he knows they won't come. They say the definition of insanity is doing the same thing over and over and expecting different results. Has the church in America lost its mind? Maybe. Let's stop this here and now and start doing things differently. My southern roots are showing, but here's a summary:

We need to quit telling the world, "Y'all Come!" Because God's Word says, "Y'all Go!"

If we don't go, we are a disobedient church.

It really comes down to this. Every single person that trusts in Christ alone for their salvation needs to pray and ask these questions: How can I be the most kingdom effective with my gifts, my skill sets, with my past and my present? How can I push back the most darkness in my lifetime?

Jesus, how do you want me to run with you to the lost?

ALL of us must GO. Some will go to their own neighborhood. Some will go to their own state or country. And some will go to the ends of the earth.

But all of us must go.

IT'S OKAY TO GET MESSY

If you are going to go where the fish are, you are going to have to get in the lake. You can't stand on the shore and beg the fish to jump out of the water and into your net. You can try to attract them out of their world and into yours, but most fish just won't come unless you go into their world to get them.

Would trying to attract them out be a whole lot less messy? Yes! Effective? No. Think about it. The Bible clearly says that Jesus came to us as fully God and fully man. The Creator of the universe had to wear a diaper. That's messy. Sometimes in our quest for the lost, we are going to get uncomfortable. As we fish, we will be out of our comfy pew, away from our comfy music, away from our comfy circle of friends who think like we do, and act like we do. And we may get cold and wet. But Jesus said the lost are worth it. Actually, He said they were worth dying for; and so He did.

Do the rave moms like going to raves, staying out all night with no sleep, getting splashed with barf as they hold an over-dosing girl in misery? Not really. But they love Jesus, and they love His Word. And so they love that girl, and they are compelled to go.

Look at Jude 1 again:

> And you must show mercy to those whose faith
> is wavering. Rescue others by snatching
> them from the flames of judgment.
> Jude 1:22-23b (NLT)

To snatch someone from the flames, you must get close to the fire. You may lose an eyebrow or two. It's okay. Jesus said people were worth dying for.

JESUS HAS ALREADY BEEN TO YOUR FISHING HOLE

In the early years of our ministry to ravers at raves, I would be asked to speak somewhere and share how it all got started. I would talk about how I felt in 2008 when the economy crashed, and all that ensued. I'd share about that first rave I went to on the job, and then how the ministry was born and how we began to get teams together to go to raves. And then I'd say something like this: "We invited God to go with us to raves."

It wasn't until a few years later that God showed me what an arrogant and incorrect statement that was. He had been going to raves all along. He invited US to go with HIM.

One afternoon, I got a call from a former raver who had recently received the gift of salvation and had been looking online to find a ministry that she could get involved with. She wanted to return to her friends, still caught up in the rave culture, and share about the PLUR that she'd found in Jesus, without the use of the drug Ecstasy at raves. She was so excited to find out about us, and she contacted us to ask if she could help.

I was so excited to hear from her! I asked her how she found Jesus. She told me that she met Him on the dance floor at a rave. I assumed that since we were the only ministry at the time doing outreach at raves, she must have run into one of our rave moms on a dance floor at some rave in one of the states where we had ministered. When I asked for location and date, I discovered that we had not been there! I asked her to explain.

Breathless, she shared how amazing it had been to hear God speak directly to her on a dance floor, while she was high on drugs! It was not a human being that had carried the Good News to her, it was God Himself, and she gave her life to Him that night, drugs and all. She got plugged into a church, began to read the Bible, and her journey with Him began.

Since then, I have heard many testimonies of people who have heard from God or seen Him while high on drugs. At times, I've silently questioned the reliability of their stories, but the resulting fruit in their lives of repentance and turning to follow Jesus have made me realize that they are walking miracles of the grace of God who goes to great lengths to seek and save the lost.

> *"If a man has a hundred sheep and one of them*
> *gets lost, what will he do? Won't he leave*
> *the ninety-nine others in the wilderness and*
> *go to search for the one that is lost until he*
> *finds it?"*
> Luke 15:4 (NLT)

Jesus, the One who leaves the ninety-nine and runs to the one, has already been to your fishing hole. He's prepared it for you. He's prepared you for it. He introduced you to it. He is going to give you everything you need to fish it.

Stay humble.

PERSONAL REFLECTION AND GROUP DISCUSSION

- Where do you go to share God's love?
- Do you remember who first went to you to tell you the good news?
- How does it make you feel to know that you can speak for Christ?
- How does it feel to know that God thought you were worth dying for?
- Do you want to share that good news with the world? Even if it means getting messy?
- Does it bring comfort to you to know that Jesus has already been to your fishing hole?

- What are some ways you can see that God has already been preparing you to fish for people?
- What are some ways we can stay humble in ministry and other leadership roles?
- Suggested verses to memorize: 2 Corinthians 5:18-20

CHAPTER 7

GET THE ORDER RIGHT AND BE NICE

GET THE ORDER RIGHT

Consider the order of events in John 8. Jesus was at the temple and a crowd had gathered around Him. He sat down to teach them, but as He was speaking, the Pharisees brought a woman in front of the crowd who had been caught in the act of adultery. They interrupted Jesus's teaching to try to make Him look bad in front of everyone. They asked Him a tricky question. They pointed at the woman.

> *"Teacher," they said to Jesus, "this woman was caught in the act of adultery. The law of Moses says to stone her. What do you say?"*
> *John 8:4-5 (NLT)*

Now I'm not the least little bit concerned for Jesus. He can handle Himself. But what about that poor woman? Oh my goodness! Can you imagine what she must have been feeling?

Did they even give her time to get completely dressed before shoving her in front of the crowd?

The first thing Jesus did was to bend down and write something in the sand. Now some scholars believe that He was just trying to avert his eyes from the naked woman. I highly doubt that. Why would He need to? It's not like that would've made Him lust! Plus, He created her! He already knew what she looked like naked, right?

Other scholars say He was probably writing a list of sins that the men who had thrust the woman in front of Him had recently committed. I really hope that's what happened, because if so, this is epic! If this was indeed a list that He wrote, one of the first items would have been the fact that by focusing only on the woman, these Pharisees were sinning by breaking the law found in Leviticus 20:10 and Deuteronomy 22:22, stating that BOTH the man and the woman caught in adultery were to be put to death.

You know what? When Jesus tells us to "check the log in our own eye" first, before focusing on the sins of others, He's really doing us a big favor. He's telling us to get the order right. Because almost always, when we judge others, we end up looking ridiculous. Here were the Pharisees trying to enforce the law that they themselves were breaking! Duh! But that is the way of judgement.

Back to the story. So, the religious leaders must have all had stones in their hands, preparing to throw them at the woman until she died. By the way, this would've also been breaking the law of the land. We see in John 18:31 that Jews were not allowed to execute anyone. Only the Romans could do that. So, Jesus started to write in the sand and the guys kept commanding Him to answer their question. They really thought they had Him with this one!

Jesus answers,

"All right, but let the one who has never sinned
throw the first stone!"
John 8:7b (NLT)

Then Jesus goes back to his writing. At this point, they were the ones who'd been had.

When the accusers heard this, they slipped away
one by one, beginning with the oldest, until
only Jesus was left in the middle of the
crowd with the woman. Then Jesus stood up
again and said to the woman, "Where are
your accusers? Didn't even one of them
condemn you?" "No, Lord," she said. And
Jesus said, "Neither do I. Go and sin no
more."
John 8:9-11 (NLT)

Check this out. First, Jesus made it clear that He did not condemn the woman. Then He told her to leave her life of sin. That's the correct order. Reverse that order, and you'll lose the gospel. You'll lose Jesus because He didn't come to condemn the world, but to give the world some super good news! There's another way to live! A way that brings life and peace! The war with God is over!

Now let's back up a bit and look at John chapter four to see how Jesus handles another sinner. This time it was a Samaritan woman who got a big surprise when she went to get water from her neighborhood well and found Jesus sitting there. She couldn't believe that this Jewish man would dare to speak to her. Jews and Samaritans didn't mingle. He really caught her off guard because He wasn't doing things according to the acceptable order of His day. He was crossing a line, violating a man-made rule. The woman asks Him point blank why He is willing to go against that order.

His answer is clear. He is willing to violate man-made orderliness and appropriateness for an opportunity to share the gospel. Jesus gives her the good news. He offers her eternal life. And she wants it! You see, to Jesus, there are no boundaries. The man-made prejudices and the "they're from the wrong side of the tracks" rules we make to protect ourselves from those who are different than us are just ridiculous to Him. He wants ALL to hear the good news, and He will break man-made rules of appropriateness and propriety and safety to get it to them. Man's order is not always God's order. Jesus got the order right.

Only after Jesus shares the good news does He confront the woman at the well about her sin. There is no condemnation here because He did things in the right order, God's order. There is an invitation to live a different way, to live an abundant life. How could she refuse? Not only does she turn to Jesus, but she runs into her town and shares the good news with them. Although this wasn't part of the plan Jesus and His disciples had made for their trip, they ended up staying there in that Samaritan town for another two days because so many people wanted to hear the good news. Jesus always does things in the right order, and the results of getting the order right are astounding.

You want to see a lot of salvations through your ministry? You want to see your friends and family and coworkers saved? You want to start a church? Get the order right. Do it like Jesus. If not, you'll do it like the Pharisees and look ridiculous.

BE NICE

So many of the instructions we have looked at involve being nice, but I wanted to give being nice its very own section, because it's so important, and yet it's a characteristic of Jesus that's so absent from so many of us today. Let the beauty of the kindness of our God wash over you again as you read this passage from the book of Psalms:

> He does not punish us for all our sins; he does
> not deal harshly with us, as we deserve. For
> his unfailing love toward those who fear him
> is as great as the height of the heavens above
> the earth. He has removed our sins as far
> from us as the east is from the west. The
> LORD is like a father to his children, tender
> and compassionate to those who fear him.
> For he knows how weak we are; he
> remembers we are only dust.
> Psalm 103:10-14 (NLT)

When we realize how much we have been given, how can that not make us a little bit nicer every day? We would do well to remember that the difficult people in our lives are only dust and to be kind to them.

Our ministry motto is "Engaging believers to engage the lost, until heaven is crowded." It comes from the parable of the great feast that Jesus told in Luke 14. Through story, Jesus paints a picture of God sending us out to invite people into His family so that heaven will be full. Our motto is just a catchy way of saying that we want to follow Jesus's example of seeking after the lost by fulfilling the Great Commission.

We can use forms of the word engage as either an adjective

or a verb to describe Jesus and what He did. *Engage* means to occupy, attract, and hold by influence or power; to involve someone's interest or attention; to bring together or interlock; to begin and carry on an enterprise; to hold the attention of; to bind someone to do something. Wow! What a word!

Engaging means tending to draw favorable attention or interest: attractive. Jesus engaged and was engaging. He spent time with the people He was trying to reach. He built relationships. He met needs. He fed the 5,000. He turned the water into wine. People followed Him around. One guy even climbed up in a tree just to get a glimpse of Him. He had to jump in a boat to escape His fans. He was nice. He asked a lot of questions and listened.

Being nice turns people toward Jesus. So be nice.

> *Don't you see how wonderfully kind, tolerant,*
> *and patient God is with you? Does this*
> *mean nothing to you? Can't you see that his*
> *kindness is intended to turn you from*
> *your sin?*
> Romans 2:4 (NLT)

PERSONAL REFLECTION AND GROUP DISCUSSION

- Have man-made rules of orderliness and appropriateness ever stopped you from sharing the gospel?
- Are there people you don't normally mingle with that maybe you should start mingling with in order to follow Jesus's example found in John 4?
- What are some man-made rules that are probably ridiculous to God?

- How does it make you feel when you have been nice to someone who really doesn't deserve it?
- How has God been kind, tolerant, and patient with you?
- Suggested verses to memorize: Psalm 103:10-14

CHAPTER 8

WORK FOR AN AUDIENCE OF ONE

John 12 gives a sad account of the many people who believed Jesus was who He said He was, but who wouldn't admit it because they didn't want to get kicked out of their religious club. They didn't want to lose their social status. Why?

> *For they loved human praise more than the*
> *praise of God.*
> John 12:43 (NLT)

Let's not be too quick to judge them. I bet some of us can relate. Have we ever been embarrassed to pray in public? Have we ever cringed when our friend started witnessing to someone, wishing we could fade away into the background? Ever kept your faith to yourself, worried that it may cause you to get overlooked for that promotion, or not get the new job?

Gonna just get real here! I am a natural born people pleaser. I was raised to please people. I was punished when I didn't and rewarded when I did. It's now my default and has gotten me into more trouble than it's worth.

When I do things the way people want me to do them, it often means that I won't be doing them God's way. Have you noticed how contrary to our ways God's ways seem to be? *Love your enemies. To die is gain. Turn the other cheek.*

A few times in the last years of ministry we have been asked to change the way we do things. People want us to charge money for things God has told us not to charge for. People want us to slow down or speed up. People tell us to say more. People tell us to say less. We've had people offer financial support with the condition that we do things their way, and people threatening to withhold financial support if we don't.

I confess that when someone tells me they ***don't like*** the way we do something in ministry, I get knots in my stomach. But I've found that waiting in line behind that person, there is always another person telling us they ***like*** the way we do it.

I have had to learn, along with Jeremiah, to disregard faces. In the first chapter of Jeremiah, when God called Jeremiah, He told him to go to the nations, do exactly what He said to do, say exactly what He told him to say. God tells Jeremiah not to be afraid of the people's faces. If we are completely focused on the countenance of the faces of those who we want approval from, we will not be able to obey God.

This should be our prayer and our hope, not just for others but for ourselves:

> *The Lord bless you and keep you; the Lord make*
> *his face to shine upon you and be gracious to*
> *you; the Lord lift up his countenance upon*
> *you and give you peace.*
> Numbers 6:24-26 (ESV)

God's smile is the only one that really matters.

> For we speak as messengers approved by God to
> be entrusted with the Good News. Our
> purpose is to please God, not people. He
> alone examines the motives of our hearts.
> Bam!
> 1 Thessalonians 2:4 (NLT – with the Bam
> added by me)

It's so important to stay in God's Word and in touch with Him, so we know what pleases Him and so we aren't tossed about by everyone else's opinion. I love this Scripture passage that can keep me on track, when I let it:

> And so, dear brothers and sisters, I plead with
> you to give your bodies to God because of all
> he has done for you. Let them be a living
> and holy sacrifice—the kind he will find
> acceptable. This is truly the way to worship
> him. Don't copy the behavior and customs
> of this world, but let God transform you into
> a new person by changing the way you
> think. Then you will learn to know God's
> will for you, which is good and pleasing and
> perfect."
> Romans 12:1-2 (NLT)

Someone once said, "If you live for people's acceptance, you will die from their rejection." We need to live only for Christ and what He finds acceptable. If I catch myself beginning to enjoy people's acceptance and compliments too much, I know up around the bend, I am going to stumble. Frankly, since

God's ways are so much higher than ours, I now find myself getting a bit nervous when too many people are pleased with me! If they are pleased with Jesus in me, then I'm safe.

When you're in ministry, you are often thrust on a stage. It can become addictive. It's too bad that people who are fulfilling the Great Commission are such an anomaly today. It's not the norm. That's why evangelists stand out. Those who offer discipleship are revered. Missionaries can become heroes. Pastors are put on a pedestal. Yet they are just doing what we all are supposed to be doing. They shouldn't be the exception; they should be the rule. But that's not how it is in our culture today. So, if we're one of those people, we must intentionally combat the misplaced attention.

After a long drive, Rob and I were once welcomed at the door of a Bible study by a man who had invited us to come. He was so impressed that we took the time out of our busy schedule to be there, and he went out of his way to let the group know that. He seemed a bit "fan-clubish" of us as well. He shared with the group how he was so happy to have such great wisdom in their midst and how he was so glad we were there to add to their time of discussion. He hung on our every word, repeatedly commenting on how blessed they were to be in our presence.

Well, I'd had enough. I waited for the right opportunity and jumped on it when it came. During an answer to one of the discussion questions, I worked in the little tidbit of truth that Rob and I had gotten in a rather loud and stupid argument in the car on the way there. This gave me the opportunity to combat the hero worship vibe in the room and share that we are just ordinary people who God has called to do extraordinary things...by His power, and only by His power!

We need to take ourselves down a few notches when others begin to think more highly of us than they ought. We do this by bringing glory to God. We also need to bring ourselves down a few notches when *we* think of ourselves more highly than we ought. We need to check in with ourselves periodically. We need to ask, has this become a show? Will we still labor in secret? When no one sees? When there's no applause? Can we work in the fields when no one's taking a photo or writing a biography about our lives?

We've got to stay humble to stay able to do God's work.

In the book of Matthew, we see two commands that appear to contradict each other until we take a closer look...

> "...let your good deeds shine out for all to see, so
>   that everyone will praise your heavenly
>   Father."
> *Matthew 5:16 (NLT)*

> "Watch out! Don't do your good deeds publicly,
>   to be admired by others, for you will lose the
>   reward from your Father in heaven."
> *Matthew 6:1 (NLT)*

The difference? Read the whole section surrounding each verse and you will see that in one case the deeds were done with the agenda of bringing glory to God. In the other case, the deeds were done in order to be admired by others. We've got to continually ask:

> *Search me, O God, and know my heart! Try me*

> *and know my thoughts! And see if there be*
> *any grievous way in me, and lead me in the*
> *way everlasting!*
> Psalm 139:23-24 (*ESV*)

PERSONAL REFLECTION AND GROUP DISCUSSION

- Has people pleasing ever gotten you into trouble?
- What have been the results when you put God pleasing over people pleasing?
- Spend some time praying over each other regarding this issue.
- Suggested verses to memorize: Romans 12:1-2

CHAPTER 9

UNDERSTAND THAT FEAR IS TEMPORARY AND QUIT WORRYING

FEAR IS TEMPORARY

Perfect love casts out fear. The only perfect love is God's love. When we love with His love, we won't be afraid of the consequences.

> There is no fear in love, but perfect love casts
> out fear. For fear has to do with punishment,
> and whoever fears has not been perfected in
> love. We love because he first loved us. If
> anyone says, "I love God," and hates his
> brother, he is a liar; for he who does not love
> his brother whom he has seen cannot love
> God whom he has not seen. And this
> commandment we have from him: whoever
> loves God must also love his brother.
> 1 John 4:18-21 (ESV)

Now we won't be perfected in loving God and others until

we are with Jesus in heaven. Until then, it's a spiritual battle to love God's way. Until then, we only experience moments of God's love flowing through us to others. It's never totally consistent. That's why the famous love chapter, 1 Corinthians 13, talks about how we only have a partial knowledge of God and His love. We don't have the whole picture. But the time of perfection will come. Until then, we wait, and we deal with our imperfection. We deal with our fears.

When I am sharing the gospel or ministering to others and I become afraid, it's often because I am afraid of rejection, of not pleasing people, of my own limitations, or of physical suffering and death. When I take a minute to notice the fear rising in me and identify where it is coming from, I can bring those feelings that do not come from God under His authority. And He takes those fears away and replaces them with His love for the lost. Every. Single. Time. It's just incredible!

Here's an example of this. When we first started ministering at raves, we frequented a rave venue that had two little clubs that adjoined on the same property called The Gotham and The Hudson. I remember feelings of extreme fear when my husband would drive me in to the parking lot with the only girlfriend I could find who was willing to go with me, and we would jump out of the car and head to the entrance. For months, on every single visit we made to this place, I would shake as Nicki and I approached the door.

We had been warned by police that there was a local gang called the STD Crew that had been frequenting the venue with infected needles, stabbing people with them as they were on or near the dance floors. Some police officers had once tried to stop us as we entered saying, "You ladies should NOT be here. It's not safe."

We had gotten similar warnings from a nearby fire department that had received so many calls for service from this address that they would wait in their truck right up the street at the ready with paramedics on board.

Once at this venue, an older man came up behind me in the dark. The speakers were blaring so loudly that I could barely hear myself think. The man quickly felt my whole body with his hands. I jumped and turned around. He was smiling. It made me sick. It made me afraid. I'm sure that was his intention. Nicki and I were starting to be regular attenders there. The predators and drug dealers who came to these events to take advantage of the kids didn't like our presence.

The dark parking lot in the back provided all kinds of opportunities for evil. According to police, stabbings, rapes, and other violent acts were common there. We had asked the megachurch directly across the street if we could park in their lot and do our outreach from there, but they said they didn't assist any outside ministries. They only worked on their own programs. Their gates would remain locked. We were left with no other options if we were to follow the calling that God had placed on us to reach these kids. We had to work from that dark parking lot. Many times I was afraid.

IN THESE SITUATIONS, I WAS EXPERIENCING FEAR OF THE PHYSICAL CONSEQUENCES OF OBEYING GOD

At this venue, we were often looked up and down by the staff at the ticket window. The lady who owned the place was pretty scary. We had the feeling she sent people to follow us to see what we were up to. I always held my breath as we purchased our entrance tickets and the transaction was complete. I just knew that the day would come when they would say they had the right to refuse us.

At the same time, I was afraid that once inside, the kids themselves would reject us. What if they mocked us? What if they tried to dose us? What if they yelled at us? We had no idea during these early months how desperate these kids were to hear good news or how welcome we would be.

IN THESE SITUATIONS, I WAS EXPERIENCING FEAR OF THE EMOTIONAL CONSEQUENCES OF OBEYING GOD

A few times outside this venue, we experienced demonic presence. It would give me chills from the top of my head to my toes. I did not like it one bit! Sometimes, men who appeared to be possessed would get right in our faces. I would be afraid.

DURING THESE TIMES, I WAS EXPERIENCING FEAR OF THE SPIRITUAL CONSEQUENCES OF OBEYING GOD

Yup! I had a lot of reason to shake as I walked across the parking lot each time we arrived. But you know what happened? We would pray. We would ask God to fill us with His perfect love for ravers. I would shake all the way from the car to the ticket window. But as soon as we entered that place, the fear left. You see, God's perfect love for these kids would replace that fear. As soon as I got to the kids, the fear was gone.

It was nothing short of a miracle.

I shared this once with a pastor friend of ours and this is what he said: "If only you could see the spiritual battle that is waged over that club whenever you moms are there. If only you could see how the demons cringe and shrivel in fear when you arrive! Then you would be able to see how BIG the One in you is, and how very SMALL the enemy is!"

DON'T SPEND TIME WORRYING

At the beginning of this chapter, we saw that 1 John 4 says our fear has to do with punishment. Since the fall of man, we humans have been afraid that God really isn't who He says He is. That He isn't really good. That He doesn't want good things for us. That He wants to punish us.

That's really the root of worry. If we believe the truth, that God is good, we will view all that happens from that perspective. Trials and sickness and death are not something we look forward to, but we can know in our hearts that God is working all things together for our good. He is good, and He knows what is best for us. We don't have to worry. He holds us in the palm of His hand. He is constantly working things out in His time. But there's the rub!

Let's face it! God usually doesn't run on our timetable. His ways are *higher* than ours. He wants us to trust Him, and He sets things up so that He gets the glory. I think that's why He waits sometimes, until we are all out of our own solutions to our problems. Then He swoops in and saves the day! An example I have seen over and over again is how God has provided for us financially at the last minute!

Once, on the day our mortgage was due, we had next to nothing in our bank account. I thought, *Well, this is it! I knew going into full time ministry that we'd probably end up losing our house. Here we go!* But don't think for a minute that when I said, "Here we go!" I wasn't completely stressed out about it!

Just a couple hours later there was a knock at our door. When I answered, no one was there. An envelope lay on our welcome mat. Inside it was a note about trusting God and a wad of cash. It was enough to pay our mortgage!

Matthew 6 tells us that our worries can't add a single moment to our life. It also says that worry is a characteristic of those who don't believe. Worry dominates the thoughts of unbelievers. Ouch!

In his book, *Worship: The Ultimate Priority*, John MacArthur said, "For some reason, we think of doubt and worry as 'small' sins. But when a Christian displays unbelief... or an inability to cope with life, he is saying to the world, 'My God cannot be trusted,' and that kind of disrespect makes one guilty of a fundamental error, the heinous sin of dishonoring God. That is no small sin."

Worry isn't some little cutesy sin in my life. I have had to deal with worry very seriously. It's a natural default for me. It's not something I can or should take lightly. It must be dealt with as sin. I confess I haven't had complete victory in that area yet.

Since that knock at our door and the envelope on our welcome mat, I worry less about our bills on our missionary budget. But like the Israelites who also saw God do amazing miracles, I slide back into unbelief that God can really take care of me. In times of worry I have learned that it helps to refocus my thoughts by asking, "Do you believe that God is a good, good Father? Because worry is fear that God may not be good." And I tell myself, "When things happen that you don't understand, remember what you do understand: God is good."

I must also remind myself that what I think should happen regarding a particular situation may not be what God thinks should happen. People who really love and serve God do lose their homes. Some make their home in a prison and lie down every night hungry, wondering if they will wake up in the morning. I'm sure some pray that they won't. But because we can bank on the fact that God is a good, good Father, we know that He will work all things out for our good and for His glory. And that's why we are here, right?

God is so kind, and He knows that to be human means we will struggle with the sin of worry. I love how He consistently gives us reminders that He is with us. Over the years of living on the edge because of ministry, I have come to find out that when you are doing God's work, He will wink at you when you least expect it, and perhaps when you need it most. He will give you the gift of little glimpses of Himself to show you that He is there and very, very real. He will show you that He can be trusted.

Very soon after starting the rave outreach ministry, God led us to create a discipleship plan specifically for ravers, where we could match up a raver who prayed for salvation with a Christian who would disciple them. We called it Hangar 33.

The "33" comes from a discipleship principal our son had learned at seminary. It's a mathematical miracle of sorts: one person disciples another for a year, then both people disciple two others for the next year. If this continues, the whole world could be discipled in 33 years!

The "Hangar" part comes from the concept of a safe, protected place where you can have your nuts and bolts tightened, your oil changed, your gas tank filled, and your wings attached to prepare you for flight.

This plan had been confirmed in many ways. The biggest way was every time we looked into God's Word and saw His heart for the lost, we saw His desire that His people become not only fishers of men, but disciplers of men. We knew we couldn't just focus on fishing without focusing on what to do with the fish once they took a bite. A few years later, God gave us the vision for Camp 33.

Not only did He give us the name for it, but God also laid out the whole weekend for us: a spiritual adventure that included a crazy, off-road Jeep drive with stops along the way to explore God's Word. It would begin in the mountains and continue down to the desert with an overnight stay at a place we'd call Camp 33, on our friend's five-acre property that they loaned us for this purpose. Ravers we met on outreaches at raves could come for free, hang out with the rave moms and dads, and learn more about this Jesus we told them about. We'd be able to be with them for a whole weekend instead of a few minutes at a party.

Rob opened his Bible and began to lay out the devotions the dads would do with the ravers out on the trail. He prayed and asked God to guide him, giving him the Scripture verses that he should cover with the campers. It took days, but when he was finally finished, he sat back and reviewed the whole thing. To his surprise, the devotions covered the subjects of peace, love, unity, and respect (PLUR); and in that order! Rob didn't even think of planning it that way. It was like God was winking! How sweet of God to do this like the ravers' motto, in the ravers' order! Oh, how He was running after them! This camp idea was going to work!

The only problem is that the cabin and outbuildings on the property hadn't felt human touch in years. The roofs were caving in or about gone. Some leaned sideways. Years ago, birds and other desert animals had moved in and now their great-great-great-great grandchildren were enjoying the fruits of their labors! Getting this place ready for Camp 33 would be a huge undertaking!

On the weekend we deemed the Extreme Camp Makeover, I was shocked as carload after carload of friends, and friends of friends, pulled off the dirt road and onto the property. A roofer, a floor guy, a painter, and representatives from almost every other trade showed up. Whole families piled out of cars. We even had a guy who said he came specifically to cook for everybody all weekend! People donated supplies. Others whipped out their credit cards every time we had to make a run into town for something. The whole weekend I was practically in tears, but the whole weekend the people pleaser in me was also practically having an aneurism!

What if this whole Camp 33 idea wasn't going to work? It was just a vision. We had no proof of concept. These people, including the owner of the property, had invested tons of time and money into this. What if we really hadn't heard from God? What if no ravers ever came? What would I say to everyone who gave so much? Out there in that desert that weekend, I could kind of imagine what it might have felt like to be Noah, building something before there was really an actual need for it. Ravers weren't exactly waiting in line for camp to open!

At the end of an incredible weekend, we said grateful good-byes to a bunch of exhausted volunteers. Rob and the property owner stood marveling at the work that had been done. The area was completely transformed! My daughter and I quickly made our final run to the home improvement store to pick up some combination padlocks we needed to secure one of the new buildings and the fuse box. While I held our spot in line, Cassie chose a package of two combination locks that were blue like the fresh paint that was still drying at camp.

Returning to the property, we handed the locks to my husband and headed home. A few minutes after we left, he almost fell to his knees when he opened the package and saw the slip of paper containing the combination to the locks we'd purchased for Camp 33, because the combination was: 33, 3, 33!

When God winks at you like, "I've got this! Just watch me!" you will never forget it.

To God be the glory! Camp 33 did work. The very first camp we had out there, a raver got saved. And then another and another. A human trafficking victim came, and her life totally transformed after getting saved on her weekend adventure with us. We really had heard from God, and all we had to do was step out and risk a little. He did the rest. All that angst for nothing!

I know we will have to get a new set of combination locks out at Camp 33 now since this story is written in a book for all to see, but I think it was worth it, don't you? Glory to God! He is so good!

In a Maui hotel in 2016, enjoying an all-expense paid vacation that was a gift from my husband's brother and sister-in-law, I got to talking with an elderly woman who had a vendor booth in the lobby. She was selling beautiful handmade jewelry and paintings. I soon found out that she was a follower of Jesus. Her name was Yonhee, and she was a Hawaiian native who had been a missionary in Cambodia. I was riveted by her story. Then she wanted to hear mine.

Before I was finished, she was overcome with emotion. I knew the Holy Spirit was right there with us. She asked if she could pray over me. I don't remember everything she said as she poured out requests to God on my behalf, but I do remember these two sentences. With the beautiful accent of the Islands, she spoke prophetic words over me, asking God to make her words come to fruition in my life: "Fearless woman she shall be; fearless journey she shall walk." She slipped a pearl ring on my finger that I'd been admiring. It was a gift I will treasure forever. The next day, I saw her again in the lobby, and she blessed me with a little painting that sits in my bedroom. A reminder of the words she spoke over me.

Months later, I decided to look up the meaning of her name. Yonhee means "gift of God." And He winked at me again.

Living smack dab in the center of God's will isn't always a walk in the park. Sometimes it does feel like a walk in the park. Central Park. In the middle of the night. Alone. During those times, you will be tempted to worry. Yes, you may go through times when you don't hear from God, but when you do, you won't be able to deny it was Him and those moments will stay with you for the times when you need it most.

When God seems silent, seek Him in Scripture. He is never silent there. His words are timeless and forever relevant. They will quench your thirst in any season. Try these words, for instance. What do they do for you?

> *Where can I go from your Spirit? Where can I flee from your presence? If I go up to the heavens, you are there; if I make my bed in the depths, you are there. If I rise on the wings of the dawn, if I settle on the far side of the sea, even there your hand will guide me, your right hand will hold me fast.*
> Psalm 139:7-10 (NIV)

Don't bow to worry! You can be a fearless child of God on a fearless journey. God's got your back.

PERSONAL REFLECTION AND GROUP DISCUSSION

- What fears do you have about obeying God?
- Do you think the one who shared the gospel with you had any fear about doing that?
- Have you ever experienced God's perfect love casting out your fear?
- What are your most consistent worries?
- How can you be free from them?
- How can the lack of worry in our lives be a good witness?
- Suggested verses to memorize: Psalm 139:7-10

CHAPTER 10

LOOK AT TRIALS AS OPPORTUNITIES

*Count it all joy, my brothers, when you meet
trials of various kinds, for you know that the
testing of your faith produces steadfastness.
And let steadfastness have its full effect, that
you may be perfect and complete, lacking in
nothing.*
James 1:2-4 (ESV)

Why in the world would James start out his famous letter by telling us to consider it pure joy when we face trials? Because every single trial in our life is an opportunity to bring glory to God as well as a chance to learn to be more like Him. Great fishers of men understand this.

We all go through various trials. Since what seems to be a trial to one person may not be considered a trial to another, I'm just going to cut to the chase here and go straight to the trial of death. I know a lot of people who aren't afraid to die, but I don't know anyone who looks forward to the process. Unless the

Lord returns first, death is the one trial that we all will face sooner or later. But even as we go through the final trial of death, we can bring glory to God.

I love the example Shadrach, Meshach, and Abednego set for us in Daniel 3. When faced with the trial of death by fire in a furnace, their attitudes were like, "Our God is able to deliver us from this, but if He chooses not to, we will still follow Him anyway!" We need to dare to be like these young men when facing all the trials of our lives.

As I was in the middle of writing this section, I took a break to return a phone call and ended up leading a twenty-one-year-old raver to the Lord. As he shared his story with me, I could see clearly how God had allowed a series of circumstances in his life to bring him to the place where he was ready to surrender to Jesus.

At the beginning of our conversation, he asked if I could explain to him why his grandmother, who was in intense pain and who the doctors said would be dead in about a week from cancer, didn't seem to be afraid. He would visit her, and she would just be praying, obviously in pain, but without any fear.

I answered his question and a few others. Then he said he wanted to have a relationship with Jesus, and I led him in prayer. He repented of his sin, told God that he believed in Him, and accepted His free gift of salvation. And just like that, as his grandmother was about to enter eternal life, Nate received the gift of eternal life. Because at her death bed, his grandmother was glorifying God by her faith and trust in Him. And it was evident to her grandson. And he wanted what she had. Whew! What an awesome writing break that was!

I've experienced a lot of death in my lifetime, and in each case I have come away from the experience with a little more understanding of God and His great love for us. One death that has affected me deeply was someone I never personally knew. The account of his death is found in the book of Acts.

Accused of blasphemy, Stephen made a long speech denouncing the Jewish authorities at his trial. He knew that this would lead to death. But as he spoke before them, he was filled with the Holy Spirit, who gave him wisdom and courage. Stephen stood there, on trial, and detailed the history of the Jews from Abraham through the prophets, concluding that the Jewish leaders had murdered the prophesied Messiah, Jesus of Nazareth. Sure enough, they stoned Stephen to death.

The faith and trust in God that Stephen showed near death as he preached the good news of the gospel brought glory to God and has affected people like me for centuries! Stephen's death was witnessed by Saul of Tarsus, a Pharisee, who later became a follower of Jesus and was renamed Paul. He wrote a huge chunk of the New Testament! Even in death, Stephen was used by God as an encouragement and instrument to bring others to salvation.

God has used Stephen's death in my life. Remembering his story has encouraged me to be brave. It has given me courage to proclaim the gospel in times when I needed it most. We've heard throughout Scripture that Jesus sits at the right hand of God, right? But what happened as Stephen finishes his speech, right before he is dragged out to be stoned to death?

> But Stephen, full of the Holy Spirit, gazed
> steadily into heaven and saw the glory of
> God, and he saw Jesus standing in the place
> of honor at God's right hand. And he told
> them, "Look, I see the heavens opened and
> the Son of Man standing in the place of
> honor at God's right hand!"
> Acts 7:55-56 (NLT)

Jesus is STANDING! Now I don't have a death wish, but can you imagine pleasing Jesus with your life and death so much that He stands as you die? Oh, how I want to please Jesus like my brother Stephen did! Even in our death, we can glorify God by being an example of one who trusts in Him to the end.

How beautifully Stephen ends his life:

> As they stoned him, Stephen prayed, "Lord
> Jesus, receive my spirit." He fell to his knees,
> shouting, "Lord, don't charge them with this
> sin!" And with that, he died.
> Acts 7:59-60 (NLT)

Stephen proclaimed his belief. He trusted in Jesus with his last words, and in the same breath, his words also gave evidence of his love for others. Perhaps this is why Jesus stood. In Stephen's last seconds on earth he was obeying the greatest two commandments. He was loving God and loving others.

Yes, great fishers of men look at trials as opportunities to glorify God by being a good witness for Him, even in death, because we really aren't afraid of trials. My favorite verse on death in the Bible is in Luke. It's the story of a widow who lived in a village called Nain. Her son had died. Jesus arrived during the burial ceremony. He sees this woman who has no husband, and now has no son. When He sees her, His heart is just over-flowing with compassion. He says, "Don't cry!" and He walks over to the coffin and raises the boy from the dead. My favorite part is:

> Then the dead boy sat up and began to talk! And
> Jesus gave him back to his mother.
> Luke 7:15 (NLT)

Jesus gave him back! God had that boy! God has us when we die! We don't have to fear trials, even the final trial of death, because God's got us!

One final thought. The biblical king of trials, Job, gives us such an important lesson in the last chapter of the Old Testament book named after him. It is his response to God at the end of all the trials he had been through. If nothing else proves to you that trials can benefit us and are something we should embrace, let this convince you:

> *Then Job replied to the Lord:*
> *"I know that you can do anything, and no one*
> *can stop you.*
> *You asked, 'Who is this that questions my*
> *wisdom with such ignorance?'*
> *It is I—and I was talking about things I knew*
> *nothing about, things far too wonderful*
> *for me.*
> *You said, 'Listen and I will speak! I have some*
> *questions for you, and you must answer*
> *them.'*
> *I had only heard you before, but now I have seen*
> *you with my own eyes. I take back*
> *everything I said, and I sit in dust and ashes*
> *to show my repentance."*
> *Job 42:1-6 (NLT)*

Trials can take us from a place of knowing about God to knowing God and seeing Him firsthand. If that's what trials can do for us, then bring them on, because there is nothing more important than knowing God and being able to make Him known!

PERSONAL REFLECTION AND GROUP DISCUSSION

- What would it look like if we adopted the attitude of Shadrach, Meshach, and Abednego in our daily lives, especially in our day-to-day trials?
- Stephen knew what he believed and was able to defend his beliefs. Are you prepared to speak with people who make verbal attacks on your faith, even if it means you might face ridicule?
- What are some ways you can prepare for these conversations?
- How important is it to love your enemies, those who instigate trials in your life, like Stephen did?
- How does it change us when we realize we don't have to fear trials, even death?
- Share with the group about a time when God turned a trial you were going through into an opportunity to share His love with someone else.
- Suggested verses to memorize: James 1:2-4

CHAPTER 11

GET THROUGH IT, BECAUSE JESUS SAYS THEY'RE WORTH IT

PRAY TO GET THROUGH IT, NOT TO GET OUT OF IT

L et's look at what was happening in Acts 4. The religious leaders were having a fit because Peter and John were preaching the gospel. They had led over 5,000 people to salvation. The gospel was false teaching according to the priests. They were super worried because Peter and John had also healed a well-known crippled man. That had really attracted the attention of the people in town.

So, the religious leaders threw Peter and John in jail for the night, then brought them out the next morning to explain themselves. Once again, Peter and John shared the gospel, saying that there was salvation in no one other than Jesus.

The religious leaders were infuriated. But they had an even bigger problem. The lame man Peter and John had healed was standing right there in the crowd for all the people to see. To make matters worse, Peter and John were saying that it wasn't really them who had healed the man. They were giving credit for the healing to the risen Jesus!

After some discussion, the leaders told Peter and John that they would be released from jail but that they could never again speak or teach in the name of Jesus. Peter and John defied their authority, claiming that the leaders had no right to stop them from speaking and teaching. They stated that the only authority over them in this matter was God Himself. The leaders continued to threaten them but, in the end, they felt they had to release them. The people were so enamored with Peter and John that the leaders worried if they kept them in jail a riot would break out!

As soon as they were free, Peter and John hosted a prayer meeting with their fellow believers. Here is what they prayed:

> *And now, O Lord, hear their threats, and give*
> *us, your servants, great boldness in*
> *preaching your word. Stretch out your hand*
> *with healing power; may miraculous signs*
> *and wonders be done through the name of*
> *your holy servant Jesus.*
> *Acts 4:29-30 (NLT)*

They didn't pray to get out of the situation, they prayed for boldness to go through it! As soon as they were finished praying these words, their meeting place shook, and they were all filled with the Holy Spirit. Even though they knew it would be dangerous, God had answered their prayers with a "yes!" They continued to preach the good news of the gospel with boldness.

When it comes to sharing the gospel, we must always pray to get through it, not to get out of it. He will give us the courage we need to share the gospel with that barista at the coffee bar, or the boldness we need to share the gospel with that gang that hangs out in the back alley. Because when we are telling others about Jesus, we are living smack dab in the center of God's will. Never ever pray for a way out of doing that!

> But you should keep a clear mind in every
> situation. Don't be afraid of suffering for the
> Lord. Work at telling others the Good News,
> and fully carry out the ministry God has
> given you.
> 2 Timothy 4:5 (NLT)

CALL THEM BY NEW NAMES

Jesus had the ability to speak life into people. He communicated their great value and worth to them. He sometimes did this by giving them a new name. Because the archenemy of Jesus is also the enemy of our souls, he likes to counterfeit everything that Jesus does. So he likes to give us names too. While Jesus calls us valuable and precious and created with purpose, Satan calls us worthless, good for nothing, the product of a cosmic accident.

We visited John 4 in Chapter 7: Get the order right. But let's go back and focus on a different part of the story. The part where Jesus calls the woman at the well a name; a nice name. People must've called this woman lots of names. They probably used many adjectives to describe her, but none of them were nice.

Here's a quick summary: Jesus is on a trip from Judea to Galilee. He stops in Samaria on the way and finds a well where he can rest because He is worn out from the walk. Along comes a local woman with a rope and a bucket to get some water out of the well. Jesus asks her to give Him a drink. She's surprised because she can tell He's Jewish. His type never mixes with her type. Jews had choice names for Samaritans, all of them derogatory.

Turns out, this woman was not only from the wrong side of the tracks as far as Jews were concerned, but also even within her own community. That's why she was at the well to draw her water in the middle of the day after the rest of the women in the community had already been there. She came alone because her sexual sins made her an outcast. Apparently, she knew a lot of the men in the community, in the biblical sense.

Yet, even though the Son of God knew all of that, Jesus addresses her as, "Dear woman." He calls her *dear*! She is precious and valuable. The rest of the community calls her disgusting and worthless. Not Jesus. Read further on and we see that His kindness and His ability to speak the truth in love led this woman, and most of her village, to repentance. Here's the golden nugget from this story:

When we show Christ-like kindness to the world, speaking the truth in love, it also encourages them toward repentance.

People are aching for purpose and value. When we call that out in them and give them names that communicate the worth that God sees in them, they change. And folks, if we don't step up and start being like Jesus, the enemy is very happy to step in and give them choice names instead.

I saw this played out so clearly one night at the rave club we frequented shortly after the ministry started. We had the bracelets God had shown us to make; similar to what the ravers make and trade with each other at raves as a sign of PLUR. Rave mom Nicki and I were walking along the edges of the dance floor in that little club, looking for kids in trouble. We found a young girl, head slumped over, and decided to check on her.

When Nicki touched her, she became alert. Nicki gave her one of our bracelets and, according to tradition, the girl wanted to give her one in return. She slipped a bracelet from her wrist and onto Nicki's. The exchange was complete. We breathed a silent prayer over the girl and moved along to check on more kids. Later that night, on our way home, I asked if the bracelet the girl had given Nicki said anything on it. Nicki pulled up her sleeve to look at the bracelet and gasped. Spelled out in alphabet beads were the words *Whore Bag*.

This became such a picture to us of what God wanted to do through our ministry. He would use our teams to give this generation a new name. The good news of the gospel was accessible through the website spelled out in beads on the bracelet that was now on that girl's wrist, instead of the name the enemy had given her. It was a sweet promise that night in the club, given to us by the God who had already been there and prepared the way for us. He would use this ministry to bring good news to these kids. New names like precious, valuable, and worth dying for, would replace names like worthless and loser. Just as we saw in John 4, *Outcast*, and probably *Whore Bag*, was renamed *Dear*.

There is power in the name of Jesus. There is power in the names He gives. May we always pray for the opportunity to share these names boldly with those He loves so dearly. Because Jesus says they're worth it.

PERSONAL REFLECTION AND GROUP DISCUSSION

- Do you pray for opportunities to share Jesus, even

though that may require courage? What has been the result?

- Share a time when it took courage to share the gospel.
- Take time to pray over each person in your group for opportunities and courage.
- Are there some hard people in your life who you should call "dear" even though they are very different than you?
- What are the names the enemy has tried to give you over your lifetime?
- What are your new names in Christ?
- Suggested verse to memorize: 2 Timothy 4:5

CHAPTER 12

STAY LONG ENOUGH AND NEVER GIVE UP

J ust for fun, let's look once more at John 4. There are so many nuggets to mine from this story! Ponder this for a moment:

> *Many Samaritans from the village believed in Jesus because the woman had said, "He told me everything I ever did!" When they came out to see him, they begged him to stay in their village. So he stayed for two days, long enough for many more to hear his message and believe.*
> John 4:39-41 (NLT)

This is what happened after the woman at the well met Jesus. He was on a road trip with His disciples necessitated by some unpleasant circumstances. His disciples were not planning on staying in this Samaritan town where Jesus encountered the woman as He sat exhausted by the community's well. But Jesus changed their plans. And so, they stayed.

How long did they stay? Long enough. Long enough for the people to hear the gospel and be changed by the Savior.

If we only work within the program, all the while checking our watches to be sure we stay on schedule, we won't stay long enough. We must be led by the Spirit as we do His work. For too long people relied on certain methods to share their faith or certain tracts to get their message out. Sharing your faith doesn't depend on certain robotic words or printed materials. It's about sharing what God has done for you and how He has changed your life. Jesus changed the life of the woman at the well. She ran and told everyone about it. Their lives changed as this changed woman introduced them to her Savior.

When Vacation Bible School is over, when the Harvest Crusade has left the stadium, do you stay? Some people need longer than a weekend to hear the message of the gospel and believe it.

Jesus didn't say, "Well, we planned to be here for just a couple hours, now it's time to go!" If He had, a whole town would've missed out on the good news. Just because the church service is finished by noon doesn't mean that's when you skedaddle. You leave when Jesus says you are done. We must learn to stay long enough, even when the program is over.

> *So let's not get tired of doing what is good. At*
> *just the right time we will reap a harvest of*
> *blessing if we don't give up.*
> *Galatians 6:9 (NLT)*

We have learned this firsthand on our rave outreaches. Some of the best opportunities have come when we were tired and thought we were finished. We'd handed out all our bracelets, we'd packed up our campsite in the rave campground. We were spent. We were done. And then a few more ravers came by, and we stayed. Convenience and staying within certain time frames are not prerequisites to sharing the gospel. Often, opportunities to share come at the most inopportune times! Staying is the last thing on our minds! I wonder who's behind that scheme?

One night outside of a rave venue, our team met to discuss leaving. We were a small team that night, just two moms and two dads. My neck was out to the point that I was nauseated. The streets were quiet. It seemed all the kids were inside the party. We'd handed out a lot of bracelets. It was okay to go.

We packed up. As we took one final drive around the venue, we prayed and asked God to show us if it was really okay to leave. Just then, a boy crumpled over and fell off the curb into the street in front of us. We knew God's answer was "Stay!"

I cringed inside as Amy and I jumped out to help the boy. Seriously? I was so close to getting home to my bed, my pain killer, and my heating pad. But what God did that night after we asked Him for permission to go or stay was incredible!

The boy was young and fragile and gay. He wore makeup and a wreath of silk flowers around his head. He had taken way too much of something and could barely walk. He wanted to get back to his hotel. We offered to drive him, but he glanced fearfully through the dark at the car and saw the silhouettes of our two rave dads in the front seat. Seeing his concern, we cancelled that plan and told him we would walk him. My heart sunk when I found out the hotel was over a mile away. With one arm across my neck and the other arm across Amy's, we half-carried, half-walked Christian back to his hotel room.

On the way we heard his whole life story. He had grown up in a strict Jehovah's Witness home. He had never been able to celebrate a single birthday as a child. As tears mixed with mascara ran down his face, he shared that some friends in junior high school snuck a cake to him during lunch in the cafeteria. That was the first time anyone had ever celebrated him.

He had no relationship with his mom. She had shunned him. He missed her so much. As he talked about this, he hugged us moms a bit tighter. I winced as he pulled on my neck. I could tell he was starving for a mom hug. "I haven't had a mom in a long time, but, tonight," he said, "I have two moms!"

We were able to share the gospel with Christian. He listened intently to every word. It was all so shocking to him. He had never heard about love like this before.

I could almost hear the "Hallelujah Chorus" when we turned into the dumpy hotel driveway. But then the music that played in my head came to an abrupt halt when Christian pointed to his room at the top of the cracking cement stairway. Up we went, each painstaking step at a time, careful not to let Christian's unsteady feet slip through the spaces between each one.

Halfway up, I asked him to show me his hotel key. I spotted the room number 223 on it. Instead, Christian stumbled to room 222. I told him he had the wrong room, but he insisted he had it right. His shoulder knocked into the door as he messed with the key. The door flew open. A very large, sweaty, red-faced drunk man wearing a tattered and stained tank top stared at us around the fat cigar sticking out of his mouth. I stammered, "So sorry, sir, we must have the wrong room!" Pulling the cigar loose he barked, "Well if you don't want him, I'll take him in here!" Then he grinned in a wide, nasty smile.

We quickly moved Christian down to the correct room. The man said, "Oh well!" as he shut his door. We prayed over Christian and made sure he had everything he needed. He said his friends would be coming back soon. He gladly promised to lock himself safely inside until they got there.

What would have happened to Christian if we had not

stayed long enough? Only God knows what Christian was saved from that night. But I am so glad we stayed. I slept very, very well that night! Knowing how long to stay is such an important part of ministry. Never leave until God tells you it's time to go.

Shirley lives in Miami and, at seventy-five, she is our oldest rave mom to date. Over the years, she has learned to discern God's voice. She walks closely with Him. I have learned a lot from this tiny-but-mighty woman. One night outside a rave in her hometown, she came across a desperate boy. She listened to his story. Then she just held him as he cried. And she held him. And she held him. She told me later that she held him until the Holy Spirit said, "He can hear you now." Shirley shared the gospel, and the young man was saved. Shirley knows how to fish for men, and she knows that fishing involves a whole lot of staying and a whole lot of waiting.

Samantha clutched her chest in apparent agony as she sat on the ground rocking back and forth on the sidewalk outside of the rave venue. Her boyfriend stood nearby, feeling helpless. Some of us rave moms gathered near her. I used my training in grounding techniques to help her through her panic attack until the paramedics arrived.

They took her right away by ambulance to a nearby trauma center. As they loaded her on the ambulance, she reached out for me. The medics couldn't allow me to ride with her, but they told me where they were taking her so I could meet them there. I took rave dad Jeff with me so that he could stay with the boyfriend in the waiting room.

Samantha nestled into my arms with Jeff's jacket wrapped around her like a blanket. For the next eight hours, I held her through IVs and tests and lots of questions. She slept most of the time. Between naps, she shared some of her story, still cuddled up close to me. As far as parents go, this twenty-year-old had lost big time. That explained the apparent craving for a mom.

As the night progressed, she began to be aware that this was taking a lot of my time. Finally, she sat up and offered to let me go home. She thanked me for showing such love to her and told me that she'd be fine waiting for the doctor's report with her boyfriend.

Oh, how tempting that was! My bed was calling me. By that time, we had been on the rave outreach for almost twenty hours. But then the Lord reminded me of all the times Samantha had been left in her lifetime. I turned to her and said, "Enough people have left you. I'm not going to be one of them." She snuggled back in and fell asleep.

What a privilege it was to *stay* that night.

Back to the woman at the well. What an amazing ministry opportunity that was for Jesus to minister to that woman! But how did Jesus happen to get there, to that town, to that well? Jesus and His disciples had to leave Judea and return to Galilee because of some unpleasant circumstances.

God can use our unpleasant, inconvenient circumstances and sudden change of plans to provide amazing ministry opportunities.

Why was Jesus at that well? Because He was exhausted and thirsty.

God can use our human weaknesses and vulnerability to provide amazing ministry opportunities.

What happened when the woman ran back to tell her community about Jesus? Many believed.

God can use our stories and our messes to provide amazing ministry opportunities.

Life is inconvenient and unpredictable, but don't try to

wriggle out of all this stuff too quickly. Stay long enough to let good come from all the mayhem. You never know, a whole town could get saved because of it!

KNOW IT'S NEVER OVER UNTIL IT'S REALLY OVER

One of the beautiful lessons we can learn from the story of the thief next to Jesus on the cross is that it's never too late to share the gospel.

> One of the criminals hanging beside Him
> scoffed, "So you're the Messiah, are you?
> Prove it by saving yourself—and us, too,
> while you're at it!" But the other criminal
> protested, "Don't you fear God even when
> you have been sentenced to die? We deserve
> to die for our crimes, but this man hasn't
> done anything wrong." Then he said, "Jesus,
> remember me when you come into your
> Kingdom." And Jesus replied, "I assure you,
> today you will be with me in paradise."
> Luke 23:39-43 (NLT)

Here was this thief, circling the drain, and minutes before death he receives salvation from his sins. Never give up, even if it seems like it's too late.

Near the exit to a rave venue one night, a young man was high and belligerent. He kept running into the crowds, trying to pick fights. He had the appearance of a gang member.

He said the wrong thing to one too many people. Someone finally threw a punch. My back was turned as I was talking with a young lady and her boyfriend. I heard a crack as the boy's jaw broke, then a horrible thud as his head hit the pavement, cracking his skull. I rushed to him and got down on the ground next to him, trying to avoid the blood gushing out of his mouth.

My rave-mom partner that night was Jeanette. She was a paramedic. That wasn't a coincidence! She knelt with us and felt for his pulse and other vital signs. She said it didn't look good. This was a serious head injury.

Bottles and other trash rained down around the three of us. This boy had ticked off a lot of people. They appeared to be glad that someone had finally shut him up. One glass bottle landed too close and rolled into me. I'd had enough.

Usually, we don't pray loudly at raves. But this was different. I found out later that two rave dads had stepped out of the RV that was parked nearby to see what all the commotion was about. They saw me stand and raise my arms as I commanded the spirits of anger and death to leave in the name of Jesus. I knelt right back down to pray over the boy, but the dads told me later that it was as if a team of angels calmed the crowd and pushed them back. Bottles and cans were set down instead of thrown. The crowd dispersed.

As I prayed over the silent young man, God told me to share the gospel with him. I looked at his limp body and felt like it was too late. I was sure he was dying. But God was very clear about what He wanted me to do. So, I spoke to the boy and shared the gospel. Then I told him if he wanted to be with Jesus when he died, he could pray after me. I led him in prayer, even waiting for him to repeat my words. It felt awkward to be conversing with a completely unconscious person, but I did it anyway.

The paramedics arrived, and Jeannette quickly gave them a rundown. They loaded him onto a gurney. His head rolled to the side. One of his arms slid and fell off the edge of the pallet, dangling down. It was so hard to watch. Just as they were lifting him in, the bottom of the gurney caught on the bottom edge of the ambulance doorway and jerked his body. His eyes popped opened, and he recited the sinner's prayer! He had heard every word I said, and he'd been praying with me!

Always, when God gives you the opportunity, share the gospel. Even when you think someone has already made their final decision. Do you think they hate God, or they're too far gone to ever come back? Share the gospel with them anyway!

It's never over until it's over. And sometimes, even when it looks like it's over, it's not. Never give up. God doesn't.

PERSONAL REFLECTION AND GROUP DISCUSSION

- Is there anyone in your life who needs you to stay a little longer?
- Who has stayed with you?
- How does the story of the thief on the cross speak to your heart?
- Have you ever known of a deathbed conversion? What does that tell us about the grace of God?
- Suggested verse to memorize: Galatians 6:9

CHAPTER 13

DON'T UNDERESTIMATE YOUR ENEMY

Now I don't want to take the analogy of a fisherman too far. All great analogies must at some point, come to an end. But as I was just beginning to read *Fly Fishing Made Easy* by Michael Rutter and Dave Card, I saw in the preface a photo of a smiling fisherman holding a rather large trout. The caption said, "No matter how long you've been fishing, you'll always feel a quiver when a fine fish takes your fly and you do battle."

Every single time I have ever shared the gospel with a kid at a rave, I have felt the quiver—the quiver of both excitement and of battle. It's as if a war is being waged over us. The Bible confirms this. First Peter 5:8 says that the enemy is roaring about seeking whom he can kill and destroy. Ephesians 6 tells us that there is a battle that is spiritual all around us. We must be prepared for it.

Always be prepared for battle when you are sharing the gospel. Know that when you get into a conversation where you will share the truth about God's love, you will be in a battle... an intense battle, whether you feel it or not.

Satan's minions won't show up if there's nothing to stop, but if there's something to stop, they will.

And the battle won't stop there. Evangelism should flow naturally into discipleship. The battle will flow right along with it. When the fish bite, a battle begins that never stops. We all know that!

One of the best ways to win a war is to understand the strategies of your enemy so that you can predict, prevent, or counter his attacks. Our teams are constantly in the war room, learning the strategies of our enemy. Here are a few I'd like to share with you.

We've seen a lot of satanic things on rave outreaches, but the worst I can remember is what happened to Ashley outside a rave club in downtown San Bernardino, California. It was her birthday. Her friends had talked her into going to a rave for the first time. They said it would be fun. Her friend Lauren had gone before and showed Ashley how to dress in typical rave wear. She also made sure they had some popular club drugs to try that night.

When two of us rave moms came upon Ashley in a dark parking lot, she was writhing on the ground, overdosing on something, wearing only a bra, a thong, and a tutu. She was viciously ripping her own fishnet stockings. She screamed, "I'm a good girl! I don't wear stuff like this!" Then she passed out.

We quickly found out that no one had called 911. Lauren begged us not to. She was afraid they would get in trouble. We assured her that Ashley's life was more important now. We signaled two rave dads, who stood across the driveway, to make the call.

As is common during overdose on some of these drugs, Ashley jolted awake. Her violent, self-harming behavior continued. She clawed at her legs. Rave mom Dana and I tried hard to restrain her as her scratches began to bleed. She fought against us yelling, "I need to bleed! I need to die! I'm a good girl. I don't do stuff like this!" And then she passed out again.

We realized that we had been given a front-row seat to watch the enemy's attack on this girl. It was devastating. Up and down she went. Dana and I locked eyes and prayed and prayed over her. We spoke words of life and hope in the name of Jesus.

We were almost relieved when she would pass out, because when she was awake she would only argue with us that she wasn't valuable enough to receive our help. She kept telling us to go home to our own kids and let her die.

When she screamed, "I need to pay!" I knew we were dealing with lies from the pit of hell. Satan was trying to negate everything that Jesus had done for Ashley on the cross. We told her the good news. Her sins were paid in full. All she had to do was believe. She stared at us. We counteracted everything she said with Scripture as the great deceiver continued to mess with her.

Unfortunately, our teams see this kind of thing repeatedly played out. The Greek word for witchcraft, or sorcery, found in the New Testament is *pharmakeia*. Do you see the word *pharmacy* in there? Drugs and demons can be partners. In my opinion, based on what I've seen as an addictions treatment counselor, there are drugs that can be very helpful when administered by a doctor, someone to whom God has given special talents and gifts, who understands how to prescribe drugs wisely.

However, drugs taken for "fun" or to try to fill that God-shaped hole in our hearts—to take the place of Jesus in our life

—can and will be used against us by the enemy of our souls. At the beginning of 1 Peter 5:8, the Bible tells us to stay alert, remain sober, because the enemy of our souls is seeking to destroy us. Ashley was most definitely not sober. The enemy was trying to destroy her. The drugs she took gave him an opportunity to mess with her. When she popped those pills, she propped a door open for him.

The strategy Satan used with Ashley is a common one. He tempted her to do something she normally wouldn't do. He got her to think it would be fun. He also used peer pressure. Ashley ended up dressing like everyone else and taking drugs like everyone else. Once he got her where he wanted her, on the ground, he swooped in and began to condemn her for what she had done. He's sick and twisted like that. Then he tried to negate the work of Christ on the cross. He hates the gospel. He wants to make us think that we must bleed and die for our own sins.

Another strategy he frequently uses is to convince us that we are not sinners; even that there is no such thing as sin. That people are naturally good. Why does he do this? Because if you're not a sinner, you don't need a savior.

Two of our rave moms happened to be standing behind a stage with a perfect view of the DJ and about 10,000 young adults on the dance floor in front of him. Once again, God was giving us a front-row seat to watch the enemy's strategy against this generation. Suddenly, the DJ stopped the music. He asked all the kids to move forward toward the stage. They obeyed him. Next, he told them to get down on their knees. When everyone was down, he said, "Repeat after me: I am not a sinner. I am not a sinner. I am not a sinner." The chant continued, climaxing into a sort of satanic worship service as the kids jumped up and danced to the lie.

We have seen that Satan is also a copycat. He takes what

God does and tweaks it in order to deceive us and draw us away from God. It was almost comical to watch what that stinkin' snake did at one rave in Austin, Texas. Our team was camping with the ravers in the campground. On our first day there, we strung some twine around the inside of our canopy to make a prayer wall. We invited ravers who visited our site to write down their prayer requests on three-by-five cards and hang them with wooden clothespins on the twine. This instigated many amazing conversations!

That first afternoon, just before the actual rave started, the promoter's film crew came by our campsite packed with kids. They stood at the edge, silently filming what was going on. We didn't think too much of it, we've been filmed lots of times as we minister inside rave campgrounds. When the rave started, a couple of us moms went inside to check out the venue and minister to the ravers. We walked the entire grounds, getting a lay of the land.

The next day, we attended the rave again. As we approached the center of the festival grounds, we were stunned to see that the giant oak tree we had noticed the day before was now wrapped in twine. A sign instructed ravers to take a three-by-five card and a clothespin and attach their hopes and dreams to the Tree of Life.

Wow! The Tree of Life! Sound familiar? What a counterfeit the enemy is. We must be aware of his strategies. We must use God's strategies to push back as much darkness as we can in our lifetime. This generation needs to know the truth and they need to hear it wrapped up in God's love!

One night we were headed to a rave in Houston called Something Wicked. A huge storm was wreaking havoc in the area. The managers of the racetrack where the event was to take place decided to cancel the rave. It was just too dangerous to host such a large event in that much rain.

We called an ex-raver for advice. She suggested we change course and head to a small club where she'd heard a promoter was hosting raves. So we headed downtown, knowing some of the ravers would end up there once they found out their party had been canceled.

When we arrived, we were shocked to find out that the promotion company was called Ministry Houston. They were hosting raves on Saturday nights in the lower level of this little club that sat next to the Buffalo Bayou. Their events were called Sacred Saturdays, their advertising featured a sexy nun.

As the rain poured and the streets filled, ravers kept arriving. The line stretched out the door. Kids were getting soaked. Many of them came to our ministry RV where it was parked across the street under an overhang at a bank that was closed for the weekend. Pretty soon, we had more kids with us than the club had in line! We fed them and gave them bracelets and blankets.

I will never forget one young man named Ruben. He came dressed as a nun. He was a regular at Ministry Houston's Sacred Saturday events. He realized we were Christians, and he was curious. We talked for a while. Then he asked me, "So, do you think it's weird that I'm out here on a stormy night like this to go to a rave party?"

I looked toward the bayou. The water was rising. So were the manhole covers on the streets around us. Just then, a firetruck arrived with a crew to begin evacuation of the clubs and bars on the street. It was getting dangerous.

I answered Ruben, "Yes. It seems pretty risky being out on a night like this for a party."

Then he asked me a question, "Would you go to your church in the middle of a rainstorm?"

I thought about it and responded, "Yes, I guess I would."

Ruben smiled. "Well then, you will understand. The rave is

my church, the DJ is my pastor, and the music is my god. You must understand; I was the kid that sat alone at the lunch tables at school. Every. Single. Day. I was an outcast because I'm gay. I come here because for one night, I feel totally accepted and loved by everyone here."

I said, "But Ruben, it's not real acceptance. They're all on Ecstasy, you're on Ecstasy when you are in there. It's fake."

Ruben responded, "I don't care. When you've never felt love and acceptance before, it's worth it."

The enemy is counterfeiting church. Family! Listen to me! We've got to quit trying to attract these people. They won't come. Our pizza parties won't cut it anymore. The parties the enemy is throwing are much more interesting. We must do what the Bible says and GO to where they are!

Time after time we see the enemy deceiving this generation, offering them a fake form of church. He knows we are made for relationship. We need community. The largest rave promoter in the world puts up billboards announcing their events with the slogan, "All Are Welcome Here." That should be what the church says. There is a way to welcome people without welcoming their sin. *Come and see! Come and see what Jesus can do! You will never be the same.*

But since that has not been the cry of our churches, since we have been louder about what we are against than what we are for, we have sent the fish swimming in the opposite direction. Satan has had the catch of his life.

One night at an Austin rave, two of us moms were ministering to a girl who had just lost her mom to a horrible disease. She had walked away from everything, packing her Volkswagen with only the essentials as she headed out on a cross-country trip to "find herself." A few states later, she saw a poster advertising the rave party, bought a ticket and there she was, smack dab in front of us on a hill overlooking the venue.

An event photographer stood nearby watching. After we prayed with the girl, he tapped my shoulder and asked if we could speak. He said he'd photographed a lot of events, but he'd never seen moms like us at a rave. Pleasantly surprised by how we were treating the kids, he asked why we were doing it. Since I love that question, I dove right in.

Soon, he interrupted me. He said, "Well, I don't believe in all that Jesus stuff, but since you do, I'd like to show you something. Last night, did you see the photos that were flashing on the giant screens on each side of the main stage?"

"Yes," I said. "I did notice."

Actually, I had noticed a whole lot more than that, because the night before our team had experienced something we'd never seen before at a rave: the DJ on the main stage stopped the music and brought a lady out who he introduced as a witch. Then she spoke an incantation over the crowd.

I shook off the memory and didn't mention all that to the photographer. Instead, I just said, "The photos flashing on the screens were moving really fast so it was hard to tell what the images were."

"Here, let me show you," he said, "I caught the images with my camera."

He seemed very proud as he showed me each of the still shots he had taken. There was one of Buddha, a couple of Egyptian gods, a couple of demonic looking beasts, and then he came to the one he really wanted to show me. "Look!" he said, "It's Jesus! As a Christian, aren't you glad they're including Him too?" He didn't wait for my answer.

Giddy, he stretched out his arm across the thousands of kids who were dancing at the bottom of the hill below us. "Aren't you excited?! Do you see what's happening here? IT'S THE FORMATION OF THE MODERN CHURCH!"

I honestly can't tell you what happened after that.

The church needs to wake up! An annual rave party in Miami refers to its venue as its "spiritual home." Another annual rave party in Las Vegas sets up a makeshift church building inside their venue, complete with stained glass windows where they offer real and fake "rave weddings."

The enemy is setting up fake "churches" that provide this generation a place to meet and fellowship and worship. And kids like Ruben are falling for it.

I am using the things we've seen at raves as an example. But the enemy is doing this all over the place, in all different ways, different settings. He will deceive and counterfeit wherever and whenever he can.

Now, after reading the stories I just shared, some of you may be thinking I'm giving way too much credit to the devil. He's just not that powerful. If that's you, I'd suggest you do a study on what the Bible has to say about him. God is bigger. God's people don't have to fear him. But that doesn't mean that he doesn't exist or that he doesn't have any power at all.

I once was asked to speak at a mainline denominational church. They asked me to come speak two times: once to the teens, and then the following week to the adults. The pastor's assistant sat in on my teen presentation. Afterwards, she pulled me aside to let me know that it would be a good idea to change my script before the adult presentation. She took great pains to be kind as she explained, "We don't talk about Satan here. We just like to stay positive, focus on nice things. We want people to leave feeling good."

I thought I surely must not have understood her correctly, so I asked, "Are you saying you don't want me to mention 1 Peter 5:8 when I speak?"

"Yes, she said. That is exactly what I'm saying."

Folks! What I saw there was another strategy of the enemy! Don't be deceived! Satan is real. He goes about like a lion seeking to kill and destroy. The Bible doesn't say to ignore him and pretend he doesn't exist! The Bible says,

> So humble yourselves before God. Resist the
> devil, and he will flee from you.
> James 4:7 (NLT)

In the story of Esther, we learn about her older cousin Mordecai, who had tenderly raised her as his own child. Mordecai's the one who overheard the sinister strategy of his enemy and uncovered his plot to destroy the Jews. As disciple makers, let's pray for Mordecai moments and then bust the enemy's plans.

PERSONAL REFLECTION AND GROUP DISCUSSION

- Have you seen the enemy's strategies at work against you or your loved ones? If you feel comfortable, share about that.
- How can you counteract the lies he spews with the truth found in God's word?
- Suggested verse to memorize: James 4:7

CHAPTER 14

DON'T CLEAN FISH YOU HAVEN'T CAUGHT YET, BUT URGENTLY CATCH THEM!

LEAVE THE CLEANING UP TO THE HOLY SPIRIT

I was selecting cheese in the dairy section of a grocery store when a lady with a thick southern accent came up to me. She told me she was very impressed with our teams of moms and grandmas who minister at raves. But she went on to explain that she herself would never be able to join us because, she said, "I'd be too disturbed by how those kids act and dress. I'd have to tell them to put more clothes on before I could talk to them."

As they say in the South, "Bless her heart!" But bless my heart too! Because I had been just like her! Since I was focused on my outside appearance, aiming to look like the great Christian I thought I was, the outward appearance is what I focused on in everyone else as well. I was missing Jesus. I'm so grateful to be a recovering judgmental church lady. I still struggle with judgement, but I know God is working on me and glory, hallelujah, He's not finished with me yet!

My favorite story in the whole Bible is one of the parables

that Jesus used to describe His Father. Pay attention closely, because His Father is our Father as well. Check out the story of the prodigal son found in Luke 15. Jesus told this parable in response to the Pharisees' complaint that Jesus hung out with sinners, even having dinner with them. Gasp!

Jesus describes a father and his youngest son. The son broke the father's heart by asking for his inheritance early and running off to party it all away. About the time the kid ran through all the money, a famine breaks out and he about starves to death. He persuades a farmer to hire him to feed the pigs. Soon, even the slop he's feeding the pigs looks good because he's so hungry! The kid starts longing for home. He realizes that even his dad's servants live better than this! The boy comes up with a plan. He will go home and admit that he's no longer worthy of being called a son. He'll ask his dad to take him on as a servant.

So, the kid heads home. While he's still a long way off, his father spots him coming down the road. The father runs to the boy who must've smelled like pigs and throws his arms around him, slop and all! He holds him and kisses his dirty, stinky face.

Notice that the father didn't stand back and give his son a quick air hug and then make him run off to take a bath before touching him! Because that's not our God.

Instead of treating him like the servant the son had hoped to become, the father treats him like a prince coming home from some amazing trip. The dad orders up a huge barbecue, and then comes my favorite line in the whole story:

> *So the party began.*
> *Luke 15:24b (NLT)*

Can you imagine what that kid must've felt like? He leaves to go party and finds out that the world's party isn't all it was cracked up to be. Then he comes home and discovers the real party was there all along.

Oh, how great and loving our Father God is! That while we were yet sinners, He died for us!

We need to fish for men and not worry about cleaning them until after they're caught. We can do our part to encourage them, but ultimately, cleaning them up will be the Holy Spirit's job. It's called sanctification. That happens after the moment of salvation: Justification by faith. Remember the woman caught in adultery? The "go and sin no more" part came after an encounter with Jesus.

I love this simple verse found in Hebrews that clearly explains justification and sanctification. Justification is what happens immediately when we accept the death of Christ on the cross for the remission of our sins. We are made perfect in God's eyes. Sanctification is what happens after that moment for the rest of our earthy lifetime. We are being made holy.

For by that one offering he forever made perfect
those who are being made holy.
Hebrews 10:14 (NLT)

An attempt to shortcut this holy process by trying to clean fish we haven't caught yet will send the fish swimming in the wrong direction. Because that's a work of man, not of God. I shudder when a kid at a rave apologizes to me for using bad language, as if my ears are holy. He's trying to make himself look good in front of me, even though he's not, so that I will accept him. It's an indication of what he's trying to do with God.

I assure nonbelievers that I can handle whatever adjectives they feel they need to use to communicate with me. Inviting them to be authentic around me enables real conversation.

Then, and only then, can we really talk about the One who died for them while they were yet sinners.

Think about this for a minute. As Christians, if we lead someone to believe that they can be "good" by not using foul language around us, wearing appropriate clothing, and doing all the outward stuff that pleases us, we are leading them into the false belief that they can be good enough for God by just adjusting a few outward things. Take them as is, like He does. Love them right here, right now, like He does, and they will see the real Jesus.

Early one New Year's morning, I sat on a curb outside of a rave venue with a precious girl named Dee. She'd had a pretty bad night, and she wanted to talk about it. As she shared, I realized she'd had a pretty bad life. Jesus came up in our conversation. The Holy Spirit gave her the faith to believe what I was telling her, and she ended up praying for salvation.

After she prayed, she started laughing. Tears of joy left her eyes and ran down her face. She felt the presence of the Holy Spirit. She was almost giddy. She said, "That's it? I'm free? Oh, my God! I'm free!" Then this recovering judgmental church lady had to hide my dismay when she shouted, "Jesus is fu***** awesome!"

Then I remembered the story of the prodigal son. Dee hadn't taken a bath yet. She had come all dirty and stinky to the foot of the cross, and Jesus had met her there, as is. He would begin the process of cleaning her up. Bless my heart! I shut my mouth and nodded my head in agreement. Jesus IS awesome!

BE URGENT

Back to the story of the prodigal son. Pretty sure it's the only time we see God in a rush, and it's for sure the only time we see God running in Scripture. You want to see God move? Go after the lost! You're smack dab in the center of God's will when you are running with Him!

> "For it is my Father's will that all who see his
> Son and believe in him should have eternal
> life. I will raise them up at the last day."
> John 6:40 (NLT)

There is nothing more urgent or important to God than the lost. So, there should be nothing more urgent or important to us.

Read this passage. Look for the urgency in Paul's appeal:

> But let me say this, dear brothers and sisters: The
> time that remains is very short. So from now
> on, those with wives should not focus only
> on their marriage. Those who weep or who
> rejoice or who buy things should not be
> absorbed by their weeping or their joy or
> their possessions. Those who use the things
> of the world should not become attached to
> them. For this world as we know it will soon
> pass away. I want you to be free from the
> concerns of this life. An unmarried man can
> spend his time doing the Lord's work and
> thinking how to please Him. But a married
> man has to think about his earthly
> responsibilities and how to please his wife.
> His interests are divided. In the same way, a
> woman who is no longer married or has
> never been married can be devoted to the
> Lord and holy in body and spirit. But a
> married woman has to think about her

> *earthly responsibilities and how to please*
> *her husband. I am saying this for your*
> *benefit, not to place restrictions on you. I*
> *want you to do whatever will help you serve*
> *the Lord best, with as few distractions as*
> *possible.*
> 1 Corinthians 7:29-35 (NLT)

It sounds to me like fulfilling the Great Commission is urgent and should take priority in our lives.

Do you pray for God's blessing in your life? Are you a person that He will bless?

> *God blesses the one who reads the words of this*
> *prophecy to the church, and he blesses all*
> *who listen to its message and obey what it*
> *says, for the time is near.*
> Revelation 1:3 (NLT)

Urgently fulfill the Great Commission and obey the two greatest commandments. You will be blessed! Don't be afraid to go tell them the good news. Be afraid not to go!

> *"We must quickly carry out the tasks assigned*
> *us by the one who sent us. The night is*
> *coming, and then no one can work."*
> John 9:4 (NLT)

Renowned for his powerful preaching in the late 1800s, J.C. Ryle said, "The highest form of selfishness is that of the man who is content to go to heaven alone." Are we content to go to heaven alone? Oh, I hope not! May your first and most urgent priority be to make sure heaven will be very, very crowded.

PERSONAL REFLECTION AND GROUP DISCUSSION

- Before you were saved, did religious people try to clean you up?
- Now that you're saved, do you catch yourself trying to do the same thing?
- What are the dangers of trying to "clean fish we haven't caught yet"?
- What are the top priorities in your life?
- What are you urgent about?
- What preoccupies your thought life? What should?
- Suggested verse to memorize: John 9:4

CHAPTER 15

RIGHTLY DIVIDE THE WORD OF TRUTH, AND RECEIVE POWER FOR WHAT'S IMPORTANT

Be diligent to present yourself approved to God,
a worker who does not need to be ashamed,
rightly dividing the word of truth.
2 *Timothy* 2:15 (NKJV)

To "rightly divide" here, means to accurately teach God's Word. In the original language, the word that is translated *rightly divide* is a single word in the Greek, and it's a form of the verb *orthotomeo*. In Bible times, this was a civil engineering term and was used when people were building roads. It's used to describe cutting a roadway in such a way that travelers can arrive at their destination directly, via a straight path, without veering off course. *Orthotomeo* was also a mining term that described drilling a straight mine shaft directly to the gold.

As an example, let's take on the biblical subject of signs and wonders, specifically healing, that needs to be "rightly divided." We must always read the Bible in context, avoiding the temptation to pull out stand-alone verses that appear to prove the point we want to make. We must strive to be balanced and accurate when interpreting the Bible.

God uses signs and wonders to bring people to salvation. That's just obvious in Scripture, and if you've been walking with the Lord for a while, it's obvious to you personally as well. Watching God do miracles is so fun. But haven't we also seen times when God chooses not to heal? How do we handle times like that? It's not so fun, is it?

God doesn't have to heal. Jesus walked past many who needed healing. We have to be okay with that. It's our job to just believe He can, lay hands on the sick, and pray. Then He chooses what He's going to do for His own glory.

We must remember that it's not the fact that we are praying for someone that heals them. Have you ever been prayed over by someone who believes healing happens due to a particular method they've found that appears to make God move? I have. They seem to believe that how they pray, what they say, or where they place their hands heals people. It's such a bummer, especially when you're the one in pain!

I once had a bad migraine during a friend's church potluck. The pastor noticed I was having trouble, and he came over to pray for me. He placed his hands tightly around my head and began to loudly pray for healing in Jesus' name. By the time he was finished, the pain was worse than when he started. When he asked me if I was healed, I shook my head no, so he started up again. By the third round of this, when he questioned me, I thanked him, and told him my pain was gone. I'm not proud of it, but I lied to this pastor to get him to stop! He wouldn't take God's no for an answer. For whatever reason, God chose not to take my pain away that night. I was okay with that. What I wasn't okay with was the guy's loud demands he made of God as he gripped my head!

The Jews of Jesus's day sought signs and wonders. That

made them miss the Messiah! When the Pharisees asked Jesus for a miraculous sign to prove to them that He was God, He called them an evil and adulterous generation. God doesn't need to prove anything to us. He's God!

Now we aren't Pharisees, we are believers, so we have every right to come before God and ask for healing for ourselves or for others. But He also has the right to say no. He will do whatever will bring Him glory. Sometimes we won't understand His decision. That's when we must rely on Scripture that tells us that everything will work together for our good when we belong to Him.

We also need to understand that God doesn't always use the flashy and fantastic to bring Himself glory. And when it comes to physical, emotional, or spiritual healing, He knows what's best. It doesn't always take a huge spectacular miracle to get people's attention on Him.

I was once approached by a leader from a church who taught a class that was focused on signs and wonders. She was teaching her students methods of healing that she believed made God move. She had heard what our teams were doing by ministering at raves. She believed her class of young people could help us out. She described her plan. She would send her students with us. We could keep doing what we do, handing out bracelets and helping kids in different stages of need. Then her students would "call down heaven" and perform signs and wonders in the name of Jesus that would "wow" the ravers. Missing legs would grow out. Ravers in wheelchairs would walk. They would see God working right there inside the rave, and they'd want salvation because of it! As I listened to her, I came to believe that this lady was very sincere. She was truly driven by a heart of love for the lost. She just wasn't rightly dividing the word of truth.

I let her finish. Then I shared with her that we didn't need to accept her kind offer of sending her students with us on outreaches. God had shown us that we are only to take teams of older moms and grandmas into the venues. We don't take young people with us. The ravers have a lot of young and cool in their lives. What most of them seem to crave is parenting. When us old ladies crash their parties, we stand out in a big way. They see our love, and they flock to us. They can't believe we would come to their party. I said, "The ravers are already seeing heaven come down. They see signs and wonders every single time our teams go to a rave." Since she knew our teams hadn't gone through her training, she was stunned and asked me to explain.

You see, it may not be real flashy or glamorous, but every single time a mom or grandma ministers to a kid at a rave, the ravers see Jesus. It's a miracle of biblical proportion that an old lady's heart would change to the point that she would say yes to God's call to go love on kids at events like these.

This generation wants to see God in action. They want to see that He can really change lives. They've already seen what religion can do, and it's fallen flat. It's not so much the amputated legs they want to see changed, although that would be spectacular. It's the hearts they long to see changed. Don't all of us want to see PLUR in our lives?

The Bible says that the world will know that we are Christians by our love. That will lead them to salvation. We don't need a whole lot of bells and whistles. Leave that up to God to surprise all of us when He thinks the time is right. Until then, we can be confident that the love of the simple Jesus who was born in a manger and rode into town on a donkey is enough.

I love the story of the jailer who got saved when he was guarding Paul and Silas in prison:

Around midnight Paul and Silas were praying

and singing hymns to God, and the other prisoners were listening. Suddenly, there was a massive earthquake, and the prison was shaken to its foundations. All the doors immediately flew open, and the chains of every prisoner fell off! The jailer woke up to see the prison doors wide open. He assumed the prisoners had escaped, so he drew his sword to kill himself. But Paul shouted to him, "Stop! Don't kill yourself! We are all here!" The jailer called for lights and ran to the dungeon and fell down trembling before Paul and Silas. Then he brought them out and asked, "Sirs, what must I do to be saved?"

Acts 16:25-30 (NLT)

The true miracle here wasn't in the earthquake, it was in the heart of Paul and Silas who stayed. The jailer drew his sword to kill himself because he knew that if he didn't do it himself, come morning, when the boss showed up and found that the prisoners had escaped, his boss would kill him himself.

Sometimes when people see signs and wonders, they turn to God and are saved. And sometimes the greatest sign and wonder from God to the lost is that His people stop to do the right thing.

One more lesson from the Acts 16 passage: God was obviously in charge of that earthquake, but there wasn't an immediate happy ending for the Christians. It was much better than being in chains, but the jailer kept Paul and Silas with him until the powers that be released them! Here we find that our desires and our comfort are not always God's goal. Even when God does a miracle, it's not always going to have the result we may have hoped for, because the goal of God's miracles is to bring glory to Himself, not glory to us.

Go ahead. Pray for signs and wonders. You're not a Pharisee. You're a Christian, so you will be asking for those signs and wonders for the right reasons. Peter and John asked God for signs and wonders to accompany their preaching. Luke spent a lot of time in Acts telling us how valuable signs and wonders are in winning people to Christ. Just let God be God. Don't be tempted into disappointment when He doesn't follow your advice and give you what you want. You will receive power to do what's truly important.

RECEIVE THE POWER TO WITNESS

> *"But you will receive power when the Holy*
> *Spirit comes upon you. And you will be my*
> *witnesses, telling people about me*
> *everywhere—in Jerusalem, throughout*
> *Judea, in Samaria, and to the ends of the*
> *earth."*
> *Acts 1:8 (NLT)*

Why does the Holy Spirit come upon us? For what purpose does He give us power? To witness! That's the goal of Holy Spirit power! That's what's truly important. If you are sharing the gospel and sharing the love of God, His power and authority will come and ride on that. Do you want to see God work? Do you want to see His mighty power? Do you want to see miracles? Witness!

I have never in my life seen God work like He works when people are ministering to the lost! It's just unbelievable. I should be a chandelier-swinging charismaniac because of all the Holy Spirit power I've seen! Folks! He's real! He does miracles today! We just don't see them all that much because the American church today is asleep. It isn't partnering with the Holy Spirit to seek and save the lost. We seem to want the miracles for ourselves, to pump us up, to make us feel good.

Back to Acts 16. Paul and Silas were mature enough to know the miracle of the earthquake wasn't for them. It was for the lost, as a witness to them. How many of us would've gone through that same experience, felt our shackles fall off, and run out of that prison, thinking that God had done this miracle for us? No, Paul and Silas understood that miracles are intended to be a witness to the lost and so they stayed. They put the lost jailer's needs above their own and that gave them the opportunity to share the gospel with not only the jailer, but with his entire family.

Pray for Holy Spirit power to witness and watch what happens! People on our prayer team are constantly amazed by all the "yes" answers God gives to our prayers. We ALWAYS get the best camping sites in the rave campgrounds or the perfect parking spots for our ministry RV to reach the most kids. Against all odds! And those times when we end up following the parking lot attendants to a "bad" parking spot, it's because two hours later a kid will go down right in front of us that we never would have seen if we'd been parked somewhere else.

You should see how many times team members just burst out laughing, slapping their foreheads over how BIG our God is! We always get to just the right place, at just the right time, for just the right purpose. Not once, not twice, but for YEARS this has happened. Because when we are praying for the right parking spot, or for money for entrance fees, or for healing, or for salvation, we are praying in God's will. Because our purpose in asking for those things is to be good witnesses, to bring glory to God. And so, God says yes. Pray in God's will and for His glory. Then stand back and watch Him do His thing!

> *Now therefore stand still and see this great thing*
> *that the Lord will do before your eyes.*
> *1 Samuel 12:16 (ESV)*

PERSONAL REFLECTION AND GROUP DISCUSSION

- What are some nuggets you have found in Scripture after you drilled straight to the mother lode by rightly dividing the word of truth?
- How do we know when we are or aren't rightly dividing the word of truth?
- Have you seen God heal someone for His glory?
- Have you seen God choose not to heal?
- What should we do with the hurt feelings that come when God disappoints us by not saying yes?
- Have you ever felt the power of the Holy Spirit come upon you as you are witnessing?
- Suggested verse to memorize: Acts 1:8

CHAPTER 16

TAKE NOTES SO YOU DON'T LOSE HEART

Sharing the gospel and discipling people can be heartbreaking. It doesn't always turn out like we hope it will. Sometimes you pour your heart into someone, and then suddenly you realize you are working much harder on their life than they are.

> *Therefore, having this ministry by the mercy of God, we do not lose heart.*
> 2 Corinthians 4:1 (ESV)

When we are tempted to be discouraged, we must remember that it's not about us. This is God's ministry, not ours. We just show up and make ourselves available. He does the work in people's hearts. If they don't submit to Him, that's their decision. We just have to be able to say that we did our job, we spoke the truth in love, we made ourselves available to be used by the Holy Spirit in someone's life and then move on, excited to see who God will bring us next.

TAKE NOTES!

God wants us to remember the things He has done for us and the impossible situations He has carried us through. Remembering these things helps us to not lose heart when we face discouraging situations. He wants us to write these things down or do whatever it will take to remember these things, because He knows that these stories of His providence and provision will help us through the future impossible situations we will face. These stories will also be a testimony of His greatness to those around us and to future generations.

In Joshua 3 we find the Israelites in the middle of a miracle. They had to cross the Jordan River. God had told their leader, Joshua, that He would perform a miracle to get them across. So, Joshua told the people, "Today you will know that the living God is among you."

As soon as their feet touched the water, the river's flow was cut off upstream. The water stood up like a wall. Just as God had parted the Red Sea, He dried up the Jordan River so the people could cross over it.

In Joshua 4, we read that God wanted His people to remember what He had done. So, He instructed the leaders to gather stones from the middle of the river that they had just crossed and use them to build a memorial. Joshua explained that God had performed this great miracle at the Jordan River so that all the nations of the earth might know that His hand is powerful and bring glory to His name. The memorial would cause future generations to ask about what happened at this place.

I love how God wanted the stones that made up this memorial to be gathered from an impossible place: in the middle of the river where there had once been deep water. They were stones that could never have been collected, except God had caused a miracle to uncover them and made them accessible.

When God pulls you out, when He rescues you, when He brings good from evil, write it down! Build stone memorials if you must! Get a tattoo! Do whatever it takes to remember and to make sure that future generations will hear these stories of the living God at work in your life. Recording this stuff will get you through when the enemy tries to mess with your calling.

My friend writes her "God sightings" on little stones and keeps them in a giant jar on her coffee table. Another scrapbooks her memories and includes God stories for future generations to see. I like journaling what God has done.

Here is one of my favorite entries:

November 5, 2016

GOD HAS WORKED A MIRACLE!!!

Our team was at a rave in Orlando. In the middle of the night, just as the event was about to let out, we found a girl named Cierra. She was sobbing. She had gotten separated from her friend.

As 45,000 kids were pouring out the exits, we were trying to find one girl in a white tutu and hot pink bra. Her name was Raven.

Cierra and Raven had rented a hotel room for the weekend. They got separated inside the rave. Cierra had all of Raven's belongings, including her cell phone, ID, and wallet. Without any money, Cierra knew Raven would never be able to get back to their hotel unless she got a free ride from a stranger. So either way, if she was still wandering around the venue, or if she was on her way back to the hotel, Cierra knew Raven was in danger.

Cierra kept crying and saying, "This was supposed to be fun."

We couldn't find Raven. Cierra was in contact with her boyfriend who was back in their home state. He was totally stressed and just wanted Cierra to go back to the hotel. She was so torn. I promised that I'd drive her back to the hotel as soon as we had spent some more time looking for Raven. I was hoping that when the crowds dispersed, it would be easier to spot her.

Cierra's boyfriend kept calling her, demanding that she get back to her hotel immediately. He was really scared for her safety. She decided to ignore him for the moment. I told her that we would go back to join the rest of our team at our parking spot and then decide what to do.

So, we took Cierra with us back to our ministry RV on the corner across from the venue. When we arrived, I saw that the team there was totally overwhelmed with ravers in various stages of need. One of them was over-dosing, and they were waiting for paramedics to get to them through the impossible traffic jams around the venue.

It made sense to keep Cierra with us, wait for the crowds to die down, help the team with all they were dealing with, and then continue to look for Raven. I knew if I

left to take Cierra back to her hotel, it would mean that
the team would be minus me and a dad because our
policy is to never be alone with a raver.

But as I quietly debated with myself, and then prayed, I
heard clearly from God that none of that mattered right
now. I was absolutely and immediately to leave and take
Cierra to the hotel.

It was so strange. I didn't blame Rob when he questioned me. This just didn't seem like a sensible plan. I
second guessed myself, questioning if I'd really heard
from God, but the answer was still loud and clear:
GOOOOOOO!

Rob came with me. We were shocked by the clear path
that remained in front of our car, while there was
complete gridlock all around us. We prayed on the way.
We got to Cierra's hotel in record time. That alone was a
miracle!

Before she jumped out of the car, we exchanged phone
numbers. I got her boyfriend's number as well. We all
promised to keep in touch until Raven was found. We
told Cierra that we would head back to the venue and
continue looking. Cierra promised to call off our search
if Raven ended up back at the hotel. I hoped that we
would find her back at the venue. No telling what shape
she'd arrive in if she accepted a ride from a stranger back
to the hotel. Or if she would ever arrive.

When Rob and I got back to the venue, we decided how

to divide the team up into pairs to go search for Raven. Just before we headed out, I called Cierra's boyfriend to see if he had heard anything. He was breathless!

He had just heard from Cierra who was just about to call us herself. The boyfriend said, "You saved Raven's life!" Then he explained.

When Cierra walked into the hotel room, she heard water running. She ran into the bathroom. Raven was down in the bathtub, totally naked and unconscious. The water was about to cover her nose and mouth. Raven was about to drown.

Cierra was able to get her up and awake. She had arrived just in time! We witnessed a miracle of God tonight!

I am so glad I wrote all of this down. It's a stone we collected from an impossible place. It helps us to remember something we learned that night: Sometimes if it doesn't make sense, it's God. Later, after you obey, it will make sense.

PERSONAL REFLECTION AND GROUP DISCUSSION

- Have you ever had to move on from someone you were ministering to because you were working harder on their life than they were? How did you get through the heartbreak of that?
- What did you learn from that experience?
- Share some of the stones of remembrance you have collected from impossible places that give you encouragement when you start to lose heart.

- How do you memorialize these things?
- Suggested verse to memorize: 2 Corinthians 4:1

PART 2

THE GEAR

CHAPTER 17

THEY'VE GOT REALLY GOOD GLASSES

We take a quick look out at the lake and see that our fisherman is still out there, totally relaxed, patiently waiting for the fish to bite. The tackle box is open at our feet. We've checked out the instruction manual. Let's rifle through the box as well as the bucket next to it and see what kind of gear this guy has brought. As we look, we learn a few things about great fishermen. They've got all the right stuff, including the right glasses!

Evangelism is simple...it begins with looking at people from God's point of view. My favorite preacher, Andrew Field, says, "See the world through gospel-colored glasses."

One of the greatest Scripture passages on evangelism is found in 2 Corinthians. It starts with this:

> *So we have stopped evaluating others from a human point of view. At one time we thought of Christ merely from a human point of view. How differently we know him now!"*

2 Corinthians 5:16 (NLT)

Yes, evangelism begins by looking at people from God's point of view. And looking at people from God's point of view requires that we have a clear understanding of who we ourselves are. And looking at who we really are begins with a clear view of who God is.

Isaiah's perspective of himself and others changed when he really saw who God was. In Isaiah 6, Isaiah sees the Lord. He was sitting on a throne and just the train of His robe filled the temple. There were angels all around Him, and they were shouting out to each other about God's greatness. It was an overwhelming thing for Isaiah to experience.

Isaiah's reaction is detailed in the same chapter. He immediately sees himself as he really is. Sometimes comparison makes us see the truth. God was so big and amazing and holy, that it caused Isaiah to see how small and sinful he was in comparison. Isaiah says, "It's all over, I'm doomed!"

But God sees his repentant heart. He forgives Isaiah. God declares that his guilt is removed and his sins are forgiven.

Isaiah's response to God is a willing heart to do His will. Isaiah says, "Here I am, send me."

That is the mark of a Christian who has seen God, and who understands what God has done for her. She is willing to go. She cares about people, because God cared about her.

> *Make allowance for each other's faults and*
> *forgive anyone who offends you. Remember,*
> *the Lord forgave you, so you must forgive*
> *others.*
> *Colossians 3:13 (NLT)*

I love to get on Google Maps and look at places I'm going to visit on vacation before I get there. It gives me the bird's eye view, the perspective from above. This is much more information than what you will see in front of you when you're actually there. I use Google Maps because I don't want to miss out on anything. In the same way, we must tap into God's perspective when we are looking at our mission field because it will give us much more information than just what we see with human eyes. And we sure don't want to miss out on that!

> *"My thoughts are nothing like your thoughts,"*
> *says the Lord. "And my ways are far beyond*
> *anything you could imagine. For just as the*
> *heavens are higher than the earth, so my*
> *ways are higher than your ways and my*
> *thoughts are higher than your thoughts."*
> *Isaiah 55:8-9 (NLT)*

When it comes to the subject of judgement, we really need God's help and His perspective! Judgement is the number one complaint we hear about Christians from non-Christians. Seriously, over and over again we hear stories of Christians hurting others by judging them in the name of Jesus. Because of this, the fact that our teams don't go to raves in judgement is the number one positive comment we get from ravers. They can't believe we are not there to condemn them. Our teams have gotten God's perspective on this, and it shows in a wonderful, glaring way to our mission field. Like they say, a little bit of light goes a long way in the darkness. In fact, God does some of His best work in the dark.

> *God sent his Son into the world not to judge the*
> *world, but to save the world through him.*
> *John 3:17 (NLT)*

I mentioned this in chapter thirteen, but it's worth mentioning again! From the thousands of conversations we have had with this generation since 2009, we have a theory that the church in general has been much louder about what we are against than about what we are for. This is not godly, and we must change that. It's sending the fish swimming in the wrong direction. What if we were really loud when we said stuff like this:

> The Spirit of the Sovereign Lord is upon me, for
> the Lord has anointed me to bring good
> news to the poor. He has sent me to comfort
> the brokenhearted and to proclaim that
> captives will be released and prisoners will
> be freed.
> Isaiah 61:1 (NLT)

In the New Testament, we read many verses on judgement. Some tell us to judge and others tell us not to. I have found that this concept stands true when held up against all the verses on judgement in the Bible:

We are to judge for identification, not condemnation. This is how I define condemnation:

Condemnation is hating someone who sins differently than me.

We are not to condemn the world but offer the good news of salvation from sin. We should not expect nonbelievers to behave. But we should love them with God's love, because while they were sinning, Christ died for them. As we live our lives out in non-judgement, we are to show the lost that there is another way to live with freedom and hope and peace. We are to speak the truth to them in love as we obey the two greatest commandments: love God and love others.

Jesus taught us how to judge for identification:

> *"Look beneath the surface so you can judge correctly."*
> John 7:24 (NLT)

One way we have learned to look beneath the surface is by having an attitude of curiosity. We love to hear the kids' stories. Some are heartbreaking and some are hilarious, but they all give us a peek at what's under the surface. And that gives us the ability to really minister to them.

Years ago, I came upon a young man who was having trouble in a parking lot outside a rave venue. He shared that he'd had a panic attack inside the rave and had to leave to calm down. We talked a bit, but unfortunately, I did most of the talking. Everything was going well as I shared the gospel with him and the hope that I've found in Jesus. But then things took a bad turn as I shared that to find this true peace in life, he would need to surrender his life to Jesus. He looked horrified.

I quickly took stock of what I'd said. Everything I'd said was true! What could possibly be wrong? I really needed that bird's eye view of this situation right now. I needed God's perspective. I changed the subject, and he gained his composure. I was so glad he didn't walk away. I began to listen for more information instead of talking so much.

Soon, I found out that he had been discharged from the military on the basis of a post-traumatic stress disorder disability. He shared that his PTSD diagnosis was the result of his recent stint overseas. He believed that he had not gotten the training he needed to be there. He shared that a gun was put in his hands before he really knew how to use it, and that he felt his commanding officer had repeatedly put him in harm's way.

As I listened to this young man's story, God gave me His perspective. In His great love for this lost one, He showed me my error so that I could correct it. God reminded me that to a soldier, surrender is a dirty word! I had completely miscommunicated the gospel to this young man. Later, after he was talked out, it was my turn. I apologized for my error and asked if I could explain it another way. He was gracious and agreed.

Instead of using the word *surrender*, I explained that he needed to place himself under the authority of a new commander; one who has his best interest at heart, one who wants life and hope and peace for him. That boy drank those words in like a thirsty man in a desert. I was able to put my arms around him and pray for him right there in that parking lot outside the rave.

But first, I had to listen to his story.

The following week, he met with my husband to drink in more of the truth that his soul had been thirsting for. Rob was also able to connect him with some resources that could help him with his PTSD.

This world is full of people like this young man. Because of various traumas in their lives, many of them are acting out. Some of us may have the opinion that they are wearing inappropriate clothes, using inappropriate language, doing inappropriate things, have too many piercings, too many tattoos, too many unnatural colors in their hair. But what is God's perspective on this?

As part of my former job as a drug prevention specialist, I was required to get certified as an addictions treatment counselor. Now I didn't mind the drug prevention side of my job. I liked to engage the community, plan town hall meetings, rub shoulders with lawmakers, partner with law enforcement, and go into schools to convince kids not to use drugs. But to sit in groups with addicts and "treat" them? That was not for me! I had no use for those people. They were too far gone. They had made their own bed and they were lying in it and that was that.

My boss absolutely would not let me work only the prevention side. To keep my job, I had to work on the treatment side as well. So, after much kicking and screaming on the inside, I reluctantly embarked on a five-year internship program. During this time, I was also running over to my teenagers' private Christian school to teach high school Bible classes in exchange for their tuition. I loved going there and teaching those kids! For the most part, they were well behaved, and I loved well behaved kids. I had three of my own, and I had spent eight years homeschooling them to see to it that they were.

God's incredible sense of humor was not lost on me when my treatment supervisor assigned me to my very first drug treatment group: teen boys.

I wish I had the words to describe these boys well. What a motley group they were! They'd all gotten into some sort of drug-related trouble at school. Most were also in trouble with the local sheriff. They were the exact opposite of the kids in my Bible class and in my home. With their arms crossed over their chests and their pants sagging down almost to their knees, they sat in a circle, glowering at me. We all agreed on one thing. We didn't want to be there.

And then God began to work a miracle. My heart grew by eight sizes. One size for each of the eight boys in that group. I began to hear their stories as the weeks went by. I discovered it's hard to be judgmental when you take the time to listen to someone's story. The walls of my judgment came crashing down, and a beautiful thing happened.

As I listened to those boys and showed compassion, their

arms uncrossed, the pants came up (just a little), and there were even some lights that came on. They ended up listening to me too. I went through the curriculum that I was given to use, but I prayed asking the Holy Spirit to be present at each group session. Although I was not allowed to mention the name of Jesus in this county treatment program, He was there! At the end of those 14 weeks, every single one of those boys hugged me as they left group for the last time. And as I exited that room, I was a very different person than I had once been.

It's harder to judge someone when you take the time to listen to their story.
So listen.

God used those boys to break my heart with the things that break His. It was during this time that God spoke to me about seeing the kids in my treatment group from His perspective, instead of mine. He used a vision to do it.

I was standing by a pool. There were lots of older people around it enjoying the day lounging on the deck in relative quiet. Suddenly, a teenager began thrashing about in the deep end of the pool. He was getting all these nice people wet as he splashed in the water. His head would break the surface. He'd yell and scream using some pretty bad language. I stood horrified by his behavior. I wished he would stop acting out. Teenagers! Geesh! Get a life! Most of them are so misbehaved all the time.

And then I got my wish. The boy quit "acting out." He became silent and still. It was then I realized that he had drowned. You see, he hadn't really meant to cause a scene, it's just that he was in the process of drowning. And instead of throwing him a life ring, I'd stood by the edge of that pool scowling, wagging my finger at him, and judging his behavior.

God showed me through this vision that many in this generation are acting out because they are drowning. When people are drowning, they're not very well behaved. We need to see the behavior as a symptom. It should become a signal to us to throw them a life ring.

Since then, I have read some research that shows that sometimes when people drown, instead of thrashing about, they get very quiet. Our society not only mocks the loud ones, we lack patience with the withdrawn ones. "Snap out of it!" we say. "What's wrong with you?"

This vision of people drowning, whether they are boisterous or quiet, has changed my human perspective to a more godly perspective. It was like putting new glasses on: the spectacles of Scripture. I hope it does that for you as well.

One more thing, lest there be confusion about what I meant above by "acting out." The examples I gave to illustrate someone who is acting out come from my own experience. I used to think that if someone was all tatted and pierced up, they were for sure, hands down, acting up. Only the "bad kids" looked like that. My world was very, very small until God changed my perspective.

Some of the most amazing, Jesus-loving people I have gotten to know over the last few years have tattoos and piercings and strange colors in their hair. They're not misbehaving. Just because it doesn't fall within normal on my "appropriate radar" doesn't mean it's a sin. Jesus loves them. I need to get over it. We human beings are a judgmental lot. Heck, we even judged Jesus when He came. His response?

> *You judge me by human standards, but I do not
> judge anyone.*

John 8:15 (NLT)

If He didn't do it, maybe we shouldn't either.

I'm so glad God had taught me these things by the time I found myself seated at a table across from a girl who was only wearing pasties and a thong.

We were on day one of a three-day outreach at a rave that offered camping. We had served breakfast to over 100 kids. The dads were pretty wiped out from flipping pancakes, cooking sausage, and telling dad jokes for eight hours straight. The moms were tired, too, but happy. We'd been able to love on all those kids and share the gospel over breakfast at the family-style tables we had set up in our campsite. The dads had just turned off the grill and sat down for a break, excited to be able to join the moms at the tables and talk to ravers. There were a couple of kids still sitting at the tables slowly sipping orange juice and chatting.

A young lady came walking into our campsite. She wore only a pair of pasties and a thong. The kids with the orange juice seemed embarrassed as they looked her up and down and then quickly glanced at the rave dads sitting at the table. Our Because Jesus Loves You sign hung behind them.

I breathed a quick, "Oh boy, here we go" sigh, and welcomed her to our table. The orange juice kids seemed to get over their embarrassment and sat back like they were about to watch a show. They totally focused on the dads, looking for their reaction.

Most of the time, when the kids are in the rave campground, they're in shorts and T-shirts or sweats. They get dressed up in rave wear right before they go into the party, but this girl was already "dressed" and ready to go, hours before the party was to start.

The orange juice kids seemed shocked as we started to treat

this girl as if she were our very own daughter. Nicole introduced herself and sat down on a chair across from me. She said she hadn't come earlier because she didn't want breakfast. She came now, just for conversation.

The small talk was brief. Nicole went deep fast. She began to share that she had just turned twenty. From the age of sixteen to nineteen, she was the sole caregiver for her mother who ended up dying of cancer. Even though she did everything she could, eventually dropping out of school, all her efforts failed. In the end, she couldn't save her mom. She wept as she described the experience. I reached across the table and held her hand.

She talked about how much she missed having parents. Her dad had left long ago, now her mom was gone as well. She also described failures at other relationships she'd had. She talked about how she had recently become a lesbian because she said she wanted someone to love her for more than just her body.

The dads at the table looked directly in her eyes and nowhere else. It was obvious that they were heartbroken for her. I heard OJ #1 whisper to OJ #2, "This is so cool!"

Nicole was a very lonely, needy girl. Because we didn't judge her, and because she was craving parenting in her life, she visited our campsite many times that weekend. We welcomed her every time. We didn't make her clean up or dress up first. She heard the gospel and saw it in action.

Our rave dads have learned to view others from God's perspective. Even beautiful girls in pasties. With His help, they have harnessed their sin nature's natural temptation to lust, and by the power of the Holy Spirit, have converted it into the desire to rescue. Because our God is a rescuing God. While we minimize the dad's exposure to this stuff on outreaches, when they do have an opportunity to minister to these kids, it's powerful. We call these times "dad moments." It is amazing what power a dad's positive comments and godly conversation can do to a wounded kid's heart.

The armor of God is on our front, to face sin and the enemy and deal with it. It's not on our back to protect us as we run away. If there's sin in your life that's stopping you from being able to minister, from being able to see others from God's perspective—lust, greed, judgment—don't just mow it down. Pull it out by the roots, get rid of it, so that you are free to minister to all of God's lost children. He wants them back. And He wants to use you to find them.

We were once visiting a small fellowship that wanted us to come and share the ministry. In the audience was a young lady that was also visiting for the first time. She wore a tank top. After the service, the pastor asked me to please go talk to her about dressing more modestly the next time she came. He explained that her clothing choices were most likely causing some of the men in his congregation to lust.

I declined. I asked my husband to talk to the pastor. The problem was with the men. He had a lust problem in his church that he needed to deal with immediately. If they couldn't handle seeing a tank top in church, what was happening to them at the mall or at their place of work?

The church in America needs to deal with this issue of lust. According to recent studies conducted among churches by Barna Research Group and Covenant Eyes, sixty-eight percent of Christian men and fifty percent of pastors view pornography regularly. Of young Christian adults, eighteen to twenty-four years old, seventy-six percent actively search for porn. And it's not just the men. Thirty-three percent of women aged twenty-five-and-under search for porn at least once per month. Yet, only seven percent of pastors say their churches are addressing this issue.

How can we see people through gospel-colored glasses

when we are secretly viewing people on a screen as objects for our own pleasure? Church! This is an epidemic in our country. It needs to stop with us! It's great that so many churches have jumped on the anti-human-trafficking bandwagon. But porn fuels sex trafficking. The church must address this.

So, we've looked at seeing people from God's point of view, but we also need to see circumstances and situations from God's point of view. When Peter was not seeing things from God's perspective, Jesus had some pretty strong words of rebuke for him!

> *"Get away from me, Satan!" he said. "You are seeing things merely from a human point of view, not from God's." Mark 8:33b (NLT)*

Looks like it's important to see things from God's point of view!

One of the all-time greatest verses on seeing circumstances from God's point of view is in Romans:

> *And we know that God causes everything to work together for the good of those who love God and are called according to his purpose for them.*
> *Romans 8:28 (NLT)*

I just can't think of a better story to illustrate this concept of God using circumstances for His will than what happened on Super Bowl Sunday 2019. Rob and I had traveled four hours to another state to help a new believer find a church. Her name was Diana. She had tried a couple of churches, neither felt like a good fit. We all thought it would be a good idea for us to go with her on her next try.

The previous year, Diana had prayed for salvation after she contacted us through our website that was spelled out on a bracelet she'd received from our rave moms at a rave. I had been discipling her every week on the phone since. We went verse by verse through the book of John, read two new believer books together, and had gone through Ephesians. She was totally growing in the Lord. She just couldn't find a church, especially one that fit with her work schedule.

We have friends in her area who have adopted eight children through the foster system. Some are special needs, some are medically fragile. They can't go to any local churches because they would overwhelm the children's department. Plus it's a huge undertaking to get a family the size of the Flynn's out the door. So, they have started a house church in their home.

On Sunday nights, they host what they call a "Family Dinner" for their church, then they meet on Tuesday nights to have church. On that night they have dinner together as well, and then they worship, have a teaching, communion, and fellowship. I wanted to recommend this to Diana, but I hesitated because I thought she'd feel more comfortable in a traditional church setting with a great young adult's program.

The week before we came, Diana looked online and found a church that she thought might work. It was very large with all the bells and whistles. It also had a Sunday evening service, which she was looking for since she worked at her retail job most Sunday mornings.

We drove in the night before and stayed at the Flynn's house. Diana took that Sunday off so the three of us could enjoy a day of hiking before we went to church that night. Before we left to meet up with Diana, the Flynns invited us to bring her back for the dinner they were hosting. We thanked them but said that by that time, we would be at the new church with her. We said our goodbyes and hugged all the kids before taking off.

Rob and Diana and I enjoyed our day. The hiking trip was amazing, but we had to cut it short to get to the church service on time. Diana double checked the meeting time online to be sure we really had to quit the hike. Reluctantly, we got in our cars. Diana followed us to the church.

When we pulled in, there was a large sandwich board sign waiting for us at the entrance that said, "Church is cancelled for tonight due to the Big Game!" Now, you need some background here. Rob and I aren't big football fans, but there are two games we watch every single year: The Rose Bowl and the Super Bowl. It's our tradition.

We weren't thinking about the date when we planned this church visit with Diana. The week before, we realized what we'd done. We'd scheduled it on Super Bowl Sunday! We were bummed, but we decided not to cancel. Diana had taken the day off, and she was way more important than a football game.

So here we were in the first car, with Diana pulled in behind us. I about had a stroke. Poor Rob's ears must've been ringing as I threw a hissy fit. I had all kinds of not nice things to say about this church and their decision-making skills! I shouted, "We have a new believer behind us who has already tried some churches! She's already discouraged! NOW THIS! This is UNACCEPTABLE BEHAVIOR for a church! Closing for a GAME? Seriously? Couldn't they at least have had an elder or deacon there to run a service just in case people showed up? How many people in this huge church could possibly like football? How am I going to explain this to Diana?" Rob tried to remind me about Romans 8:28 but I would have none of it!

I got out of the car and walked back to Diana, trying desperately to cover up my bad attitude on the way. By the time she rolled down the window, I was able to speak sweetly. I said something like this, "Now is the time when we practice what we have learned from our study of Scripture. We must take the log out of our own eye, before removing the speck from our brother's eye. Cancelling church for a game is a speck. It's not necessarily a sin. It's an opinion. I disagree with it, but we just have to let it go."

Diana smiled at me. She knew me enough by then to know that this mama wasn't happy! We talked a bit and realized that it would be too late to try to find another Sunday night service to visit. Then, suddenly, I remembered the Flynns' invitation. I said, "Hey, how about we make the best of this and take you to our friends' house for their church fellowship dinner night?" Diana agreed, and she followed us to the house.

Diana stepped foot in that house and was surrounded with kids greeting her. The adults gave her welcoming hugs. They made her go to the front of the food line. They all wanted to sit near her. She felt what we feel every time we step foot in that house! Love lives there. Jesus is alive there.

Just over a month later, Diana and I were having our weekly discipleship call. She had been going to the Flynns' house church for weeks by this time. We were discussing something in the book of Acts and she turned to read chapter two. She was reading how the believers met together in homes, devoting themselves to the apostles' teaching and to fellowship and to prayer and communion together. She gasped. "That's just like the Flynns! It's church!"

I said, "Yes, you are right."

Then Diana laughed and said, "I've finally found my church! It's not in a church building, but it's my church!"

The Flynns go live on Facebook on Tuesday nights. Sometimes I tune in just for fun, and there, usually somewhere in the front, is Diana.

You can make many plans, but the Lord's
purpose will prevail.
Proverbs 19:21 (NLT)

Diana is the one that pointed out that verse to me. She said it reminded her of what happened on that Super Bowl Sunday.

God is good, and He does work all things together for His glory! I'm so thankful that a church made the (stupid 😊) decision to close on Super Bowl Sunday and so regretful that I spent time having a fit in the car that night! God had this!

I hope I remember this story next time I need God's perspective on circumstances.

PERSONAL REFLECTION AND GROUP DISCUSSION

- What is God showing you to change about your perspective of others?
- What is God showing you to change about your perspective on circumstances?
- Suggested verse to memorize: John 3:17

CHAPTER 18

THEY WEAR THE RIGHT CLOTHES AND AREN'T AFRAID TO GET WET

WEARING THE RIGHT CLOTHES

Back in the day, you could tell a lot about a person by their laundry line. My gram had one out in her garden. If you'd peeked over the fence on a Monday, you would have seen that she and my gramps had dressed up for church the day before. You'd also be able to tell that Gramps was a hard worker and liked to do things himself around the house. You'd see grease stains on his shirts and paint on his work pants.

If Christianity had a laundry line, you would see love, joy, peace, patience, kindness, goodness, faithfulness, gentleness, and self-control hanging there. The armor of God would be on the line as well. This is essential clothing for fishers of men.

The parts of this armor are described in Ephesians 6. We are supposed to put on this armor so that we can stand firm against the strategies of the enemy. The Greek word that is translated, "put on," is *endusamenoi* and it means to clothe or be clothed, in the sense of sinking into a garment.

> *Finally, be strong in the Lord and in the strength*
> *of his might. Put on the whole armor of God,*
> *that you may be able to stand against the*
> *schemes of the devil.*
> *Ephesians 6:10-11 (ESV)*

We need to sink into this armor every single day. We should never dream of leaving home without it. It should be more important to us than the actual clothing we wear. We wouldn't think of leaving home without that, right?

This armor includes the belt of truth, the breastplate of righteousness, shoes of peace, the shield of faith, the helmet of salvation, and the sword of the spirit. In Isaiah 59:17, we see that even Jesus wore this armor.

They say that the two "kill spots" on the body are the head and the chest. Shots to other parts of the body are often survivable, but people rarely survive shots to those critical areas. It's interesting that in the list of armor in Ephesians, the head is covered by salvation and the chest is covered by righteousness. This is intentional.

We know salvation protects us. We will survive eternally. What about righteousness? Every rule that God gives us to live by is for our good. None of them are frivolous. He's not the giant party pooper in the sky. He wants us to enjoy life while we are here on this earth, and He wants good things for us. His boundaries protect that. When we make choices to sin, when we compromise, when we don't seek God's best for our lives, we are lifting that breastplate of righteousness off our chests and opening ourselves up to the enemy's potshots. It will lead to consequences that God does not want us to have to face. He wants us to live abundantly by following His commandments.

Keep your clothes on, Christians!

DON'T BE AFRAID TO GET WET

In 1 Kings 18, we find the account of Elijah coming to visit King Ahab with a message. There had been a great drought in the land. Elijah, at the Lord's direction, had come to tell the king that God would soon send rain.

When Ahab saw Elijah, he greeted him with these words: "So, is it really you, you troublemaker of Israel?" Elijah responded that it wasn't he who had made trouble for Israel, it was Ahab himself! He went on to explain that because the king and his family were worshipping Baal instead of the Lord, they were reaping the consequences: drought and famine.

Elijah told the king to gather all the prophets of Baal and the other godless prophets in the land, as well as all the people of Israel. When they were all together, Elijah called the Israelites out for "hobbling between two opinions," because they were trying to worship God and Baal at the same time.

So Elijah sets out to make the people decide once and for all which one they would worship, because they couldn't worship both. He tells the prophets of Baal to make an altar and put pieces of beef on top of the wood. Elijah said he would do the same. Neither he nor the prophets should light up their barbecues because they were to leave that job up to the one they worshipped.

So the prophets of Baal did as Elijah instructed. They spent hours calling on the name of Baal to set fire to the wood, but nothing happened. Then Elijah, growing sarcastic, finally begins to mock them. "Maybe you need to call a little louder. Perhaps your god has left to go to the bathroom and he can't hear you! Or maybe he's daydreaming or on vacation."

So the prophets got even louder trying to summon their god. They even cut themselves with knives and swords to try to get their god's attention. And now we hear about raves for the very first time in history. Verse 29 states "they raved all afternoon until evening" but they got no reply from Baal.

Now it's Elijah's turn. He called to the people of Israel to come watch. He builds the altar with 12 stones. Then he does something totally crazy, but God was telling him what to do. Elijah digs a trench around the altar big enough to hold three gallons of water. He piles wood up in the middle and sets the steaks on top of that. But before he asks God to light it up, he tells the people to fill 12 jugs full of water. They are to pour it over the whole thing so that it gets completely wet and spills over, filling the trench!

God was wetting down the wood! He was creating an impossible situation so that He could prove Himself to be the only one true God. When He lit up the altar, the people would see the truth. Have you ever seen God wetting down the wood? I have. Many times. And sometimes that wood is me! He puts me in these crazy situations, like going to raves in the name of Jesus, along with all these old people, so that the lost will see that He is real.

Like one raver said one night after praying with us, "I can't believe God came to a rave to find me!"

From a human point of view, God does the crazy, the impractical, the impossible, the inappropriate, the reckless, so that He will get the glory and people will see that He alone is God.

You know what happens next! God sends fire down from

heaven. He not only cooks the steaks, but incinerates them, as well as all the wet wood, the stones, the water in the trench, and even the dirt. Bam! God is very thorough in His communication with mankind. He's on a mission, and no other god will stop Him from seeking and saving His own.

Don't be afraid to get wet. Don't try to get out from under the water when He's wetting down the wood! When the impossible happens, remember that God is in control. He is working all things out for His glory.

God's writing an amazing story, and you're one of His characters! (Some of you more than others.) When God is doing the impossible, He often calls us to do things that don't make sense. The rave ministry doesn't make sense! It's impractical for old people to stay up all night at these crazy parties listening to music that sounds like a car alarm going off. But it's impractical because God wants to do the impossible! Just like wet wood on a barbecue is not a good plan, neither is marching around the city of Jericho or Gideon's army only numbering 300! What's impossible to us brings glory to God.

Let the problems come. Let the engine die and the tires go flat, the dishwasher break and the power go out. Be faithful in times of trouble, and you will see God work! He's just wetting down the wood.

PERSONAL REFLECTION AND GROUP DISCUSSION

- If someone could see your "laundry line" what would they see?
- How has following God's rules protected you?
- Share a time when you believe God was wetting down the wood in your life.

- How does Elijah's barbecue give you a fresh perspective on trials?
- Suggested verses to memorize: Ephesians 6:10-11

CHAPTER 19

THEY ARE PREPARED TO STAY LONG ENOUGH

Great fishers of men are in it for the long haul, so they are prepared to stay as long as it takes to get the job done. In chapter twelve, we looked at John 4 and saw how Jesus stayed long enough to minister to the people of the Samaritan town. Now, I want to investigate the principle of staying a bit further and focus on the heart preparation that is required to enable us to stay long enough.

Years ago, I knew a woman who was zealous to share the gospel, but she didn't seem to want to do it if it messed with her schedule. She wasn't sensitive to the Spirit, and she wasn't willing to wait on His timing. She hurt a lot of people in the process.

After shopping together for our groceries at Costco one time, I was in a long line with her. When we finally got to the front, she decided that was the perfect time to witness to the checker. She launched into the story of the death and resurrection of Jesus while the line continued to grow behind her. People waited. They craned their necks to see what the holdup was, rolling their eyes, and commenting loudly. The checker seemed frantic, not quite knowing what to do.

When we finally got to the car, I shared with her that by witnessing that way, it was obvious that she had caused others to stumble. She said she didn't care. "What if today is the day of salvation for that checker?" she retorted.

I responded, "Well, if God is telling you that, then it's worth it to cancel the rest of your day, let your groceries defrost, and wait until she gets off work."

You pay the price; don't make others pay. Be prepared to stay long enough in order to put others' needs above your own. What you have to share is really good news! But don't hurt your message by giving it at the wrong time just because that's what's convenient for you.

> A loud and cheerful greeting early in the
> morning will be taken as a curse!
> Proverbs 27:14 (NLT)

Our precious rave mom Cindy is such a beautiful picture to me of a Christian whose heart is always prepared to stay as long as it takes, even though it means she will pay the price for it later. She and her husband are older, and the all-night outreaches can be challenging. Toward the end of a long night in Houston, Cindy found a boy laying between two empty parking spots in the middle of the dark parking lot. People were still leaving, cutting through the lot to get to the nearest exit. We were so grateful she had found him and moved him to safety near the ministry RV. He surely would have been run over!

We called his family, and they agreed to come get him. Cindy spoke softly to him and prayed over him while the rest of us packed up to leave. An hour went by. Since we had more than one vehicle, we suggested that Jerry and Cindy head back to the hotel so they could get rested for outreach night two. I told her I would take over with the boy so they could leave. She declined, saying that she felt she should see this one through to the end.

Another half hour went by and still, the boy's family hadn't come. I made the offer to Cindy once again. Politely but firmly she said, "I'm staying! I'm not leaving until he does." She continued praying over the boy who was now sound asleep in one of our chairs.

When the family came, they loaded up the boy. They were grateful and wanted to exchange contact information. They said they would let us know how he was doing the next day. The boy reached for Cindy to hug her goodbye. After they left, we folded up the chair the boy had been sitting in and found his prescription glasses tucked in the corner. Cindy called the family.

The next day, the boy walked into our hotel lobby to get his glasses from Cindy. He thanked her again for staying with him. He remembered that she had stayed! He was too disoriented for Cindy to share the gospel with him the night before, but now she had the opportunity as she walked him out to his car. The boy's family got out of the car to join him and Cindy, and they were able to hear the Good News as well.

God is good, and Cindy stayed.

For the sake of the lost, be prepared to work within God's timeframe, on His schedule, no matter how long it takes.

> *Do nothing from selfish ambition or conceit, but*
> *in humility count others more significant*
> *than yourselves.*
> *Philippians 2:3 (ESV)*

PERSONAL REFLECTION AND GROUP DISCUSSION

- Have you ever experienced the joy, like Cindy did, of working with God on His timetable?
- How can we put others first when we are witnessing?
- Suggested verse to memorize: Philippians 2:3

CHAPTER 20

THEY INVITE MINISTRY IN BECAUSE THEIR HEARTS HAVE BEEN BROKEN

THEY INVITE MINISTRY INTO THEIR HOMES, PERSONAL LIVES, AND CHURCHES

In Luke 16, we find the parable of the shrewd manager. What a powerful verse we find at the end of the story:

> *"Here's the lesson: Use your worldly resources to benefit others and make friends."*
> Luke 16:9a (NLT)

I've been on the receiving end of someone using their worldly resources to benefit others and make friends. Once at a Christmas luncheon, I ran into an acquaintance. We greeted each other. While we made small talk, I noticed she was wearing a unique bracelet. I complemented her on it and without even blinking an eye, it was gone from her wrist and onto mine; a gift I will never forget. We went from acquaintances to friends that day because of that gesture. Our relationship changed in that moment.

It so impacted me that a couple of months later, when a young newlywed visiting my home mentioned that she liked a decorative piece that sat on a shelf, I followed my friend's example and gifted it to her. She was thrilled. I was blessed. So much so, that I've repeated the scenario a few more times. The blessings I have received from giving these things away far outweigh the blessings I got from having this stuff in my house. There's no comparison!

Further down in Luke 16, we find that when Jesus finished telling the parable of the shrewd manager, He gave some explanation. The response of the Pharisees who were listening to Him is not surprising. They ridiculed Jesus for what He said. But what catches my attention is what the Bible lists as the source of their bad attitudes. Check this out.

> *The Pharisees, who dearly loved their money,*
> *heard all this and scoffed at him. Then he*
> *said to them, "You like to appear righteous*
> *in public, but God knows your hearts. What*
> *this world honors is detestable in the sight of*
> *God."*
> *Luke 16:14-15 (NLT)*

They dearly loved their money. I believe this is the source of many problems in the church in America today, and it affects our attitude toward evangelism and discipleship. We just flat out love our money too much! We have created these attractive churches, giant machines that need to be oiled, so we keep creating programs that have little to do with evangelism and discipleship to attract the "right" kind of people who will bring in the money we need to be sustainable. This has created church members who feel they have done what God requires by donating to the building fund or the new parking structure instead of meeting the needs of the lost and hungry and hurting.

A few years ago, we ran into an old acquaintance who had become an elder at his church. He had no idea how God had flipped us upside down and called us into full time ministry, so we filled him in. We shared a few stories with him of how God was using the rave outreaches. He responded by saying that he loved what he was hearing. He said he would love to introduce us to his church's missions board so they could consider supporting us, but unfortunately, we didn't fit into the parameters the board had. Our focus is on eighteen to twenty-four-year-olds. Their church had decided that ministering to college age people wasn't for them. He seemed embarrassed when he said they had decided to focus only on ministry to young families because that's who would give money to the church. He repeated what the missions board had told him, "College kids don't tithe."

It wasn't too much later that we ran into him again. He told us that his church had failed. It was no longer able to sustain itself. I don't know all the details, but it sure seemed that their priorities were not in the right place. They had to sell their church building. God allowed a faithful, missions-minded fellowship to take over. They are very evangelistic, and the church is growing with new believers. They may just have to do some construction to add more room to accommodate all of them. Now that's a great reason for a building fund!

Faithful people will use their resources to impact people's lives for Christ. They will use the stuff God has given them and their finances to introduce others to Jesus. They love people more than they love their stuff or their money. I have met multi-millionaires who decided to place a reasonable cap on their income. They said, "Enough is enough" and they give all the rest of their money away to mission work. They choose to live modestly for the sake of the gospel.

Using my stuff for the Kingdom used to be a big issue for me. Someone once said, "Everything in your house is either a tool or an idol. Unfortunately, I've had some experience with idol worship in my house. There have been many times in the past, before my heart was broken with the things that break God's heart, where I didn't allow ministry to take place in my home because I didn't want things to get messed up. "Their kids are maniacs. They'll run amuck and break something." "Well that's the last time I'll have the youth group over! They spilled soda on my favorite couch!" I spent many years putting things above people.

God has a sense of humor. Now I host Camp 33 in my home. Just last week, we had twenty people eating in my house, and some of them slept there as well. I had cleaned my house from top to bottom in preparation for the weekend, but three days later after they all left, I had to clean it all over again! It was kind of a bummer.

Then I read this verse, and it ministered to me so much:

> *Without oxen a stable stays clean, but you need*
> *a strong ox for a large harvest.*
> *Proverbs 14:4 (NLT)*

If we want our lives to be all shipshape and tidy; if we love our stuff and our money too much, we will never be able to do what it takes to fulfill the Great Commission. People are messy. Ministry is messy. Sometimes it's very expensive. But we will see a harvest that we'd otherwise never see if we are willing to die to ourselves and share our lives and our stuff with others.

GREAT FISHERS OF MEN HAVE A BROKEN HEART

Jesus did! In Genesis 6, we see that humanity's sin broke God's heart. It separated us from Him. But He made a way to redeem us. And when Jesus finally hung on the cross, scientists say His heart literally broke.

My heart has been broken over the things that break His. First and foremost, my own sin. Staying aware of my own sinful state helps me so much when I am faced with the sin of others. I've seen some pretty dark stuff out there, but because my heart is broken over my own sin, that motivates me to move with compassion.

I was outside a rave venue in the middle of the night when I saw two young men and a young lady dressed only in strips of leather and wearing handcuffs. They were on the street corner simulating violent sexual acts. I felt repulsion boiling up in me. I was literally sick to my stomach. Then I made a conscious effort to remember who I am. I am nothing except for the grace of God in my life. At that moment, I was filled with compassion for those three human beings and remembered that Jesus thought they were worth dying for. That motivated me to cross the street and talk to them.

Another thing I have found so helpful when I am having a hard time having compassion on people is to remember that when people are sinning, they are often just trying to acquire something that they think will be good. Sin is often an attempt to add value to their life. But just like Eve in the book of Genesis, they've been duped by the enemy. It wasn't the evil side of the tree that Eve was attracted to, it was the good side.

There is a "good" that will lead people away from God. Eve just wanted knowledge and wisdom. That sounds good, doesn't it? Satan is the great deceiver. He often wraps evil in a good-looking package.

*The woman was convinced. She saw that the
tree was beautiful and its fruit looked
delicious, and she wanted the wisdom it
would give her.*
Genesis 3:6a (NLT)

Skip on down and you will find that the fruit was still in her mouth, the juice probably still on her lips, when she suddenly felt shame for the first time. It's just so tragic. In one bite, her relationship with God was broken. Sin entered the perfect garden. I wonder if all of creation knew at that point. Did the flowers, suddenly wilting, and the sparrows, suddenly feeling pain for the first time, turn their little heads toward Eve as if asking, "Why?" I just can't imagine her shame. Or maybe I can. It's heartbreaking.

It was heartbreaking enough to God that He set out to repair the broken relationship with mankind. It was an unthinkable, ghastly plan. To put Himself in our place to pay for Eve's sin and those of the rest of humanity. Every despicable, evil, nightmarish thing we would ever dream of doing to each other, He took on Himself. He paid for every rape, every murder, every act of adultery, every lie, every evil thing that man could ever invent. The scarlet cord of His plan to redeem man is woven all throughout the Old Testament. At the beginning of the New Testament, His plan is fulfilled in the death and resurrection of Jesus.

And this is why Jesus came not to condemn the world, but to save it. He came with a broken heart. He was moved with compassion for people.

*Jesus traveled through all the towns and villages
of that area, teaching in the synagogues and
announcing the Good News about the*

> *Kingdom. And he healed every kind of*
> *disease and illness. When he saw the*
> *crowds, he had compassion on them because*
> *they were confused and helpless, like sheep*
> *without a shepherd. He said to his disciples,*
> *"The harvest is great, but the workers are*
> *few. So pray to the Lord who is in charge of*
> *the harvest; ask him to send more workers*
> *into the fields."*
> Matthew 9:35-38 (NLT)

Wow! Jesus is broken hearted over what He sees. Just what did He see? Let's look at what it means to be a sheep without a shepherd. I found the account of a sheep farm owner online who shared that several times he has been called out to gather up flocks that have been left unattended by a shepherd. He said it's a sorry sight. They are weighed down by their dirty, unsheared wool. It's full of parasites bothering them. They are sick with infections that stunt their growth and threaten their survival. Their uncared-for hoofs are so long and infected that they can't walk, and their knees are inflamed. The weak ewes don't have enough milk for their babies, so the little ones die of starvation and exposure.

This is my mission field. They are weighed down with the cares of the world. They feel alone in the world, often with no one to care for them. Many share that their parents are so busy trying to survive themselves that they have no time to really invest in them. They are often immature. Thirty seems to be the new eighteen. At the end of the party that they thought would bring them peace and happiness, they are often left stumbling, barely able to walk in the parking lot. Sometimes, they die of exposure to the heat or the drugs, or whatever Satan has thrown at them.

When Jesus saw this, what did He do? He called me to pray for workers to go into this mission field. Then He called me to be one of the answers to my own prayer. He's calling you as well. He may have a different mission field planned for you, but His heart is broken over it, and it's waiting for you. Please say yes.

The Great Commission resulted from Jesus' broken heart; from His compassion. Consequently, the best ministries, churches, and mission organizations have originated with a broken heart. They are started by people who could care less about becoming famous or wealthy. They are people who have broken hearts for the things that break God's heart. They care about the one. They are moved by compassion for people. They have seen the confused and helpless and have said, "Here I am! Send me into the fields to work." Get involved with these ministries. They have the heart of Jesus.

PERSONAL REFLECTION AND GROUP DISCUSSION

- What are some ways we can use our "stuff" to impact people for Christ?
- Are there any material items you own that you love too much? What should you do about it?
- Have you ever known Satan to wrap something evil up in a good-looking package?
- How does remembering your own sinful nature help you to have compassion on other sinners?
- What is something many people consider to be "good" that can lead people astray?
- How different would things be in our world today if Jesus had come to condemn it and not to save it?
- Suggested verses to memorize: Matthew 9:36-38

CHAPTER 21

THEY HAVE GUARDRAILS
AROUND THEIR LIVES

I live in the mountains. We've got guardrails; they keep us on the road that leads home. These guardrails are often dented–a sign that they've done their job and kept a car from plummeting over the side of the mountain. When we are following Jesus and fulfilling the Great Commission, we've got invisible guardrails around our lives. Like brackets or parenthesis, they keep us contained, set apart. Like my gram used to say, "Others may, but you may not."

After Moses gets the Ten Commandments written on two stone tablets, I love how he instructs the people to stay in their lane, inside the guardrails God has placed around them.

Moses told the people:

> So be careful to do what the Lord your God has
> commanded you; do not turn aside to the
> right or to the left. Walk in obedience to all
> that the Lord your God has commanded you,
> so that you may live and prosper and

prolong your days in the land that you will
possess.
Deuteronomy 5:32-33 (NIV)

Let's explore some of these guardrails. We won't be exhaustive here. But let this section encourage you to discover the guardrails God wants around your life.

When you pray for God to inhabit your life, He will rearrange your lifestyle to fit His eternal plan! When that happens, your friends and relatives may not be able to relate to you anymore. When people are focused on the "American Dream" it may be hard for them to connect with people who are making life choices, especially financial decisions, that appear reckless. You may be one of those people in their lives. Some of my friends and some of my extended family are not real supportive. They question what God has called me to do. I'm pretty sure they think I've gone off the deep end.

At some point, you may have to learn to be okay with people who just don't view life the same way as you do. Even though you are on a different path, you can still honor people as friends and family without seeing eye to eye on everything and following their advice. Though it may cause awkwardness in our relationships, or worse, we must follow God's calling on our lives. His calling is our guardrail. What our friends and family think is not.

Think of how American history could have changed if Paul Revere had a mom with whom he didn't see eye to eye, and she questioned his mission. What if he'd listened to her and changed his plan? What if late one night she'd said, "Listen here, Paul Revere! I don't care where you think you have to go right now, young man. Nothing good happens after midnight! You need to stay home!"

If we are to take the Great Commission seriously, we must be focused on it as our highest calling. We must make our life decisions accordingly, no matter who tries to persuade us otherwise. Don't be surprised when you're mocked or ridiculed by people who aren't going the same way you are. They don't have those same guardrails around them.

The guardrails are always there. Not just when we are ministering. Fulfilling the Great Commission is a lifestyle. If we are followers of Jesus, we need to be followers of Jesus twenty-four/seven. This isn't a job we clock in and out of. We must always remain aware of our calling . Obviously when we are sharing the gospel, or are on an outreach; but also when we are at the grocery store, when we are out on a date, when we are in line for a movie, or the super tough one... when we are at home. We will be watched. Being aware that people are watching you and that you belong to Jesus is one of the guardrails that will hold you accountable to stay on the right road.

This is super important to God. Why else would He command that church leaders be especially kind to others? Not just when they are serving at church, but outside the church, in the community. First Timothy 3 lists the qualities God wants to see in church leaders. As well as being able to teach, not lovers of money, or drinkers of too much wine, God wants them to be people who enjoy having guests in their home and to be well-liked in the community. How cool is that? He wants His people to be NICE, both inside and outside of the church walls. People are watching.

While beginning to write this chapter, God gave me a great example to use! I was on an airplane seated across the aisle from someone that I'd eventually be witnessing to during the flight. She noticed that I was writing and asked me about it.

This led to a conversation where I was able to share the gospel. What if I'd cut in line in front of her? Or if I'd been rude to the flight attendants?

Then there's the guardrail given in Romans 14: loving others. This is not the only place in Scripture we see this guardrail, but Paul gives us some very good examples here of how we should love others!

We need to be very, very careful about how we party, how we eat and drink. He tells us we shouldn't be condemning each other or looking down on each other for our differing beliefs in this area, but he also tells us we should be willing to give up our practices if they are distressing to someone. In verse 15, he literally says, "Don't let your eating ruin someone for whom Christ died."

Wow! What a responsibility that is! Our behavior can ruin someone? There's no food or drink or activity I enjoy that much! If we really love others, it won't be a big deal to adjust our lifestyle to keep from harming our witness to them.

> *Don't tear apart the work of God over what you eat. Remember, all foods are acceptable, but it is wrong to eat something if it makes another person stumble. It is better not to eat meat or drink wine or do anything else if it might cause another believer to stumble. You may believe there's nothing wrong with what you are doing, but keep it between yourself and God. Blessed are those who don't feel guilty for doing something they have decided is right. But if you have doubts about whether or not you should eat something, you are sinning if you go ahead*

> *and do it. For you are not following your*
> *convictions. If you do anything you believe*
> *is not right, you are sinning.*
> Romans 14:20-23 (NLT)

Christian family, if you believe God has given you the freedom to drink alcohol, would you please consider keeping your drinking of it between yourself and God and not on Facebook or Instagram? In this world of social media, you just can't know who is watching you. You have no way of knowing if that photo of you holding up that glass of wine at that party is going to stumble someone. It's just not worth it. Too many people struggle with alcohol addiction, too many have lost their lives over it.

> *For the Kingdom of God is not a matter of what*
> *we eat or drink, but of living a life of*
> *goodness and peace and joy in the Holy*
> *Spirit. If you serve Christ with this attitude,*
> *you will please God, and others will approve*
> *of you, too. So then, let us aim for harmony*
> *in the church and try to build each other up.*
> Romans 14: 17-19 (NLT)

Speaking of social media, we can apply these same principals to what we post or how we comment publicly. Many have expressed shock about what people say on social networking websites, Christians included. It's like we think we can say whatever we want there, and we say it as if we won't be held accountable for it.

I was reading through a string of comments on a Facebook post from 2018 that was praising retired Senator Bob Dole for his salute over George H.W. Bush's casket, his former rival. With absolutely no provocation, an older man commented, "Take note, younger generations, that don't know what respect is anymore. This is what respect and honor look like... a true class act."

A few minutes later, a young person reacted with her own comment, "Pot meets kettle. Just go ahead and assume younger generations as a whole don't understand respect, all while being disrespectful yourself."

It's sad what my generation has done to this generation by not staying inside the guardrail of loving others.

A few years ago, some Christians decided to get themselves all in a knot over the fact that the popular fast food coffee company, Starbucks, came out with their annual holiday cup, printed in a rather plain, red ombre design with a little green on it. The company explained the simplicity of that year's cups was intended to "usher in the holidays with a purity of design that welcomes all of our stories" (aka: be more inclusive).

Now this company has never claimed to be a Christian company. The CEOs have never claimed to be followers of Jesus. They sell coffee, not Bibles. Their previous holiday cups didn't herald the birth of Jesus. This new cup was simply red and green. But even so, an internet "evangelist" decided to make a video that went viral. On the video, this guy, dressed in his Jesus T-shirt, rails against the coffee chain for trying to keep Christ and Christmas off their cups. He goes on to encourage Christians to "prank" Starbucks.

He didn't like the way Starbucks referred to Christmas as merely a holiday. It angered him that company employees would say, "Happy Holidays" instead of "Merry Christmas." So, he told Christians to go place their orders, telling baristas that their name was "Merry Christmas." Then, the baristas would have to write that name on their order and call out

"Merry Christmas" instead of their real name when the coffee was ready.

The result that year was that at practically any given time, you could go into Starbucks and hear baristas shouting, "Merry Christmas" as they distributed beverages to people waiting in the pickup line.

These Christians may have thought they were being funny, or they may have thought they were crusading for Christ, but either way, according to Scripture, this broke God's heart. I could almost hear Him say, "Father forgive them, for they know not what they do." They were jumping outside the guardrails God has placed around our lives.

That season, I went to Starbucks a lot. I don't normally frequent the place, but I was filled with compassion for the baristas who were sent swimming in the opposite direction of God, by God's people. Most of these Starbucks employees were the same age as my mission field, so maybe that's why God put it so strongly on my heart to go to them.

I can't tell you how many amazing conversations came about because I ordered my coffee, gave them my real name, and then apologized for how my Christian family was treating them. I used social media to encourage other Christians to do the same and, although my post didn't go viral, others agreed to join in the fun. Yes, it was fun to be a good witness. And it didn't hurt that it entailed a peppermint mocha!

I love how the guardrails God gives us are usually not unwelcome additions. The Bible says that He gives us the desires of our hearts. In this way, He helps us to want what He wants. When we walk with Him, we become willing to do things His way. The guardrails are comfortingly desirable. The guardrails cause us to live differently, and often, God has changed our hearts to the point that we don't mind these boundaries.

My husband and I have watched many of our friends enjoy amazing trips to the Holy Land. We live vicariously through their photos and Facebook posts. Someday, we'd love to go there and experience it for ourselves, but we joke that we will have to wait to see it after Jesus returns, during the thousand-year reign. It's not that we think it's wrong that our friends go, it's just that we have a different calling on our lives. We have guardrails around us that don't allow for a trip like that. It could change. But for now, we have made choices with our finances and our time that would make it impossible. So, we will gladly stay put. If God ever shows us differently, we'll be the first ones to board the plane!

Goodness is a guardrail. Being full of the goodness that can only come from God and bragging on His greatness is a form of evangelism. We are to be vessels that communicate God's awesomeness!

> *Give thanks to the Lord and proclaim his greatness. Let the whole world know what he has done. Sing to him; yes, sing his praises. Tell everyone about his wonderful deeds.*
> *Psalm 105:1 (NLT)*

Proclaiming His greatness means that we get to show the world that our God is good. He is loving and generous and kind. When our actions seem to indicate that we serve a miserly God who is somber and moody and deeply cares about the design on our disposable coffee cups, we bring insult to His name.

I will never forget what happened when I ran into a restaurant to pick up a to-go order while my husband stayed back at our ministry booth nearby at a pastor's conference. This conference was very popular, it drew pastors from around the country.

As I stood waiting for the host at the front to pack up my order, a server from the floor walked up. She didn't see me standing to the side. She rolled her eyes, shoving her latest "tip" into the host's hands. It was a gospel tract. I cringed as I saw the cover: "Take a Tip." This tract starts out something like this: "Here's a tip that's worth more than money—Christ died for your sins..."

Mortified, I interrupted the two, expressed my shock, and apologized for the situation. The server said, "Oh, trust me! This isn't the first time. There's a pastor's conference in town, and I get stuff like this in place of money every time they're here." I was glad I'd left my conference name badge back at the booth!

The host handed me my order. Before I left, I put some money in the server's hand. I asked her to please forgive my Christian family and told her that's not what Jesus would do. I gave her one of our rave bracelets and left.

I started my car to head back to the conference. Before I let myself get too angry at the pastors that did this, I thought back over my time as a Christian, living outside the guardrails. I wondered how many times God had to send someone else to clean up *my* mess?

The sooner we learn to live within our guardrails, the better.

PERSONAL REFLECTION AND GROUP DISCUSSION

- What are some guardrails that God has put around your life?
- Is there anything about the way you live or speak or

behave that you need to change so that
nonbelievers around you aren't stumbled?

- What are the guardrails you keep wanting to jump?
- How can you know what your guardrails are?
- Suggested verses to memorize: Romans 14:17-19

CHAPTER 22

THEY HAVE COUNTED THE COST

Obeying the call of God on our lives to fulfill the Great Commission wherever we are in the world is costly. It's costly in many ways. We need to come to grips with that.

In his book, *The Cost of Discipleship*, Dietrich Bonhoeffer declared, "When Christ calls a man, He bids him come and die."

Jesus used some extreme comparison to get His point across as He challenged us to consider the cost of being His disciples in the book of Luke. We must love Him so much that, by comparison, it almost appears as if we don't love anyone else! This can be a hard passage for us to swallow, but keep in mind that God tells us the two greatest commandments are to love Him and love others, and so we must interpret what Jesus is saying here correctly, keeping all of Scripture in context as we approach these verses:

> *"If you want to be my disciple, you must, by comparison, hate everyone else—your father*

*and mother, wife and children, brothers and
sisters—yes, even your own life. Otherwise,
you cannot be my disciple. And if you do
not carry your own cross and follow me, you
cannot be my disciple. But don't begin until
you count the cost. For who would begin
construction of a building without first
calculating the cost to see if there is enough
money to finish it? Otherwise, you might
complete only the foundation before
running out of money, and then everyone
would laugh at you. They would say,
'There's the person who started that
building and couldn't finish it!' Or what
king would go to war against another king
without first sitting down with his
counselors to discuss whether his army of
10,000 could defeat the 20,000 soldiers
marching against him? And if he can't, he
will send a delegation to discuss terms of
peace while the enemy is still far away. So
you cannot become my disciple without
giving up everything you own."*
Luke 14:26-33 (NLT)

Bottom line here, discipleship is costly. God wants us to love Him and others, but when all is said and done, love Him the most, and spend our time, energy, and resources as if we really do.

Go figure! I didn't plan it this way, but I happen to be writing this section as I sit beside my two-year-old granddaughter's hospital bed. Her twin sister is also here, down the hall in another room. They both got a nasty flu and developed pneumonia. They will get through this, but right now they need help to breathe. I thank God that we can be here.

Just a couple of months ago, I spoke with a grandma who is a missionary far, far away from her grandbabies. She is grateful for the Facetime feature on her phone. I can't imagine having to rely on that right now. But that is the cost of her calling. She said yes, knowing what that meant. God is giving her, and her family, the grace they need to live that out.

As for this Grammy, we had just finished up our largest rave outreach of the year at the largest rave in the world in Las Vegas, Nevada. There was an estimated attendance of 465,000. There was an entire week of rave events in the city culminating in a three-day party called the Electric Daisy Carnival. We were spent. We were just packing up, looking forward to an empty calendar for seventy-two hours. Then we got the call that there was an ambulance coming to take our granddaughters to the hospital.

We packed the car and drove across state lines straight to them. Four hours and a lot of prayer later, we got to hold them in our arms and pray over them in person. We finally left the hospital late that night, got home, and fell into bed exhausted. But our sleep was cut short when our phone rang at 5:30 a.m.

The call came on our "call a rave dad or mom" hotline on our website. We knew it was a raver that needed to talk. Weary as ever, but relieved it wasn't an emergency call about our granddaughters, we answered the phone. For the next two hours, we shared the gospel with precious Rosie, answered a whole lot of questions, dealt with some demonic presence she was experiencing, and then led her in prayer for salvation.

I share all of this not to make you feel sorry for me, or to get you to pat me on the back, but to illustrate how there is a cost to living out your calling. Sometimes you must answer that phone or get to that meeting with that one you've been witnessing to when really, you just want a break. Your calling never goes away. As we discussed in the last chapter, you are "on call" twenty-four/seven. Fulfilling the Great Commission is not a nine to five job.

I honestly used to think that if I was living smack dab in the center of God's will, things would go well for me. My reasoning behind this was that since I was fulfilling His Great Commission, He would make my way easy. I didn't consciously think this through, but my reaction to bad things happening in my life showed me that this was the way I thought. I would be so shocked, and sometimes even had hurt feelings, when I was doing God's work and bad things still happened. I don't really know where those beliefs came from. Many before me have suffered and even died for fulfilling the Great Commission. I don't know why I thought I was so special. The fact that anything good ever happens in my life is an absolute gracious gift from God. We are fallen people. We live in a fallen world. God owes us nothing. We owe Him everything.

When I read Scripture to see what it says, in its entirety, without picking and choosing only the feel-good verses, I find that God doesn't care so much about keeping us comfy, but He cares a whole lot about developing our character. It's necessary in our sanctification process. It's all a part of our redemption. God is a redemptive God. He will do what it takes to make our character more like His. He redeems us for His glory and to partner with Him in spreading the good news of the gospel to others.

As Christians, this is the calling He has placed on every single one of our lives. Running from this process is not a good idea. In fact, look at Jonah in the Old Testament. When he decided to run from his calling, God made him very, very uncomfortable to get his attention. That guy sloshed around in the stomach acid of a fish while he figured it out.

Every single day God is working on my life, making me more and more into His image. And that's not always a fun process. It costs me something. While I may never have to swim in stomach acid, I've gotten plenty on me as young people get sick from the drugs they have taken. It's not fun, but God is making me into someone who loves the lost enough to risk them barfing on me. After all, He thought they were worth dying for.

There's also cost involved simply because we are sinful people, living in a sinful world. Bad stuff just happens. On top of this, when we are living in the center of God's will, there are evil forces constantly at work against us. Satan hates us and hates the impact we are making as we push back the darkness. God is greater, but we still feel all that going on.

When I am sharing the gospel, I can sense the battle. Almost always, the days before and after an outreach are challenging. It's costly. I have just come to accept this and ask God to work it all together for the good because I know that I am called according to His purpose. The whole reason I am here on this earth is to worship God and to bring glory to Him. Period. That's it. Here's that verse again:

> *And we know that God causes everything to work together for the good of those who love God and are called according to His purpose for them.*
> Romans 8:28 (NLT)

Often people take this verse to mean that everything will work out like we think it should. Yet, the guy who wrote this, Paul, died a horrible death because of his faith in Jesus. Depending on the scholar you prefer, he was either decapitated or crucified. I think you would agree that Paul loved God and was called according to His purpose! So, we must understand that "working together for good" doesn't mean we won't experience something awful or tragic, even death. But it does mean that in the end, we will be with God forever. It does all work together for good!

Just days after resigning from my drug prevention job to do rave ministry full time, I found myself in a Texas hospital room with the baby daughter of a raver who we had been ministering to. This baby and her twin sister, who had died five days before, had been in a tragic drowning accident. This little one didn't survive either. So there I was with her mommy as they took her off life support.

I've never felt such pain as I watched this young mother grieve the unimaginable. After the machines went quiet, the nurses put the baby in Barbara's arms and let her rock Sabrina for the last time. Then Barbara asked me to take a turn.

As I took Barbara's place in the rocking chair and received Sabrina's lifeless little body, I felt anger welling up in me. This was not what I had signed up for! Rocking a dead baby was not part of the agreement I'd made with God when I decided to quit my job and go into full time ministry! My head pounded as I internally shouted out to Him, "Why didn't you heal Sabrina? Couldn't you have at least let this young mom keep *one* baby?"

For days, this brand-new believer, Barbara, and I had prayed for a miracle, but God's answer was no. It was devastating.

For Barbara's sake, I calmed myself enough to sing "Jesus Loves Me" over the baby. I brushed her hair away from her face and traced the outline of her little nose. Her mommy and I sobbed and sobbed. God spoke clearly in those moments. "I have called you to a drowning generation. Will you go?"

The cost of discipleship is not to be taken lightly. Jesus wants us to go into it with our eyes wide open. He wants us to know what we are getting into. Then He wants us to say yes.

In the years since Sabrina and her sister, Savannah, left us, Barbara has come to deeply know and love and walk with Jesus. She leads prayer groups and Bible studies. She shares her testimony, giving others hope in the midst of tragedy. You see, I didn't get the miracle I prayed for, but God gave us another miracle. He has those babies safely in His arms, and their mama is leading others safely to Him as well.

Serving Jesus is serious stuff. Being a "Sunday Christian" won't cut it. It isn't a game He wants us to play. Time is too short. We must give up our evil desires. We must put aside anything that we used to do for fun that would be a bad witness to others as we follow Christ. We must even be willing to rock dead babies.

> This is all the more urgent, for you know how
>   late it is; time is running out. Wake up, for
>   our salvation is nearer now than when we
>   first believed. The night is almost gone; the
>   day of salvation will soon be here. So remove
>   your dark deeds like dirty clothes, and put
>   on the shining armor of right living. Because
>   we belong to the day, we must live decent
>   lives for all to see. Don't participate in the
>   darkness of wild parties and drunkenness,
>   or in sexual promiscuity and immoral
>   living, or in quarreling and jealousy.
>   Instead, clothe yourself with the presence of
>   the Lord Jesus Christ. And don't let yourself
>   think about ways to indulge your evil
>   desires.
> Romans 13:11-14 (NLT)

Did you hear the wake-up call? When Paul wrote this, he

said that time is short! Folks! It's 2,000 years later! If time was short then, think how short it is now! We better do what he says. WAKE UP!

I saw those words on the front of a raver's T-shirt one night, except they were punctuated with the "f" word in the middle. "Wake the F*** Up" was in bold, block letters down the front of this raver's shirt. Drug paraphernalia hung around his neck as he stumbled in front of rave mom Bonnie. I was standing at a distance and snapped a quick photo. What a picture that was for the church! I wish I felt I could appropriately show that photo when I speak to church groups. There is a dying world out there, and we don't even know it.

When someone makes us aware of it, we don't do anything about it because we often think it's just too expensive, too messy, too dirty. It will take too much of our time. It will cost us too much. If we call ourselves Christians, followers of Jesus, we need to get our spending priorities in order. And I'm not just talking about money. I'm talking about how we spend all our resources, including our time.

I picture the passage from Romans 13 like an inventory Paul is asking us to take, to cut costs in some areas in order to free us up to increase costs where they should be increased. He's telling us what to take off and what to put on. He's asking us to throw our efforts into what will pay off and quit doing stuff that will not be profitable. Notice that he considers quarreling to be just as harmful as sexual sin.

Church! We spend so much time arguing with each other, that a whole world is dying around us and we don't even see it. We are so wrapped up having church meetings over the color of the carpet in the sanctuary or whether we should sing hymns or contemporary worship songs or over who offended us at Bible study the other day, that we have lost our purpose. We go to all our cute little gatherings and sit on our comfy pews. We are not here for all of that! We have fallen asleep. The world is wasting away while the enemy sings us a lullaby, *"Go to sleep, go to sleep, go to sleep little church."* While we get all wrapped up in taking care of ourselves, he is gladly taking care of the world.

I don't care for the way the message was worded on that raver's T-shirt, but somehow, that message needs to get across: WAKE UP!

Fulfilling the Great Commission will cost you everything, but the joy you get from serving the Lord will far surpass the joy you once got from everything you lose.

PERSONAL REFLECTION AND GROUP DISCUSSION

- Have you felt the "pay-off" from doing the Lord's work?
- Have you felt the cost of doing the Lord's work?
- Was it worth it?
- Suggested verses to memorize: Romans 13:13-14

CHAPTER 23

THEY'RE NOT AFRAID OF HARD WORK, AND THEY MAKE THE MOST OF EVERY OPPORTUNITY

GREAT FISHERS OF MEN WELCOME HARD WORK

First Thessalonians starts by giving three marks of a true believer: Faithful workers, laboring in love, and having steadfast hope in Jesus. In this section, we will focus on the first two which involve work and labor. Now please don't get your undies in a bunch over this. I'm not talking about working hard to get salvation. That's impossible. Remember, I'm talking about people who are already saved: believers.

Some of us believers have gotten all comfy as we've hunkered down under grace. We've bought into the lie that our lives should be easy now that we're saved. We've got it made! We don't have to work for it, so we can sit back and enjoy. We've forgotten that the grace of God isn't anti-effort. It's anti-earning. That is, though we can't earn our salvation, we must "work out" our salvation.

The Greek word for labor, in 1 Thessalonians chapter 1, is what we would describe as laboring to the point of exhaustion. Deuteronomy 6 tells us to love the Lord our God with, among other things, all of our strength. That's exhausting. Because we love Jesus, we should be willing to labor in the mission fields for Him. To the point of exhaustion.

Remember? He calls us to labor:

> Then he said to his disciples, "The harvest is
>   plentiful, but the laborers are few; therefore
>   pray earnestly to the Lord of the harvest to
>   send out laborers into his harvest."
> Matthew 9:37-38 (ESV)

The stereotypical Christian church in America is lazy. We have more retreats than we know what to do with. If we're not laboring on the front lines, what do we need to retreat from? I know of someone whose whole idea of the Christian life was to go from one Bible study to the next, one worship concert to the next, one conference to the next, one luncheon to the next, one retreat to the next, but she never did anything about the Great Commission, even with all the knowledge and good feels she'd accumulated. I know her well, because that gal was me.

In Jeff Iorg's book, *Is God Calling Me?* he writes, "Many Christians complain about the slightest inconvenience. Where is our willingness to sacrifice? Radical environmentalists, homosexual activists, and religious fanatics all around the world are giving their lives to advance their causes. Even more should be expected of us, who claim to have the message of eternal life for the world."

Iorg relates an inspirational story of sacrifice from the book, *The Cry of the Kalahari* by Mark and Delia Owens. Here is Iorg's edited excerpt that describes the lengths to which Mark and Delia went to get to Africa, and the great sacrifices they made all along the way:

Delia and I met in class at the University of Georgia, and it didn't take us long to find out that we shared the same goal. By the end of the semester we knew that when we went to Africa, it would have to be together.

We decided to take a leave from the university and earn the money needed to finance the expedition. Once a site had been chosen, we thought someone would surely grant us the funds to continue.

But after six months of teaching, we had saved nothing. I switched jobs and began operating a stone-quarry crusher while Delia worked at odd jobs. At the end of another six months, we had saved $4,900.00, plus money for airfares to Johannesburg. But it was still not enough.

Trying desperately to raise more, we piled everything we owned—stereo, radio, television, fishing rod and reel, pots and pans—into our station wagon and drove to the quarry one morning, just as the men were coming off the night shift. I auctioned it all away, including the car for $1,100.00.

A year after we were married, we boarded a plane with two backpacks, two sleeping bags, one pup tent, a small cooking kit, a camera, one change of clothes each and $6,000.00. It was all we had.

Here's the thing. Mark and Delia gave all they had to study the brown hyena! Wow. Just wow. Is not the gospel worth more than a pack of hyenas?

Get out there! Work in the fields for Jesus. Don't be

surprised if you break a sweat doing what He has called you to do. Do you call yourself a servant of the Lord? Then serve Him. Servants sweat.

GREAT FISHERS OF MEN MAKE THE MOST OUT OF EVERY OPPORTUNITY

> Live wisely among those who are not believers,
> and make the most of every opportunity. Let
> your conversation be gracious and attractive
> so that you will have the right response for
> everyone.
> Colossians 4:5-6 (NLT)

We need to love God and jump on every opportunity He gives us to love others. That's our purpose here. May I suggest that part of doing that would be to notice God and notice others?

So many opportunities to share the gospel go by unnoticed because we weren't watching out for them. We need to be wide-eyed, aware, and curious. What people did God bring into my life today? Why did I see that person for the fourth time this week? How did God speak to me? Where was He present?

Paul is such an example of one who knew how to make the most out of every opportunity. Many times, we see him arrested and thrown in jail or standing before the courts in his own defense. And each time, he uses it as an opportunity to share the gospel.

Become a noticer of people and a noticer of opportunities!

When our youngest daughter was about fourteen, she and her dad were driving home from the grocery store. Just as a they came around a bend in the road, Cassie noticed a car parked in a turnout. Out of the corner of her eye, she noticed a woman in the driver's seat with her head in her hands, as if she was crying. She asked Rob to turn around.

Cassie approached the car and gently knocked on the window. Cassie saw that the woman had indeed been crying. She rolled her window down. Cassie told her that she had noticed her as they drove by, and she had asked her dad to turn around. She told the woman that Jesus loves her and that whatever she was going through, He could help her. The woman was stunned. Cassie offered to pray for the woman, and she agreed.

After she was finished, Cassie told the lady, who was still weeping, that she wanted to give her something. She went back to the car and asked Rob for one of our PLURway.com rave bracelets. Cassie gave it to the woman and asked her to go to the website on the bracelet and listen to the hope she would find there. The woman wiped her tears. She hugged Cassie. She was so grateful.

A few days later, Rob and I got an email through the contact page on the website from the bracelet. A woman was writing to tell us about a young girl that had given her one of our bracelets along the side of a mountain road. The subject line of her email was, "Touched by an Angel."

She went on to tell the story of how she had been reeling from all that had recently happened in her family, including some marital problems and her sister's recent cancer diagnosis. She was feeling desperate, like she just couldn't go on. Too much was happening all at once. She pulled into a turnout to cry and contemplate what to do. And then a young girl tapped on her window, and everything changed. She felt God's love. She was interrupted by hope. She was noticed.

I had to wait until my daughter got home from school that

day to hug her neck! What a blessing she had been to that lady. God only knows what could have happened if Cassie hadn't noticed her.

Children seem to be such better noticers than adults. They are naturally curious. Maybe they aren't so wrapped up in the cares of life as we are, so they have more time to notice things. A trip to the zoo with children is so much different than when you're just with adults. When I go without the grandkids, I am looking at everything that is in front of me, from about five feet on up. When my grandbabies are there, they point out a whole new zoo that's just inches above the ground. We see every little bird and squirrel running around trying to steal the food from the animal enclosures. We see the butterflies and bees and lizards enjoying the landscape. It's amazing how they notice and point out details that I would've missed.

We can get so busy and have such tunnel vision that we don't notice people around us in our rush to get to the next thing on our to-do list. We miss so many opportunities that God has for us.

I once sat in a conference on human trafficking where I heard a survivor share her story. When she was a young girl, she stayed at home for hours on end, taking care of her little brother while her mother worked multiple jobs to make ends meet. Her father had left years before.

She shared about looking out the window at her neighborhood, wishing she could live life like many of her neighbors' children did. She was often hungry as she tried to make do for herself and her brother with the few canned food items that sat in nearly empty cupboards. No one around her seemed to notice as they went on with their busy lives.

Until one day. When someone finally noticed. She and her brother were walking to the park and a man who lived at the end of the street came out and offered to take her out for a cheeseburger. The thought of a burger was all it took to make her say yes. That was the beginning of her life as a human trafficking victim. It all started with someone noticing her need and offering to meet it. Except it wasn't the nice ladies that lived up and down the block who noticed her. It was the evil guy on the corner.

Predators are noticers. They make the most of every opportunity. It's what they live for. Everyday normal decent people go about their own lives, minding their own business. We need to change that.

PERSONAL REFLECTION AND GROUP DISCUSSION

- Is there something God has called you to do that you've worried might be too much work?
- Describe someone you know who has the marks of a true believer.
- If someone could watch a documentary on your present-day life, would they know you are a follower of Christ?
- How can you make the most of the opportunities God gives you to share the gospel?
- What are some ways you can slow down and be a good noticer of people?
- Share about a time when God pointed out someone to you who needed to hear the gospel.
- Is there someone you have noticed in your neighborhood, or at work, or even at church, who "needs a cheeseburger"?
- Suggested verse to memorize: Colossians 4:5-6

CHAPTER 24

THEY PRACTICE SPIRITUAL DISCIPLINES AND COMMON SENSE

SPIRITUAL DISCIPLINES

One who practices the spiritual disciplines reminds me of a good sailor. She has learned how to trim her sails to catch the wind when it comes. She understands that she can't create the wind, but she is prepared to be moved by it because she has put herself in the correct position.

In his book, *Spiritual Disciplines for the Christian Life*, Donald Whitney puts it another way. "Think of the Spiritual Disciplines as ways by which we can spiritually place ourselves in the path of God's grace and seek Him, much like Zacchaeus placed himself physically in Jesus's path and sought Him."

We must watch our heart's agenda when practicing spiritual disciplines. These aren't items we need to quickly check off on some daily honey-do list from God. Whitney said, "So while we cannot be godly without the practice of the Disciplines, we can practice the Disciplines without being godly if we see them as ends and not means."

There are many spiritual disciplines of the Christian life.

Among them are serving, meditating on God's Word, evangelism, worship and stewardship. The three I'd like to focus on here are taking a Sabbath, fasting, and praying. This will by no means be an exhaustive study of these disciplines. They will warrant further study. However, here are some things to consider.

PRACTICING THE SABBATH

Someone once told me that to have a great roaring fire, you need to allow gaps between the wood. That's such a great illustration of taking a godly rest. Our schedule needs gaps in it. Observing the Sabbath is one of the ten commandments, yet, as we often do with the Great Commission, we seem to think that taking a Sabbath is a suggestion, not a command.

Even Jesus Himself took breaks. When God created the earth, He took a rest on the seventh day. The Bible is clear about not wasting time by arguing over which day to take. But it's clear we are to take one! For six days, we are to labor, and then on the seventh day, we are to rest and use that day solely to enjoy God's creation and worship Him.

What this means to you and to me may be different, but the thought behind a Sabbath is that we take that day to refresh ourselves intellectually, physically, and spiritually. Worship corporately with other believers on that day. Take a nap. Go for a walk. Ride a bike. Refresh so you are ready to get back to work, serving Jesus with all your strength.

Sundays are often workdays for us. We speak at churches or we are ministering at raves. Getting legalistic about practicing the Sabbath doesn't please God. It's okay to pick another day that works for you. It may be a different day each week.

I have been guilty over the years of not obeying God in keeping the Sabbath. I've paid dearly for it. It doesn't happen all at once, but it creeps up on you. Don't ignore the importance of rest as a disciple of Jesus.

FASTING

Jesus prayed and fasted before going into spiritual battle. We must follow His example. We ask our teams to do this before outreaches. An interesting fact I read lately about fasting is that when your body isn't using all its energy to digest food, your brain gets more of the energy. I'm no doctor, but this makes a lot of sense to me. Perhaps fasting helps our brains to be sharp when we need to discern the lies of the enemy as Jesus did in Matthew 4.

Fasting keeps us focused on praying. When I am fasting and I feel that rumbly in my tumbly, it reminds me to pray! How often do we get busy, finding ourselves at the end of the day with the realization that we took no time to speak with God? Fasting helps us keep focused on the things we should. During the hours we fast, we spend the time we would normally use for eating to pray instead. We are replacing physical nourishment with spiritual nourishment.

Be careful that you don't get religious about this. Don't fast more than what is healthy for your body. Long fasts should be done under proper medical supervision. Be sensible. Do it for the right reasons, in the right way, for the right amount of time.

There is a kind of fasting that involves denying ourselves more than just food. Check out Isaiah 58. The people were fasting to please themselves. They were trying to look good and missed the whole meaning of fasting. The Lord called them on it, saying:

No, this is the kind of fasting I want: Free those
who are wrongly imprisoned; lighten the

> *burden of those who work for you. Let the*
> *oppressed go free, and remove the chains*
> *that bind people. Share your food with the*
> *hungry, and give shelter to the homeless.*
> *Give clothes to those who need them, and do*
> *not hide from relatives who need your help.*
> Isaiah 58:6-7 (NLT)

Pray about how God would have you fast. A fast might include taking the time we would normally spend on ourselves and spending it on others. It may mean we skip just one meal in a twenty-four-hour period and give that meal to someone else. It may mean we spend time doing prison ministry or working at a homeless shelter instead of taking the time for a pedicure or to watch a ballgame. It may mean that before we rake our own leaves, we go rake the leaves of that irritating uncle or annoying mother-in-law. Fasting to serve puts our heart in the right place.

PRAYING

Before our teams go out to minister, we meet to worship and pray. We always close our time with Ephesians 6. If someone were to look in the window at just the right time, they might think we look quite silly. As someone reads the passage on the armor of God, we stand, literally making the motions of putting on the armor: the helmet of salvation, the belt of truth, the breastplate of righteousness, the shoes of peace, et cetera. It's a team tradition and it helps so much to have that picture fresh in our minds before we go out into the spiritual battle that surrounds the events where we minister. We are entering Satan's playground. We must armor up for that.

However, God has shown us that we should be armoring

up for the spiritual battle that is all around us every day. Not just on outreach days!

One night, my husband and I were in a hotel near a conference where we had a display to introduce the ministry to conference attendees. Compared to what we do on outreaches, these kinds of events almost seem like vacations. My heart had been light as we'd checked in.

We'd had a roller coaster of a week! A raver who had been a prodigal, coming back to God after attending Camp 33, was going to be baptized. That week he had announced the date. My husband and I cleared our calendars to be there. But then, that same week, we found out that another raver we had ministered to, also a prodigal who eventually returned, had been killed in a car accident. Ryan's funeral would be on the same day as Darrien's baptism. In tears, we changed our plans. In a couple of weeks, on the same day, Rob would be going to a baptism and I'd be going to a funeral. This conference seemed like a welcome respite!

So, there we were in that hotel room, feeling like we were taking a little break. But in the middle of the night, I woke with a horrible pain in my throat and chest. Assuming it was heartburn, I jumped out of bed to get some water.

As I found my way to the bathroom in our hotel room, I heard a voice in my head say, "Ryan wasn't supposed to die." I knew right away that the voice was not from the Lord because He alone decides when it is time for someone to leave this earth. I knew the enemy was messing with me, questioning the authority of God. That was confirmed when I tried to take a sip of water. My jaw was locked. Again, I heard the same voice. This time it said, "And I can shut your mouth!"

I began to pray. God immediately gave me peace. He began to speak to me. He told me that I am on the front lines all the time. Everyday. Not just when I'm on an outreach. I need to armor up daily to withstand the fiery darts of the enemy. I went back to bed. My jaw released within minutes.

The enemy HATES those who fish for men! Not only are you living smack dab in the center of God's will when you are partnering with Him in the Great Commission, but you've also got a target on your head. You know what to do. Greater is He that is in you than he that is in the world. Armor up! There is a spiritual battle going on all around you. Don't start or end your day without taking up your sword and standing firm on the truth of God's Word.

Pray continually throughout each day. This is an essential spiritual discipline! Actually converse with God. Wait for Him to speak back to you.

> Don't worry about anything; instead, pray about
> everything. Tell God what you need, and
> thank him for all he has done. Then you will
> experience God's peace, which exceeds
> anything we can understand. His peace will
> guard your hearts and minds as you live in
> Christ Jesus.
> Philippians 4:6-7 (NLT)

Spiritual disciplines are so important. I see them as necessities and ask people to hold me accountable to being disciplined in these areas. Prayer, fasting, meditating on God's Word, practicing good stewardship, taking a Sabbath... all these things are vitally important when you are serving on the front lines, fulfilling the Great Commission, and pushing back as much darkness as possible in your lifetime.

THEY PRACTICE COMMON SENSE

We've talked a lot about how following God can seem crazy sometimes. But it's crazy enough without bringing some of our own self-inflicted crazy along! Whenever possible, practice common sense. Pour over the book of Proverbs. There's a wealth of common sense in there.

> *My child, do not lose sight of common sense and*
> *discernment. Hang on to them, for they will*
> *refresh your soul. They are like jewels on a*
> *necklace. They keep you safe on your way,*
> *and your feet will not stumble. You can go to*
> *bed without fear; you will lie down and*
> *sleep soundly. You need not be afraid of*
> *sudden disaster or the destruction that*
> *comes upon the wicked, for the Lord is your*
> *security. He will keep your foot from being*
> *caught in a trap.*
> *Proverbs 3:21-26 (NLT)*

A few common-sense things based on Scripture stand out when it comes to discipleship ministry and Christian leadership:

1. Don't put people in leadership too soon. This just makes sense. It has nothing to do with age, but everything to do with maturity. There are so many pitfalls that face leaders, don't cause a new believer to stumble by putting him in charge (1 Timothy 3:6). And please! Can we not put them in a lead teaching role in Sunday School? Children will swallow everything they're told—whole! They

don't have the discernment to check what they are being taught against Scripture. Let the adults have the newer teachers if you must. Give the children our best.

2. Minister out of a place of healing. Be sure that your wounds are healed before you attend to another's wounds. Learn the lessons God wants you to learn in the broken places, and then use it for His glory. We require recovering addicts to be clean and sober for a minimum of five years before they can join our outreach teams. They will be super effective when they get to that place.

3. When you are hydrated, people will know that you know where the water is. Fishers of men need to be practicing what they preach.

4. Minimize temptation. Do whatever it takes. Our rave dads are required to have Covenant Eyes on their computers along with a board-approved accountability partner because we can't have men out on our mission field who are struggling with porn at home. Look at your particular situation, on your particular mission field. Choose appropriate safeguards.

5. Place people in positions according to their strengths and gifts. It won't always be like this, but since Rob and I have both quit our jobs, we run a tight ship that's on the verge of financial ruin every month, so we do almost everything the ministry needs in-house, between the both of us, without paying staff, whenever possible. At first, I was doing all the accounting. What a joke! That is NOT my strength. It's not even my weakness; it's flat out not even on my radar. We used QuickBooks, and my

password was I HATE ACCOUNTING 123. We had to be real about our strengths and weaknesses and assign jobs accordingly. It's the same on our outreach teams.

PERSONAL REFLECTION AND GROUP DISCUSSION

- What are some spiritual disciplines that you regularly practice?
- How do you believe that has helped you in your day-to-day life?
- What are some spiritual disciplines that you need to pay more attention to?
- What does it mean to you to minister from a place of healing?
- How can you stay hydrated?
- Suggested verses to memorize: Philippians 4:6-7

CHAPTER 25

THEY DON'T FORGET WHERE THEY CAME FROM, AND THEY KNOW WHO THEY ARE NOW

WHERE DID YOU COME FROM?

Not everyone has the same background as you or I have. We must remember that we all have different experiences, engrained prejudices, and opinions. We don't come from the same place, so we sometimes see things very differently. Some of us were abused, some of us came from ideal Christian homes, some from plenty and some from want. When we "get this," we come to see that not everyone begins where we did, and our tiny world can enlarge to include and love more people.

Our backgrounds give us reference points from which we stand to view the world. How we were raised, what we were taught with words, and even more so by deeds, will affect how we naturally respond and react to the world around us. Some people call this our "hidden script." They are our defaults. My hidden script includes the default to judge because I was raised in a legalistic, religious, abusive home. As a child and well into early adulthood, I was consistently judged. Now I automatically go there. I must consciously work not to hold others hostage to my past. What I hated most about my life, I do to others. "Mirror, mirror on the wall, I am my father after all."

Yet, there is potential here to flip this all around. What power there is when we give our broken past up to Jesus and ask Him to redeem it, to use it for His glory! This is what makes my husband such a great fisher of men. He often tries to explain what it feels like to be on one of our outreaches: "I know what I went through as a teenager, and so, in a sense, I'm rescuing me."

Have you ever met someone before they became a believer who was a relatively nice guy? Then he got saved and turned into a mean-spirited, judgmental human being? I have. Unfortunately, sometimes these people were a lot nicer B.C. (before Christ). It's because after they got saved they started living right. They got all puffed up about it, starting to judge others for the way they themselves used to live. They have forgotten from whence they came. It's time for them to hear the gospel again, to be reminded of who is the sinner and who is the Savior of the world.

After we get saved, we must remember that we are still here on earth. We're not in heaven yet. It's not time to rest in peace. The body of Christ in America sure does a lot of soaking without doing a whole lot of ploughing. Our attitude should be, "My master wants me out working in the fields because they are ripe for harvest and the time is short. So no matter how hard it is, I'm going to hit the fields and get to work."

Soaking is for those who've been out ploughing all day! The Christian life isn't all about going from one retreat to the next, one Bible study to another. Those things are great, but they need to be done for the purpose of fortifying ourselves to fulfill the Great Commission. Don't be so heavenly minded that you're no earthly good. Remember where you came from, that others are still there, and get to work!

Now that we are saved and have been around other Christians for a while, we've picked up on a whole new language. I call it Christianese. We need to remember that where we once came from, they don't speak that language. When I'm meeting someone for the first time in the shuttle on the way to the airport and I want to share the gospel with them, I ought not speak like this: "Have you been washed by the blood of the lamb and become part of the body of Christ? Hallelujah if you have. If not, I'd love to tell you what I've been learning at my missional life group. The leader is so anointed! Anyway, here's my contact info. Safe travel mercies! And in my next quiet time, I'll be praying a hedge of protection around you!"

The bottom line is that knowing and remembering where we came from helps us to have an attitude of gratitude. That will help us to be good representatives of the Lord. It will give us compassion and empathy.

> *And whatever you do or say, do it as a*
> *representative of the Lord Jesus, giving*
> *thanks through him to God the Father.*
> Colossians 3:17 (NLT)

WHO ARE YOU NOW?

Who did God create you to be? What are the things He has made very important to you? Your core values? Integrity? Mercy? Justice?

> *Take delight in the Lord, and He will give you*
> *your heart's desires.*
> Psalm 37:4 (NLT)

What are the desires of your heart? The Bible says that if you delight yourself in the Lord, He will give you desires. He will lay on your heart the things that please Him. You will want to do those things. Before you got saved, the desire of your heart may have been to pursue the American dream, a big house, an amazing car. But since you have surrendered your life fully to Jesus, those desires have been replaced with kingdom things. If you are fully surrendered to Jesus, look at the desires He has placed in you. They are there because He thinks they will be a valuable resource for His mission to reach the lost.

When my husband and I finally had to leave our jobs because the ministry was growing and needed more of our time, I thought we would have to get rid of all the things we had acquired in our past life. Our dock and our boat were two of those things. Well guess what? God had other plans. As soon as our hearts had released those things, and we were willing to give it all up, God showed us that He had plans to use those things for His glory. We cashed out all our savings and our retirement plans to make ends meet, but He had us keep some of our other things, knowing that He would be using them in the future to bless ravers who came to Camp 33. Back when we were pursuing the American dream and had purchased the dock and boat, we had no idea they would be used for kingdom work!

Who we were then and who we are now are, for the most part, different. But God is the same. He is the constant. His mission is the lost. He will use us as He sees fit to reach them, with our past and with our present and with our future.

What are your gifts and talents? How can you use these things to serve Him as you fulfill the Great Commission? Are you an IT guy that's super good with computers? Maybe God wants to use that talent to reach the lost somehow. Are you extra sensitive to people and how they are feeling? Maybe God wants to use you in a counseling role, give you opportunities to meet people in their broken places and introduce them to the Mighty Counselor, the Prince of Peace.

God is super creative in His quest for the lost. Never underestimate that your character traits, preferences and talents—no matter how unusual, farfetched, or obscure—can be used by God to reach people. As I write this, I'm sitting in the motorcycle shop attached to a biker church across from a rave venue. I am killing some time as I wait for our team to arrive. The church loves what our ministry does and lets us use their shop to worship and pray with our team before we outreach at this venue. There are motorcycle parts everywhere, along with a coffee bar. A cross made of an old trailer hitch hangs on the wall in front of me. On the wall next to me is a dart board and, if you lift the panel on which it is mounted, there's a knife and axe throwing wall underneath that the church uses for men's events. The pastor is talking to my husband at the other side of the shop. He's got a black bandana tied around his head. His arms are covered in tattoos, and he has silver skull rings on almost every finger. A chain loops down from his belt across his leg. A bunch of bikers are coming and going, prepping a trailer that they call their "battle wagon" to go on an outreach of their own at a local bike night event. They are so excited, talking amongst themselves about their opportunity to share the gospel with fellow bikers tonight. Yes! God is creative. He uses everyone and anyone who is willing.

We have a friend who is an amazing entertainer and bass looper. He has opportunities to go to places most Christians don't or can't. He has been able to get all-access passes for our teams at giant music festivals. At one rave event, we were able to go wherever we wanted, whenever we wanted, and we even ate amazing gourmet meals backstage with that weekend's headliners. All because God has given this guy some quirky talents that he takes on the road, looking for opportunities to use them for the kingdom.

Another couple we know and love go to goth clubs to share the gospel. Their bent toward this culture is being used for kingdom purposes. What used to be their passion is now their purpose. They are some of the most effective apologists we know.

When people get saved, their whole personality usually doesn't change. If they were an introvert before, they are probably still an introvert. As they die to self and experience the fruit of the Spirit in their life, their personality comes under the authority of a new boss. Their natural gifts or talents usually don't change, but how they use them does. Great fishers of men know how God can use them right where they are, who they are. When all of who and what they are answers to Jesus, life gets really exciting!

PERSONAL REFLECTION AND GROUP DISCUSSION

- Share your testimony and what God has done for you.
- What are some talents that God has given you that can be used for His kingdom?
- What are the desires God has placed in your heart?
- Suggested verse to memorize: Colossians 3:17

CHAPTER 26

THEY KNOW WHERE THEY ARE ON THE MAP

Like that "You are Here" dot on the map at the mall, know where you are currently placed to minister. Work on your ability to connect with the culture where God has placed you: your fishing hole. When I found my dot on the map and realized it was smack dab in the middle of a rave party, I became a student of the rave subculture. For me, engaging the people of that culture was a necessary part of fulfilling the Great Commission. Understanding their culture was imperative!

It became clear to me that God had not called me to rescue a culture but to rescue people. People ask me all the time why I don't march on city hall, tell them what I've seen and demand that they shut raves down. My response is that spiritual problems cannot be solved politically. The culture will change when people's hearts change, not the other way around.

**When we jump to solve spiritual problems
solely by creating new laws, we are choosing**

temporary fixes that will ensure permanent problems.

According to the Dorling Kindersley *Encyclopedia of Fishing*, "The best anglers are also good naturalists, who learn the habits of fish, and study currents, tidal flows, bankside vegetation, submerged weeds, the underwater topography, and a host of other natural and artificial underwater features that indicate where the fish are likely to be and what they will be feeding on. You can build up an enormous store of useful knowledge while you are fishing simply by observing what is going on in and around the water and noting how the movements and feeding habits of the fish vary with the time of day, the weather, and the light conditions."

Wow! Great fishing has a whole lot to do with understanding the environment. And great fishing for men has a whole lot to do with understanding the culture those people are in. I am always surprised when someone involved in evangelistic outreach of any type refuses to watch or read mainstream news or get on social media like Facebook or Instagram. We must understand what is feeding our mission field. We have to understand what makes them tick. We must understand their worldview in order to engage them well.

Notice here that I said engage, not agree with or become. Thank God that I don't have to dress in typical rave wear—a tutu, a bra, and a thong—to reach ravers! The very fact that I come into their world looking completely different attracts them to me! I can be culturally relevant without being identical.

Because I have a deep understanding of their culture, my attitude toward them shows that while I look nothing like them and act nothing like them, I am actually in touch with them. I can carry on an informed, intelligent conversation with them. I assume this would be the same if a white girl like me were ministering in a jungle in Uganda. I may not look anything like them, but I can still be in touch with who they are and understand their needs and mindset.

Being relevant doesn't equal compromise. We don't have to BE them to minister to them. I didn't have to become an addict to become a great addiction treatment counselor. I did, however, do a whole lot of listening. Client after client thanked me for being a part of their journey to freedom and recovery. They still come up to me, years later, in grocery stores or the mall, to thank me. All I did was listen, offer compassion, hope, and tried and true counsel.

My ministry leadership coach, Rebecca Badry, says, "Relevancy creates a receptivity to the gospel. And you can only become relevant by listening." She and I have discussed at length how important listening is in fulfilling the Great Commission.

You must listen to your mission field until you find something you can relate to or personally connect with. Then you will find the entry point to sharing the gospel. It's those, "I do that too!" or "Oh, my goodness, I feel the very same way!" moments in a conversation where you become relevant to the one to whom you are listening.

However, we must be sincere in our listening. Sharing the gospel isn't some activity that we engage in to check off some box on our to-do list or to get some brownie points with God. There are times we may listen and not end up sharing the gospel. We must trust the Holy Spirit to give us that opportunity. And if it doesn't come, we must trust that we were just tilling the soil of that heart to prepare it for the next person who will come along and plant the seed.

Many times, in our ministry, I have sensed that God has

used us to be the very first positive experience a young person has ever had with a Christian. And God may be using that to get their heart in the right place to receive the gospel at a later time. There have also been kids I've listened to who have asked if we could meet again and talk some more. They are so drawn by the fact that I listened to them the first time with sincerity because I truly cared and had no other agenda.

> *Understand this, my dear brothers and sisters:*
> *You must all be quick to listen, slow to*
> *speak, and slow to get angry.*
> James 1:19 (NLT)

Over and over again, I have seen the incredible wisdom of this advice James gives on listening. It's interesting that James not only says how important it is to listen, but how we must not be easily angered by what we hear as we listen.

I once had the opportunity to sit down inside a casino in Las Vegas with a thirty-something tourist from England. It's just one of those crazy God stories. He wasn't there for the rave that was in town, but he couldn't help but notice all the ravers coming and going from all the hotels. We were in the same line for coffee when he asked me if I knew what was going on. I told him why I was there. He was baffled. And that was the start of a very long conversation.

His nickname was Brain; that's what was on his name badge at work. He was an Organic Medicinal Biologist with a PhD from Oxford. He quickly shared that he was an atheist. I could tell he was looking for my reaction.

He was probably a bit disappointed because if my face said what my heart was feeling it was, "Perfect! Only God could arrange this!" What an unlikely meeting this was: the missionary and the atheist in a casino.

We had an incredible time as we shared our stories. He heard the whole gospel as I explained the colors on the bracelets I wore on my arms. He was very skeptical. I asked him to consider reading the Bible and praying that God would reveal Himself to him. Brain said that he would NEVER in a million years do that! He was very kind, but firm.

As we continued to talk, he shared that he had never been able to have a loving, respectful conversation with a Christian before. He was shocked to be having one now. He said all the Christians who had ever talked to him were hateful and angry and aggressive once he started sharing his viewpoint.

He asked if we could continue talking, so we did. We talked about all sorts of issues, some little, some big, like how he'd had too much to drink the night before, terrorist attacks in America, the possibility of intelligent design in nature, and how he'd just lost $300.00 in the slot machines. After a while, he felt comfortable enough to take a risk.

Like tiptoeing through glass, he carefully shared that where he lived they all think Christians are idiots to believe what we believe. He said he'd be laughed out of his hometown if they knew he had spent this much time talking to me! He waited for my response.

I also took a risk. I carefully shared that I thought it was funny that he thought I was an idiot for believing in Jesus, while I think throwing $300.00 in a slot machine is quite likely the very definition of an idiot!

We both laughed and he said, "Well done. I guess you're right!"

Before we went our separate ways, I asked him if I could pray for him, and to my surprise, he said yes. When I finished in Jesus's name, he looked at me incredulously and said, "Wait a minute! What is going on here? I'm covered in chills."

Explain that Dr. Brain!

God is relentless in his pursuit of Brain and millions more like him. This was his very first contact of many with the living Jesus, loving through Christians. I can't wait to see him in heaven someday, and when I do, I may just have to say, "I see they let idiots in here!"

I hope one of the lessons you take away from this story is that if someone like me could find common ground with Brain, you can find common ground with anyone! Our intelligence levels didn't match, our nationalities didn't match, we weren't close at all to the same age.

As I've ministered to young people across the country and spoken to groups of people my age to encourage them to engage the lost of this generation, I have learned firsthand that Satan whispers lies to us older people, making us think that we can never reach the generations after us because people have to be as young and cool and hip as they are in order to reach them. He discourages us by saying we are out of touch, because he knows that us older people being in touch with the younger generation is what they need. It's what they crave.

The truth is, being in touch with the next generation has nothing to do with our ages, but we do have to know where they are at on the map! The only way to discover this is by listening to them. That will lead us toward becoming relevant and relatable, even to someone like Brain.

Being relevant has more to do with knowing where someone is and then adjusting ourselves, than about being like them in some way or similar in age. If you are the boss and you want your employee to do a particular job, you need to give that employee instructions. To do this well, you need to consider any prior training or experience that they've had so you can know how best to communicate the instructions to them.

Parents do this all the time. Think about telling a child to "dust this room." If they have no prior experience or knowledge of what dusting a room means, then you might just end up with the wrong result! In our culture, dusting a room means removing the dust. But if they don't understand that, you could end up with more dust in that room than you ever imagined!

I've overheard Christians trying to share the gospel with people. Sometimes the words they use make it obvious that they are assuming that the people they are sharing the gospel with know the basic story of Jesus's death and resurrection. This approach is outdated. Many years ago, we could have assumed that if you were born and raised in the United States, you would know about Jesus. But in our culture today, we can no longer make those assumptions.

Good fishermen don't make assumptions. They know their fishing hole, know the type of fish that reside there, and what type of bait they respond to. In William Tapply's book, *A Fly-Fishing Life*, he shares how, as he gets to know the area where he is fishing, he becomes better at it: "I have learned to slow down and pay attention to the way water moves and insects reproduce and fish behave. I have watched and listened to other fishermen. I have tried to learn the hard lessons that fish teach."

Just like that expert fisherman, we need to slow down and observe the culture of our mission field before we barge in thinking we know what they need to hear. I once saw a hilarious video on missionaries who do just the opposite. It was highly exaggerated to make a point, but it confronted the North American mindset that we have a higher way of living and need to share it with others. In a roundabout way it used humor to depict Americans barging into other cultures to try to share the gospel AND teach them to live like Americans at the same time, as if that's the only godly way to live.

There are many cultures that are unscathed by the greed

we experience in the United States. They are okay with paying cash for things, living simply. They think it's ridiculous that we take out loans and mortgages to get the things we want. If we go over there to plant a church, we may not need to have a huge building fund like we see here in the United States with the latest and greatest architecture and all the high-tech bells and whistles. They may just want a simple structure where they can gather out of the rain. We need to learn these "hard lessons that fish teach."

Coming in on a white horse to save the day may make us feel good, but it isn't always what a community needs. They may need us to come alongside them, live with them, gently enter into their culture instead of attempting to change it to make it more like the culture we are used to. The goal of that would really be to make ourselves more comfortable, wouldn't it?

We have experienced a few people at raves being offended when we say we are there to help them. These people don't feel they need help. Now when they see how we take care of those whom they agree need help, those hurt feelings go away. But we must be careful how we communicate our mission to them. No one is ever offended when we say we are there to show God's love to them, not shove it down their throats.

We once found a girl at three a.m., coming down from a drug trip, sitting in just a thong and a bra on a corner in front of a gas station down the street from a rave venue in a notoriously dangerous city. She was on the phone getting directions from her friends who were waiting for her in a parking lot two blocks away. Two of us rave moms approached her and told her we would help her get to her friends. She told us she didn't need help. She informed us that she was twenty-four years old. To her, that meant she was totally able to safely get herself to that parking lot alone.

So we tried a different approach. We apologized saying we didn't mean to treat her like a child. We told her that we were moms who were here to show God's love to people by keeping them company when they were alone. We told her that we could just follow her at a distance, and we wouldn't need to talk. We gave her a bracelet, and she agreed. So, it worked. We were able to follow her to safety, we just had to word it the right way. More hard lessons that fish teach.

I believe some of the most effective ministries in the United States are those that target a particular subculture, because their focus has slowed them down. They are learning about that subculture and how to approach it. This is one way that God is so creative in His quest for the lost. And these days, He seems to be ramping up, putting people in place to minister by showing them the needs of a culture and then showing them how to create an experience of community within that culture in this world that so lacks community.

People in these fast-paced, online, text-instead-of-talk days are starving for it. One ministry takes a portable cappuccino machine to malls and soccer fields. Another goes to laundromats to wait with people who sit there with time to kill. Still another takes elderly women to bars and clubs when they close, and they offer flip flops to the young ladies who come stumbling out in stiletto heels and walk them to their cars or Ubers. Our ministry is to millennials and post millennials. We set up a family-style campsite in the middle of rave parties and offer pancakes and conversation with loving parents and grandparents. We sunblock them in the heat and wrap them in blankets in the cold. We meet them at their need. Then they ask us why we are doing this. Getting to answer that question is what I live for.

Culturally, this is sometimes like being in a canoe on white water with one oar in the current of my own cultural past and one oar in the current of the rave culture. It's not always smooth sailing, but God meets me and the kids I am ministering to in the churning foam. This always keeps me aware that I cannot do this in my own strength and that's good!

I know where I stand, where my dot is on the map. I know my mission field. Millennials are the largest generation our nation has ever known. There are seventy-eight million of them. I know that sixty-five percent of them think that they are Christians, but sixty-five percent of them rarely or never attend church. Eight million of them believe the American church is irrelevant—and, for the most part, I'm with them on that. Less than twenty percent—that is twenty percent of seventy-eight million!—have a Biblical understanding of Jesus and matters of salvation! The generation that comes after them is similar. This means that over sixty million of our nation's young people are dying in their sin.

In the middle of all that is my fishing hole! I know that there's something called PLUR that is very important to my mission field. It's the ravers' motto. It stands for Peace, Love, Unity, and Respect. I know they don't often find it, but they crave it. They are willing to use drugs like Ecstasy to experience it, even for just a few hours. I know they won't come to church, so I go to them, where they are, to offer them lasting PLUR, because I know they will only truly find it in Jesus.

God, in His great mercy, redeemed my story when He called me. He tapped into my own heart hunger for kind parenting. I could identify with the generation He called me to. And that's called beauty for ashes. I get to introduce a generation that asks, "Who am I?" to the great "I Am."

As I've studied, immersing myself in this mission field, I've also learned that they are a very spiritual generation. They talk openly about spirituality. They don't mind being asked where they are at on their spiritual journey. They want input.

Recently, we had dinner with an executive from one of the top communications companies in the world. He'd just returned from a team-building retreat for the sixty higher ups in the company. He shared that the event coordinator was instructed to get a speaker on spirituality. He tried for the pope, the Dalai Lama, and had to settle for Oprah Winfrey. So, she came and sat on a couch in front of them and shared everything she has learned on her own spiritual journey. My heart hurt as I pictured these wealthy, accomplished, genius-level business-people sitting at Oprah's feet to gain wisdom on spiritual matters. Think this generation isn't open to spiritual things? Think again! People are hungry.

> *"In the last days, God says, I will pour out my*
> *Spirit on all people. Your sons and*
> *daughters will prophesy, your young men*
> *will see visions, your old men will dream*
> *dreams."*
> Acts 2:17 (NIV)

Folks! This is happening. We see it a lot as we minister to this generation. And they don't know what to do with it! This is an opportunity for the church to direct them to the giver of the visions. But instead, the church seems to be afraid of this stuff. When we run into a twenty-something who wants to tell us about the dreams and visions they are having, or the sixth sense they seem to possess, we run the other way thinking that they are demonic or unclean somehow. We run from this stuff that gives us the heebie-jeebies instead of facing it and talking about it. When we push these kids away, we send them right into the open, waiting arms of Wicca and other contemporary pagan religions.

Have you noticed how interest in eastern mysticism has

risen in this generation? I think the way the church has treated these kids accounts for some of that. Greater is He that is in us than He that is in the world! Let's quit being so scared of all this stuff. Let's have open dialogue about it!

Dannie was the name of a girl who came to get a mom hug from me at a rave in the summer of 2017. I'll never forget her. After she hugged me tight, she held my face in her hands and said, "You are love and light and nothing can destroy you." Then she put a beaded necklace around my neck that she had made to give away that weekend. Spelled out in the beads threaded on the elastic cord were the words PLUR Warrior.

This girl had a prophetic gift. She also had the gift of discernment. She had no idea who I was, yet her words were accurate, just a bit misguided. I am not love, but the God who lives inside me is. It is true, nothing can truly destroy me. I have eternal life. And it's true, I am a warrior with a message of PLUR to ravers.

Remember, Satan is the great counterfeiter. I believe he can mimic godly gifts and use them to trap people. We need to arrest his plans. When we run into kids like this we need to address their giftings and show them how to place them under the authority of the Greater One.

I explained this to Dannie. She allowed me to pray over her and claim her and her gifts for the Lord. God is good!

PERSONAL REFLECTION AND GROUP DISCUSSION

- What are some good questions you can ask next time you are with someone who is very different than you?
- Have you ever been in a situation at work or school

where you had to learn to get along with another culture or subculture? What did you learn?

- Would you like to be the first positive experience someone has ever had with a Christian? How can you make sure that happens?
- Suggested verse to memorize: James 1:19

CHAPTER 27

THEY ARE AUTHENTIC

od created you. He gave you gifts and talents. He wants you to use them for His glory. If you are an extrovert, use that for His glory. If you are an introvert, use that for His glory. If you don't speak well or if you're an amazing speaker, use that for His glory. In our weakness, He is made strong; He is glorified.

A WORD TO THE YOUNG

Jeremiah thought he was too young to do God's work. The Lord called him on it:

> But the Lord said to me, "Do not say, 'I am too young.' You must go to everyone I send you to and say whatever I command you. Do not be afraid of them, for I am with you and will rescue you," declares the Lord.
> Jeremiah 1:7-8 (NIV)

We use everything we've got, and then He gives us the rest. He'll rescue the parts of us that won't make it. He will come alongside us when we are not enough.

A WORD TO THE OLD

If you're over forty, I'm talking to you. Yes, you are now old. This generation has a lot of young, cool, and hip in their lives. Just when they need parenting most, their parents try to be their friends. They don't need friends. They need parents. And when they don't get what they need at home, they need you to fill in the gaps.

Our rave moms and dads don't try to act cool or hip. We try not to. And for some of us that's easier than others.

All kidding aside, I think it's one of the great tragedies of our culture that we try our hardest to maintain our youthful appearances and actions. In past generations, gray hair was a sign of wisdom. Age was attractive. It meant this wasn't your first rodeo. You had a lot of experience and maturity.

Now I'm not saying we ladies should all quit dyeing our hair and the men shouldn't work off that belly. I'm just saying we should let our age show. We shouldn't work so hard on blurring the lines between the generations.

This generation wants sincerity and authenticity. I recently heard about a church who let all their older leaders go. They wanted a church that attracted millennials, so they thought they needed an all-millennial leadership team. I'm not sure how that will work out for them. I pray they haven't made a big mistake. It's not the model for ministry that God has given to us.

Because we have found that this generation is vastly unparented, our rave moms and dads are older parents and grandparents. It's what God showed us to do early on. Oh, trust me, we fought the idea. But God hadn't made a mistake. The young people at raves love us. The older the better. They treat us grandmas like rock stars. They ask for photos with us. They hang out with us. They ask us to visit them at their jobs. They want us to come to their soccer games and their birthday parties. They call us in the middle of the night for advice.

From what we can gather, the thousands of college-age people we have ministered to over the years wouldn't think fifty-year-old pastors—wearing their skinny jeans and trying to act and speak like they're twenty-five—are attractive. As long as they aren't judgmental, they are attracted to old people who are acting their age; sincere and authentic.

A Fuller Youth Institute study of 250 congregations found that young adults want substance rather than style, hip pastors, or big budgets. The gospel is very simple. It's also amazing all on its own. No bells or whistles (or clanging cymbals) needed. Gospel. Period. That's it. The world is craving good news. Feed it to them in love.

> *If I could speak all the languages of earth and of*
> *angels, but didn't love others, I would only*
> *be a noisy gong or a clanging cymbal.*
> *1 Corinthians 13:1 (NLT)*

The first time we invited human sex-trafficking survivors into our home to experience a weekend similar to Camp 33, I was a bit nervous. I'd been through numerous training courses in my former job that were required to identify clients who might be victims of trafficking, and our Camp 33 team had also been given a crash course in ministering to these girls, but the rubber was about to meet the road in my own home. It was scary.

I didn't want to say the wrong thing and trigger them. I

wanted them to feel loved with no strings attached. We'd been warned that they are master manipulators and triangulators because of their past trauma. I wasn't sure how all that would play out.

Finally, minutes before they arrived, I just started baking pie. They say "desserts" is "stressed" backwards. That worked for me. So, I pulled out the sugar and flour and began to peel and slice apples. An amazing thing happened. One by one, these tough girls ended up in my kitchen. They were drawn to the sights and smells of an old lady doing what old ladies have done for hundreds of years. Except these girls had only seen glimpses of it on TV, never in real life.

The conversations slowly started and continued throughout the whole baking process. One girl was thrilled when I asked her to measure the sugar. Another asked to cut a little heart shape in the top of the pie. She was so proud as she slid her masterpiece into the oven. Here was just normal little me having life changing conversations with young ladies who had been robbed of their childhood. It was real, and authentic, and it wasn't the least bit scary after all.

Scary stuff would have happened if I'd tried to be something I'm not. Because then I would have had to keep that act up all weekend. That would have been impossible. Faking it can work from a stage in front of hundreds of people for an hour, but it won't work living with people for a weekend. And it won't work at your job or your school or in your home. Jesus is real. We must be real too.

The church owes this generation a great big thank you for shaking us up! They are demanding authenticity from us. They don't want a system or a method. To engage this generation, we are having to learn again as a church how to live like Jesus. Revival is coming!

PERSONAL REFLECTION AND GROUP DISCUSSION

- Are there opportunities in your life to "parent" young people, even young adults, who are lacking parenting in their lives?
- Are there some changes you can make to embrace your age, whether you are young or old, and use it for the kingdom?
- Is there someone in your life who might enjoy simple things like baking a pie or playing a board game with you?
- Suggested verse to memorize: 1 Corinthians 13:1

CHAPTER 28

THEY ARE NOT OVERWHELMED BY THE LOST

The Bible tells us that when Jesus was here on earth, He had compassion on the crowds. The Bible also tells us that He was *moved* with compassion. Compassion energizes us. It sets us into motion. Compassion says, "I see where you are, and I can help."

Great fishers of men are filled with compassion. I, too, have had compassion on my mission field, but I've also experienced being overwhelmed by it. While compassion is invigorating, becoming overwhelmed shuts us down. I believe a root of feeling overwhelmed by the lost—especially the vast numbers of the lost in our world—is a lack of hope. It's a tactic of the enemy to get our focus off the gospel, away from the Great Commission. He'd love to incapacitate us with this feeling.

This story will help me explain. One night during the first year of the rave ministry, three of us were at the little rave club we frequented. To this day, we are grateful for that place. God taught us so much there about the rave culture. We were such a small team, but the lessons we learned from those nights of ministry became the basis for much of the training manual we still use today for our new rave moms and dads.

That night at that little club, God taught us the lesson of the importance of not becoming overwhelmed by the lost. Rob secured a spot in the parking lot to worship, intercede in prayer, and remain at the ready in case we encountered any problems. Nicki and I headed toward the venue. We had no money for entrance fees that night, so, instead of going in Nicki and I decided to stay outside and hand out all of the bracelets we had brought with us to the ravers who were in line waiting for the club to open.

When the last bracelet was given out, Nicki and I felt led to stand off to the side, by the entrance. We prayed silently for every single person as they entered. There were 1,500 kids there that night. Forty-five minutes later, Nicki was still fervently praying, but I'd had enough.

As I had watched hundreds of faces go by, I began to be overwhelmed by the lost. There were so many! The things they were saying to each other as they walked past me, the drugs they were popping into their mouths or snorting or smoking, combined with the way the boys were treating the girls, it was all just too much after a while.

This was a small rave! There were much larger raves being held all over the country in every major city. How were we ever going to reach all these kids? And I still could only find one mom to go with me! This was crazy. I needed a break!

As I turned to tell Nicki, God stopped me cold! This is what I heard Him say: "I have called you to stand here and pray for each one of those kids. I expect you to do it! Who do you think you are? I am the One who will save them, not you! This is not too big for me! Get back to praying right now. Do not be overwhelmed! There are future missionaries and pastors and godly husbands and wives, moms and dads passing by you right now! Pray for them! Tonight will be a part of their future testimony."

Instantly, I had hope instead of despair. Compassion kicked in. Nicki and I finished off the night, praying for every single one of those kids. To this day, every time I hear that a raver has gotten saved and gone on to become a missionary or a pastor or a godly mom or dad, I wonder if they were in the line that night all those years ago.

> *For this is what the Sovereign Lord says: I*
> *myself will search and find my sheep. I will*
> *be like a shepherd looking for his scattered*
> *flock. I will find my sheep and rescue them*
> *from all the places where they were scattered*
> *on that dark and cloudy day.*
> *Ezekiel 34:11-12 (NLT)*

For many more months, we continued to minister at that club. Each time we were there, we prayed over those kids. We also prayed over the promoter and the staff; everyone involved in that little club. On nights we couldn't be there, we met with another couple, Wes and Peggy, on our knees in their living room, crying out to God for the salvation of these precious people.

Peggy had severe neck problems. Some nights she was in too much pain to meet in the living room to pray. On those nights, we literally gathered around her bed instead. She just wouldn't quit. She was overwhelmed by her pain, but she was not overwhelmed by the lost because she had compassion for them. Night after night, we simply prayed in faith, with great hope and expectation that God would someday answer our prayers with a "yes."

Just a month before writing this chapter, we welcomed a

new volunteer to our Camp 33 staff. We knew Trino was an awesome Christian and a godly husband and dad, but we had no idea about his past. On his first Camp 33 weekend, God used him to make a huge impact on the ravers that came. One of those ravers who got saved after that weekend said Trino was one of the reasons that he was drawn to Christ. It was evident that God had sent Trino to us!

We had some time to talk on Trino's second Camp 33 weekend. My jaw about hit the floor when he shared that the same year that we began to minister in that little club, he had been the rave promoter there! We pieced our stories together and realized that he had been there that night that Nicki and I had prayed over the line. He was there all of the other nights we prayed over that place, including the nights we couldn't be there when Wes and Peggy and Rob and I prayed over the promoter and the staff.

All along, we had been praying for Trino; we just didn't know his name.

But God did.

Wow! Just wow! Our new Camp 33 volunteer was a former rave promoter at the very club where God had trained us! He has a radical testimony. You just can't make this stuff up! Never, ever, ever think that someone is too far for the hand of God to reach. Don't be overwhelmed. We can trust Him to reach the lost! That's His business. We are just along for the ride.

Andrea is one of my favorite GRITS (girls raised in the South). She is on our prayer team, and she shared with me that she has watched what God has done over the years in this ministry. She said that every time we go out, she sees Him give us the Four P's: Protection, Placement, Priority, and Provision. She is so right! How can I possibly be overwhelmed when God has done this every single time? God gives the Four P's to everyone who is about His business. We can trust Him. Our hope is in Him!

He loves these kids more than I do. He loves your mission field more than you do; your family more than you do. He's got this. And we don't have to get it. We just have to do it. Trust and obey, for there's no other way, to fulfill the Great Commission, but to trust and obey!

PERSONAL REFLECTION AND GROUP DISCUSSION

- Have you ever felt overwhelmed by the lost as you watch the news or read Facebook?
- How does understanding the gospel and the God who saves change that feeling?
- Is there someone in your life who appears to be too far gone, too lost? Is that true, or is that a lie from the enemy?
- What specific things are you going to pray for them?
- Suggested verses to memorize: Ezekiel 34:11-12

CHAPTER 29

WHAT'S IMPORTANT TO GOD IS IMPORTANT TO THEM

Then the Lord said, "You feel sorry about the
plant, though you did nothing to put it there.
It came quickly and died quickly. But
Nineveh has more than 120,000 people
living in spiritual darkness, not to mention
all the animals. Shouldn't I feel sorry for
such a great city?"
Jonah 4:10-11 (NLT)

Jonah ran away from God's call to take His message to the people of Nineveh. It's kind of a funny story, but when a plant dies, Jonah was really upset. God gets on his case for caring more about a plant than about people. Because people are of utmost importance to God, people are of utmost importance to good fishers of men.

After we presented the rave ministry at a church women's group, some ladies gathered around me to ask questions. An older lady stood back. When everyone was gone, she came up to me and said, "I really admire what you do, but I just don't have time to help you. I have my own ministry. I rescue cats."

I cannot for the life of me remember what I said, but I hope I was kind. She may be an extreme example, but a whole lot more people are thinking like her these days. This may be unpleasant, but we need to wrestle with how we will conform or not conform to what has become very acceptable in our culture.

God made plants and animals. He asked us to take care of them. He doesn't want us to be cruel to them, and I believe He made some of them specifically for our enjoyment and our protection. While He cares about animals and according to the Bible, He knows when every sparrow falls, the Bible also says:

> "...you are more valuable to God than a whole
>   flock of sparrows."
> Matthew 10:31b (NLT)

Why? Because people have souls. They were created for relationship with God. They are more important than trees or animals or the angels. They are made in God's image. He thought they were worth dying for. No matter how much we may love her, Jesus didn't suffer and die on the cross for our beloved Fluffy.

I am trembling as I type because I know this will be hard for some people to accept. It may even be offensive, but animals are not people and not nearly as important as people. "Dogs are people too" is a cute but very inaccurate statement. If you disagree, look in Scripture. See if you can prove me wrong. I am confident that you cannot.

I have loved my little Buddy as much as anyone should love their dog. But I love people more. Proof of that is, if he had ever hurt anyone, he would've been escorted over the Rainbow Bridge. Sorry, but that's a fact.

I live in California. In the last few years I have seen an increase in people treating their pets like humans. It was funny at first, but there is something very wrong with a society that has successful pet bakeries and pet clothing stores when their foster system is so full of children that it's about to crumble. According to the American Pet Products Association (APPA), Americans spent a record-breaking $72.56 billion on their pets in 2018. This is more than the combined Gross Domestic Product (GDP) of the thirty-nine poorest countries in the world.

I don't claim to have any easy answers for this, but I do know that people who follow Jesus must keep what is most important to Him, most important to them. And that's human beings. Maybe Fido could go without that raincoat this year and a foster child could get a raincoat instead. It's a start.

I remember the sick feeling that came over me, accompanied by chills, as I sat in on a high school youth group gathering in my community one night. It happened in the middle of a fun ice-breaker game where the youth pastor gave the kids two choices. They had to run sit on one side of the room or the other, based on their choice. It was all fun to experience until he asked the question, "Would you rather have the power to talk to animals, or the power to talk to people in any language?" Almost the whole room picked animals over people and gathered on the right side, while one other mom and I sat on the left.

As an evangelist, I would give my right arm to be able to speak in any language! For a second, it felt like the walls of that youth room were closing in on me. It was so eye opening. This is where we are right now in our society. People just aren't that important anymore. The amazing privilege of sharing the gospel is taken for granted.

We need to change that.

I mentioned my dog, Buddy. He was a great dog. He protected our home and our kids and let us know when someone was at the door. He was a big help most of the time, but never more than when we took him on rave outreaches with us! The ravers loved him. He'd hang out in the ministry RV in the parking lot until he was needed. Then we'd bring him out to sit with a young man who was having a really bad night or a young lady who was experiencing anxiety from the drugs she had taken. Buddy was great at calming people down. He was used by God in many situations.

A friend of ours is on the front lines in the war against terrorism and trafficking. He has a trained guard dog that goes everywhere with him. That dog is being used to protect a modern-day hero of the faith. Good for him!

When our youngest daughter was nine, she ended up in the hospital for five days after an emergency surgery. She didn't smile until the day a beautiful Christian woman came in with her adorable therapy dog, who immediately proceeded to join Cassie on the bed, gingerly stepping around all the heart-monitor cords and IV tubes. He was such a blessing that day to our family. If I didn't believe in God already, I just might have that day when that lady and her therapy dog came in and shared His love with us.

If you love your pets, look for ways to include them in ministry. What a great way to put pets and people in the right order. God was creative enough to invent the puppy and the goldfish. He's creative enough to show you how to use your pets for His glory.

PERSONAL REFLECTION AND GROUP DISCUSSION

- What are some ways you've experienced animals being used for God's glory?
- If you had an extra twenty dollars in your budget this month, how could you use it for the Kingdom?
- How can we better care for God's creation?
- How can we better care for human life?
- Suggested verse to memorize: Matthew 10:31b

CHAPTER 30

THEY LEAVE A LEGACY

*O God, you have taught me from my earliest
   childhood, and I constantly tell others about
   the wonderful things you do. Now that I am
   old and gray, do not abandon me, O God.
   Let me proclaim your power to this new
   generation, your mighty miracles to all who
   come after me.*
Psalm 71:17-18 (NLT)

Everyone will leave a legacy, something we leave for those who come after us. Some of these legacies will be positive, some will be negative. Either way, how we live now will affect the generations that come after us.

There is nothing more damaging to the spiritual development of a young person than for a Christian mom or dad to live one way outside the home and another way inside. Loving people in Jesus's name outside your home, then treating your kids and your spouse as anything less makes a mockery of Christianity. I'm not pointing fingers here. I hate to admit it, but the fact is, I have had to ask forgiveness of my family for the way I have treated them many, many times, but I have rarely had to ask forgiveness of someone on my mission field. I am on my toes when I am out representing Christ. But shouldn't I also be representing Christ at home?

Family must be our first mission field. What good is it if I spend my life reaching out to ravers but by doing so I create a new generation of ravers in my own home? What good is it if I volunteer to teach Sunday School every week but I don't teach my own kids at home? Please don't create a whole new mission field by not caring for your kids.

Our oldest daughter, Joscelyn, is the funniest person I know. She can make me laugh till I literally get sick. Her experience the last few years as a pastor's wife and mother of twins has made her even funnier. She has a lot of material to work with! Recently, she sent me a hilarious text when I had already told her that a prior ministry commitment wouldn't allow us to meet up with her family for a spur of the moment trip to the zoo. Here's what her text said: "I met you at a rave last month. I really need to talk. I am going to be at the zoo today. If you meet me there, I'll probably become a Christian."

I laughed so hard I about fell off my chair. It made me look again to be sure I couldn't work it into my schedule, it was just so cute. But in all seriousness, I think there are many kids out there who act like the people their parents are ministering to in an attempt to get their parents' attention. We need to be so careful with these tender ones. They need us!

Fish with your kids! Engage them, don't leave them out. Take them with you or include them in the work you do as much as you can. Be sensitive to the Spirit on this. If you're going to teach your kids about the two most important commandments and the Great Commission, you need to be living out those things in front of them and with them.

I'll never forget the impact a quick missions trip made on our son, Matthew, when he was only ten years old. We headed down to Mexico for the day and asked God to use us. Matt came home shirtless because he met a little boy at the border who had no shirt. Matt's heart was broken that day. He acted on that broken heart. Our kids need to be on the mission field in some way at an early age.

I am so glad to see that more and more missionaries are taking their children onto the field with them. Back in the day, there used to be boarding schools for missionaries' kids. The fallout from this was devastating. These days, families are staying together on the mission field. For those families who are doing it right, it's not hurting the kids one bit. In fact, a whole new generation of missionaries are rising up because of it.

A friend of mine who is a missionary in South Asia is the mommy of an adorable little girl. Recently she shared that she was wrestling with some questions like, "Is our calling to live and work in multiple locations and countries adversely affecting our daughter?" These thoughts were on her mind a lot lately because she and her husband and daughter had been home on furlough. They had thoroughly enjoyed visiting family and friends in the States. When it was time to fly back overseas, her little girl didn't want to leave.

During the trip back, on a layover in some airport some-where, my friend shared that her little girl lit up when she spotted a table full of Legos in a corner shop. Two little girls were already there playing with the plastic blocks. My friend's daughter immediately engaged the girls, asking their names and introducing herself. Laughter and giggles ensued, making the layover quite an enjoyable experience.

Watching them play there in that airport, my friend heard the Lord whispering to her mommy heart, "The very thing you worry and wonder about negatively affecting your daughter is the exact thing I am using to form, shape, mold, and make her into a resilient, adaptable, friendly, caring, kind-hearted lover of all, and this will all be used for good in her life to make her who I desire her to be."

God is so good!

Our outreach teams know that we have a strict "family comes first" policy. If something serious comes up in their family, an illness, a moral failing, a death, a major life change, we tell them not to be afraid to take time off to minister at home. In fact, in many cases, we insist they do. Our families are our first calling. When you need to minister to them, God will fill in the hole that you leave behind on your mission field. Remember, it's not about you. The bottom line is you are replaceable, and God is very, very big.

Years ago, some friends of ours came off their mission field overseas temporarily when their relatives were involved in a horrific car accident. A mother and father were killed. Their five children were spared but orphaned. At first, the extended family came up with a plan to care for the children, but soon it became very apparent that this missionary couple were the only ones in the family that had what it would take to raise these children.

They agonized over this decision at first. It had nothing to do with their love for the children, but it had everything to do with the people of their mission field that they had served for years and had come to love with all their hearts.

I will never forget a conversation I had on the phone with them. I encouraged them to joyfully leave their mission field, to come home permanently to raise these children who needed so much love and care to move past their trauma. I shared that I believed they would make more advances against the kingdom of darkness in their lifetime by raising these children to be warriors for the Kingdom of God than they would ever make as just the two of them on the mission field. And sure enough, from a distance, I watched these children as they grew, going on to take major ground against the enemy!

God is so big.

We not only have legacies we pass down to our families, but we pass them down to our Christian family. Be sure that you are always aware that, as a good steward of the ministry God has given you, you must prepare your replacement. You aren't going to be able to do this forever. Don't let your ministry die with you. Bring others in on what you're doing. Show them your favorite fishing hole, pass on the lessons you have learned while fishing there. In this way, prepare the next generation to take over for you.

Are you praying for the babies being born right now, that one or more of them will carry the torch you've lit? Take every opportunity to share with younger people what God has shown you. Let them see how amazing life can be when it is lived smack dab in the center of God's will. We must be intentional about this because the enemy is intentional about doing the opposite.

The night before our grandson was born, God gave me a picture of a wave washing over the entire globe. It started small, then built and built as it covered the whole world. He showed me that this was a picture of this generation being birthed right now. They will grow up to spread the love of Jesus like a wave across the entire globe.

I believe this generation growing up right now will be the one to finally take the gospel to the ends of the earth. In their lifetime, they will finally reach everyone. These kids will have a passion like never before to complete the Great Commission. It will be a burning in their hearts. They will sense it when they are still young.

I saw this vision as I was praying for my grandson, who I

didn't expect would be born the very next day. He came early. My husband and I were in two separate states, and I would celebrate my fifty-fourth birthday before we were together again. We met at the airport, going straight to see the new baby. Our first grandson. What a treasure. I couldn't help but think of the vision God had given me when I held him in my arms. I made a mental note to share it with Rob on our drive home.

I never had the chance to share it with him though, because I slept through the whole drive. When we finally arrived, we carried our luggage into the house and sank wearily into living room chairs. What a long, wonderful amazing day. Just then, Rob realized that he hadn't given me my birthday gift yet and ran to get it. He handed me a little box. I gasped when I opened it. Inside lay a sterling silver ring in the shape of a wave.

It was like God winked.

Please pray for these young ones. If my vision is even halfway accurate, they have a great and awesome task. Pray they enjoy their childhood. That they get to play and imagine and wonder. Pray that they don't have to grow up too fast. That they are shielded and protected and nurtured and loved while they are young, because I believe their adult years will require strong foundations to withstand the holy battle that lies before them.

If God calls you to child-related ministry, spend a lot of time on your knees. Give it your all. If you are a decision maker at your church, be sure the children get your best. Be sure the best teachers in your church are the ones teaching the kids. They should have the A team, not the B team.

Teach your children and your grandchildren Bible stories with a fresh passion. Tell them about David and Joseph, Ruth and Esther. Don't forget the woman at the well, the prodigal son, three men in a fiery furnace, and Paul in prison. These stories will guide them.

Sing songs of worship with them, old and new: "A Mighty Fortress Is Our God," "It Is Well with My Soul," "How Great Is Our God," "This Little Light of Mine," "So Will I," "Good, Good Father," "Jesus Loves Me This I Know," and many others. These songs will encourage them.

Live and love out your faith in front of them. This will be your legacy. Refuse to judge the world. Be kind. Give sacrificially. Give cups of cold water repeatedly. Obey Jesus. Spend copious amounts of time in the Word, praying, and worshipping in front of them. Please don't kick them out of church to a separate room to play silly games and color, at least not for the whole service. They need to see us worship. This example will train them.

Treat them with respect. Heap blessing on them. Don't exasperate them, but lovingly disciple them. Teach them by your example to die to self. This discipline will shape them.

Carpe Diem, seize the day! Time is short.

PERSONAL REFLECTION AND GROUP DISCUSSION

- Do you welcome children into your worship service, even if it's a bit inconvenient sometimes?
- If you're a parent, what are some ways you can include your kids in evangelism and discipleship?
- When you are praying for this generation, what are some specific things you pray for them?
- Has God ever winked at you?
- Suggested verses to memorize: Psalm 71:17-18

PART 3

THE BAIT

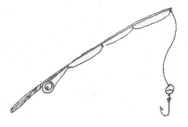

CHAPTER 31

GOOD WORKS

WHAT'S THE HOOK?

I n Part One, we talked about how Jesus came to the lost to fish for lost souls. He went where the fish were and got into the lake! To continue using this analogy of a fisherman that Jesus uses to describe evangelism, we need to see what He used for bait and how He expects us to fish. Let's get a closer look inside that tackle box and see what our good fisherman has to put on his hook. As we dig around, the first thing we find is good works.

Titus 3:1-8 says it best:

> Remind them to be submissive to rulers and
> authorities, to be obedient, to be ready for
> every good work, to speak evil of no one, to
> avoid quarreling, to be gentle, and to show
> perfect courtesy toward all people. For we
> ourselves were once foolish, disobedient, led
> astray, slaves to various passions and

> *pleasures, passing our days in malice and*
> *envy, hated by others and hating one*
> *another. But when the goodness and loving*
> *kindness of God our Savior appeared, he*
> *saved us, not because of works done by us in*
> *righteousness, but according to his own*
> *mercy, by the washing of regeneration and*
> *renewal of the Holy Spirit, whom he poured*
> *out on us richly through Jesus Christ our*
> *Savior, so that being justified by his grace*
> *we might become heirs according to the*
> *hope of eternal life. The saying is*
> *trustworthy, and I want you to insist on*
> *these things, so that those who have believed*
> *in God may be careful to devote themselves*
> *to good works. These things are good and*
> *profitable for people. (ESV)*

Why would good works be profitable for people? Is Paul just talking about good works being profitable for Christians? Or for everybody?

Check this out:

> *"You are the light of the world. A city on a hill*
> *cannot be hidden. Nor do people light a*
> *lamp and put it under a basket, but on a*
> *stand, and it gives light to all in the house.*
> *In the same way, let your light shine before*
> *others, so that they may see your good works*
> *and give glory to your Father who is in*
> *heaven.*
> *Matthew 5:14-16 (ESV)*

Our good works are profitable for everyone, because they bring glory to God! We were created for this! The two most important days of your life are the day you were born and the day you found out why.

> But you are not like that, for you are a chosen
>   people. You are royal priests, a holy nation,
>   God's very own possession. As a result, you
>   can show others the goodness of God, for he
>   called you out of darkness into his
>   wonderful light.
> 1 Peter 2:9 (NLT)

A popular ice hockey team near my old hometown would celebrate wins by lighting a lamp outside of their stadium that would shine over the freeway for all to see. The community would know that their team had won the game. After the final goal was made, fans inside the stadium would yell, "Light that lamp!"

Well let me encourage you with the same words! Light that lamp that God has given you! He wants those of us who have believed in Him to be careful to maintain good works. Because it causes others to see who He is! Through Him, we are winners! Light that lamp!

The world likes to make fun of us. Some of us Christians give them plenty of material to work with! We have also given the world too many reasons to gossip about us, to be angry with us, to judge us, and to run from us.

One rave at a time, our teams are trying to change that perception. And it's not that hard. "Why are you here? Why are you doing this? Why do you care?" These are some of our favorite questions because they show us we are on the right track. Our good works are showing. That gives us opportunities to tell them about the One who sent us.

> *It is God's will that your honorable lives should*
> *silence those ignorant people who make*
> *foolish accusations against you.*
> *1 Peter 2:15 (NLT)*

We once met a group of young men outside a rave whose ringleader wore a ship's captain hat. We were in front of our ministry RV when they walked by, headed to the entrance. Some of the moms gave them bracelets. Captain must have run into us before, because when he saw the bracelet, he threw it down and stomped on it. "I don't want to hear any of this Jesus sh**!"

They all walked away. Well, that wasn't the last we saw of Captain that night, because one of his friends had had way too much to drink, started throwing up, and they all got kicked out of the venue. They came back to our RV because they weren't sure where else to go to get help for their friend. To make matters worse, they couldn't remember where they'd parked their car. Captain's hat was slid halfway over his eyes as he walked toward us, hanging his head. He was the last one of the boys to reach us. When he did, we acted like we were greeting a long-lost friend.

We hugged them and invited them to sit. We fed them, gave them blankets, and cleaned up the drunk one. Eventually, we got them to their car. They were all wearing bracelets when they left, even Captain. The next week we got an email from him, apologizing for his behavior. He thanked us for showing Jesus's love to him and his friends.

When people's lives please the Lord, even their
enemies are at peace with them.
Proverbs 16:7 (NLT)

Our behavior matters. Others will either be turned toward
Jesus because of it or turned away. You choose.

PERSONAL REFLECTION AND GROUP DISCUSSION

- Before you came to Christ, did someone's behavior
  delay you from making the decision to follow Him?
  Share about that without naming names.
- Has someone's behavior ever pointed you toward
  Christ?
- How important do you think our behavior as
  Christians is? In the world? At home?
- Suggested verse to memorize: Proverbs 16:7

CHAPTER 32

KINDNESS

Jesus wants us to be kind! We touched on this in Part One in Chapter 7: Get the Order Right and Be Nice. But this is so important that I want to camp on it a little longer. Kindness is bait to a world who wants to know if Jesus is really real and if He really has the power to change the heart of a human being. Because of that, it is imperative that we are kind to our mission field, kind to our community, and kind to our fellow fishers of men.

JESUS WANTS US TO BE KIND TO OUR MISSION FIELD

There was a young man I'll call Tom who hated Christians. We'd met him at a rave. He just couldn't handle our message. Every time we saw him after that he would call out to us and tell the people we were talking to that we hated ravers. We even ended up at the same funeral for a raver. He just couldn't bear to hardly look at us.

When we started doing our rave camping outreaches, his friends all came for pancakes and sausage, but he stayed away, except for the few times he walked by to taunt them for hanging out with us. This continued for a couple of years. He must have shown up at seventy-five percent of the local raves we went to! Then last year, an amazing thing happened. He walked up to the dads serving breakfast in our campsite and said, "I've tried so hard to hate you people, but I just can't. You're just so nice!"

Rob's response was, "Have some breakfast!" And with that, he handed Tom a plate full of pancakes and sausage.

I didn't see all of this going on. I was at the tables with a bunch of happy ravers who were eating their pancakes. I didn't see the face of the young man who pulled out the empty chair directly in front of me until he had already slid into it. I looked up, and there was Tom!

I tried to hide my shock with, "Welcome! How's the breakfast taste?" Before too long, we were talking and laughing like old friends. And that was it. He's never said a derogatory word since!

> *Now, who will want to harm you if you are eager to do good? But even if you suffer for doing what is right, God will reward you for it. So don't worry or be afraid of their threats. Instead, you must worship Christ as Lord of your life. And if someone asks about your hope as a believer, always be ready to explain it. But do this in a gentle and respectful way. Keep your conscience clear. Then if people speak against you, they will be ashamed when they see what a good life you live because you belong to Christ.*
> *1 Peter 3:13-16 (NLT)*

Remember the story I shared in Part One about the guys with the megaphones? They weren't explaining their hope as believers in a gentle and respectful way. They weren't kind. As they blared half-truths and unkind things over their megaphones, it was like they were fishing but using a shark for bait. Those fish just weren't going to bite. In fact, they swam away as fast as they could, far away.

Evangelism must be done with kindness.

JESUS WANTS US TO BE KIND TO OUR COMMUNITY

I wrote this to fit the church when I saw a similar story on Facebook that was directed at AA meetings. It illustrates the destruction that is caused when we aren't kind to those right next to us: our neighbors, our community members, our church family.

His phone rang in the middle of the sermon at church, during the most serious part.

People turned around with scathing looks.

The deacons admonished him afterward for interrupting.

His wife continued to lecture him for his carelessness all the way home.

You could see the shame, embarrassment, and humiliation on his face.

He never stepped foot in that church again.

That evening, he went to a bar.

He was still upset and trembling.

He accidentally spilled his drink all over his shirt and the counter as well.

The bartender apologized for his trouble and gave him a napkin to clean himself.

The bus boy mopped the floor.

The manager offered him a complimentary drink.

She also gave him a hug and said, "No worries. Who doesn't make mistakes?"

He has never stopped going to that bar since.

JESUS WANTS US TO BE KIND TO OUR FELLOW FISHERMEN

Our mission field is watching how we treat each other. We will cover this some more later, but think about this for a few minutes. When Christians compete in ministry, when they don't play nice, that's probably a good indication that they aren't doing what they are doing for the right reasons.

There are other ministries that have popped up here and there since we started. They haven't done things the way that God showed us to do them. One time, after we presented the rave outreach ministry to a church, they decided they wanted to outreach at the raves in their city their own way, instead of partnering with us.

I'll be honest. It bothered me. First, they hadn't even thought of doing this before we came. Plus, they didn't understand the culture. The way they wanted to reach ravers was, in my experience, not going to work.

But I had to step back. I had to take my emotions, my feelings of ownership out of this. The ravers are God's mission field. He loves them more than we do. He invited us to that fishing hole. He showed us how to fish for them. He is big enough to show others too. He is also big enough to reach ravers even if someone isn't doing it the "right way." If I'm in competition with other fishers of men, that's an indication that I'm doing this because of what I am getting out of it—attention, good feelings, self-worth—instead of doing it solely for God's glory.

The great poet, Edgar Guest, wrote a cute little poem on fishing. Read it with evangelism in mind. Although he didn't intend it to be a tool to teach spiritual concepts, it sure spoke to my heart, especially considering the concept of being kind toward our fellow laborers.

"Out Fishin'"
by Edgar A. Guest

A feller isn't thinkin' mean,
Out fishin';
His thoughts are mostly good an' clean,
Out fishin';
He doesn't knock his fellow men
Or harbor any grudges then;
A feller's at his finest, when
Out fishin'.

The rich are comrades to the poor,

Out fishin';
All brothers of a common lure
Out fishin';
The urchin with the pin an' string
Can chum with millionaire an' king;
Vain pride is a forgotten thing,
Out fishin'.

A feller's glad to be a friend,
Out fishin';
A helping hand he'll always lend,
Out fishin';
The brotherhood of rod and line
An' sky an' stream is always fine;
Men come real close to God's design
Out fishin'.

PERSONAL REFLECTION AND GROUP DISCUSSION

- Did the kindness of a Christian originally make you want to find out more about Jesus?
- Can you think of some people who are probably watching you and your behavior?
- Suggested verses to memorize: 1 Peter 3:13-16

CHAPTER 33

GENEROSITY

*And all the believers met together in one place
and shared everything they had. They sold
their property and possessions and shared
the money with those in need. They
worshipped together at the Temple each day,
met in homes for the Lord's Supper, and
shared their meals with great joy and
generosity—all the while praising God and
enjoying the goodwill of all the people. And
each day the Lord added to their fellowship
those who were being saved.*
Acts 2:44-47 (NLT)

Hmmmm. Sounds like a formula for church growth to me! And it didn't involve having a better worship team than the church up the street or a larger-than-life kid's program. It didn't involve sheep stealing from other congregations. They were adding nonbelievers to their fellowship, not disgruntled, pouty Christians from other fellowships that weren't doing things exactly as they wanted. The people of the church here in Acts were living in such a way that they attracted others. They were living generously and meeting some basic needs of the people.

Perhaps one of the most touching examples of generosity in the early church was Tabitha, whose name in Greek is Dorcas. Her story is in Acts 9. She was always doing kind things for others, showing generosity toward the poor.

When she suddenly died, many mourned her death. Peter was in a nearby town. They sent for him. When he arrived, he was met by a roomful of devastated widows who showed him the coats and other clothes that Tabitha had made for them. She had made a huge difference in the lives of these women who were a marginalized segment of society.

Are you so generous that your death will be mourned by the people you helped? The answer will be yes if you practice God-honoring generosity. It changes people's lives. And not only that, it changes us. You see, the story of Tabitha didn't end with the mourners. Peter prayed over her body and she came alive. Now we might not physically be brought back to life when we die, but spiritually, we come alive when we practice generosity. It does the heart good.

Generosity can be an evangelistic tool in the hands of loving Christ followers. In the hands of a good fisher of men, it is bait.

We are finding with this generation that we often need to meet needs, physical and emotional, before we they will listen to us. We are seeing this globally as well, as mission works provide water and employment opportunities for a village. Then they are invited to share why. We love the question, "Why are you doing this?" as we give sunblock and water, wipe faces and tears, and serve pancakes. The answer is, "Because Jesus loves you." Powerful after a need has just been met. We must be willing to meet the physical needs of our mission field.

> *Whoever is generous to the poor lends to the*
> *Lord, and he will repay him for his deed.*
> *Proverbs 19:17 (ESV)*

> *The point is this: whoever sows sparingly will*
> *reap sparingly, and whoever sows*
> *bountifully will also reap bountifully.*
> *2 Corinthians 9:6 (ESV)*

IF YOU WANT TO BE A SUCCESSFUL FISHER OF MEN, BE GENEROUS

My husband and I recently led a young lady to the Lord after she'd been on a bad drug trip at a rave. She contacted us through the "call a rave dad or mom" hotline on the website on one of our bracelets she had gotten at the festival. After a long conversation, she prayed for salvation.

One month later, she came to Camp 33. There, she shared more of her story with us. It was powerful to see how God had been drawing her to Himself over the years. She had seen Him at work in her life many times, she just didn't recognize Him. But now that she was saved, she could look back, clearly seeing that it had been God at work many times in her life, pursuing her.

She shared the story of how God had once used a plumber to save her life. To this day, that man doesn't know what he did. He was just being generous. Someday in heaven, he will find out.

Bubbling over about the goodness of God, this young lady, who I will call Holly, shared how she had struggled many times with suicidal thoughts. She had grown up in a chaotic, dysfunctional home. Her mom left her dad for another woman. Her dad took on two jobs to replace his ex-wife's salary so he and his daughter could stay in the same rental house.

Eventually, her dad hooked up with another woman. He decided to move to another state with her and her children. Holly was devastated. She had just received a scholarship to attend a local college. Determined, she decided she would do everything she could to stay put in that house so she could go to college. Taking on multiple jobs, working herself to the bone, life became overwhelming. She was all alone.

One day, her water heater broke. She was without hot water. So she let the landlord know and rushed off to work. Everything seemed to be falling apart. Two days later, she decided it was time to end it all.

Holly found an extension cord in the basement of the house and began to make a noose. There was a hook she had noticed screwed into the ceiling in the corner that would be just right. She hung the cord from it, stood on a chair, put the noose around her neck and jumped. But she hadn't correctly tied the knot. She landed on the floor. She tried again. The same thing happened. Frustrated, she got on her computer and looked up, "how to tie a noose."

Holly had finally tied the noose correctly. It would work this time. She even tried it once, holding onto it with her hands and swinging from it to double check that it would work. She had just placed it around her neck when there was a knock at the door. Frustrated again, she stashed the cord with the well-tied noose behind something and answered the door.

It was the plumber that her landlord had sent to fix her water heater.

As they talked about the problem and the solutions, Holly asked how much it would cost. The man asked her if she would be the one responsible to pay the bill. She said that was the agreement she and her dad had made with the landlord. Then she explained that her dad was gone, so she would be paying the bill herself. The plumber was curious and asked enough questions to get the whole story out of her.

I'm sure you've guessed the end of the story by now. The plumber would not take any money from Holly. He fixed her water heater and told her he was proud of her that she was so determined to finish school.

After the plumber left, Holly untied the noose and returned the electrical cord to its place in the basement. She lived that day because someone was generous at a time when she thought she was all alone in this world.

Be generous.

PERSONAL REFLECTION AND GROUP DISCUSSION

- Share a time when someone's generosity changed the course of your day or your life.
- Is there someone in your life who could use a dose of generosity? What is a practical way you could meet that need?
- Ecclesiastes 5:13 says that hoarding riches harms the saver. What are some ways you can be generous with your riches?
- Suggested verse to memorize: Proverbs 19:17

CHAPTER 34

PARTYING ON PURPOSE

The week after we met a raver who we'd camped next to inside a rave campground, she invited our team to her birthday party. She'd heard the good news of the gospel for the first time that weekend as we ate together in our campsite. She was attracted to us.

She told us she didn't really know what to believe about God. She'd been to church with her mom a few times. She couldn't stand it. According to her, they judged her from the minute she walked in. She'd never heard the things we had told her about Jesus from the preacher there. This girl was a lesbian. She was not welcome in that church. The things she told me made me sad, but frankly, I doubted they were all true.

Four of us rave parents drove up to her party being held on the driveway in front of a garage at an apartment complex in a really bad part of town. I quickly surveyed the situation. Could the group of guys standing on the curb drinking tequila have gang affiliations?

We had brought our youngest daughter along to minister with us. I shocked myself as I quickly gave her instructions. You see, I felt compelled to tell my fifteen-year-old that if a fight broke out, or if there was gunfire at any time during the party, she was to immediately run to the bar at the end of the street and seek shelter there until we could meet up. I pointed out the shabby looking building with broken windows, lit beer-brand signs blinking like a beacon of hope. Well, that was a first for this mom! I'd never dreamt I'd tell my daughter to take refuge in a bar! God really has a sense of humor. Ministry sure is messy sometimes!

But what happened that night at that party changed my life. Our little raver girl welcomed us to her party and led us to the table where she had saved us some seats. We were treated like guests of honor. Mariachi music blared as we began to introduce ourselves to the others at the table. It soon became apparent that raver girl had seated us at the gay table.

Her mom and her mom's friends were at another table in the corner speaking Spanish. I kept noticing them stare at us, as if they were watching to see how we would handle these sinners. I was watching us, too. I prayed that God would use us.

We gave raver girl a beautiful Bible with her name engraved on it that night. The crowd hushed as she opened it. She had tears in her eyes as she thanked us. It was a divine moment.

We made friends with many of raver girl's friends that night. To this day, they still come up to our house to play on the lake or in the snow. We've had them up for Thanksgiving dinner. Her mom ended up coming too. I made turkey, she made taquitos. It was perfect.

We have had multiple opportunities to share the gospel with them. All because we went to their party. There were no gunshots or fights. Instead, I learned a Latin dance, courtesy of one of the girls at my table. Years before, if you would've told me that one day this judgmental church lady would be dancing the Rumba with a lesbian at a party in the ghetto, I would've told you to get lost.

People may judge me for including my teenage daughter in the festivities that night, but let me tell you that months later, when raver girl's partner suddenly lost an aunt, we were the ones they called. The young couple was banned from attending the funeral. They were devastated. We came up with a plan. We would have our own funeral service for the beloved aunt.

I'll never forget the sight of my teenaged daughter, standing behind a newly engraved tombstone on a sunny day at a cemetery a few miles from the ghetto. A whole group of raver girl's friends were gathered, watching intently as Cassie played her guitar and sang songs about our Savior. Then my husband stepped to the front and gave the entire message of salvation to these precious ones who were not welcome at church. All because we went to their party.

Jesus went to parties too. You can read about them in the New Testament. He performed His first miracle at a wedding reception. He went to people's homes, sinner's homes (gasp!), and they threw Him dinner parties. He partied on mission. He partied on purpose. Because parties provide divine appointments.

When Jesus met Zacchaeus, He didn't invite the little guy to the temple or to a prayer meeting with His disciples. He went to his house, where Zacch lived, into Zacch's world. Why did Jesus invite Himself to Zacchaeus's party? Let's look at Jesus's own answer to this question.

> *When Jesus came by, he looked up at Zacchaeus*
> *and called him by name. "Zacchaeus!" he*
> *said. "Quick, come down! I must be a guest*
> *in your home today."*
> *Zacchaeus quickly climbed down and took Jesus*

> *to his house in great excitement and joy. But*
> *the people were displeased. "He has gone to*
> *be the guest of a notorious sinner," they*
> *grumbled.*
> *Meanwhile, Zacchaeus stood before the Lord*
> *and said, "I will give half my wealth to the*
> *poor, Lord, and if I have cheated people on*
> *their taxes, I will give them back four times*
> *as much!"*
> *Jesus responded, "Salvation has come to this*
> *home today, for this man has shown himself*
> *to be a true son of Abraham. For the Son of*
> *Man came to seek and save those who are*
> *lost."*
> *Luke 19:5-10 (NLT)*

Jesus goes to parties to seek and save the lost. Why should we go to the world's parties?

> *But when the teachers of religious law who were*
> *Pharisees saw him eating with tax collectors*
> *and other sinners, they asked his disciples,*
> *"Why does he eat with such scum?"*
> *Mark 2:16 (NLT)*

Why should we be like Jesus and eat with scum? Because things go bad at the world's parties, very bad. And if we are there when things go bad, God will use us to pick up the pieces. He is glorified through that!

God invented the party. He designated seven specific feasts that Israel was to celebrate each year. These feasts often began and ended with a Sabbath rest. God commanded the Jews not to do any of their normal work on those days. They looked forward to these events. All of God's parties were a foreshadowing of the greatest celebration of all that was yet to come. When His son would crash Satan's counterfeit party with the gospel.

And that is the example we follow in our ministry today. We go to dark places with great news, sharing it with those who are starving for a good party because they are left empty and wanting after the world's parties.

Sometime after two a.m., a young foreign exchange student from Thailand roamed desperately through the almost-empty rave parking lot in one of the most dangerous cities in America. His "friends" had left him, taking his wallet and his phone back to Los Angeles with them, almost a two-hour drive away.

Can you imagine what that would feel like? Still coming down from the drugs you used, in a totally foreign place, barely able to speak English.

Then imagine walking up to an RV full of rave parents packing up after a night of outreach, only to find out that YOU are exactly why they are here!

Rave mom Teri wrapped her arms around that young man. She was able to communicate to him that she would help him. She called for an Uber, then got him something to eat.

The boy was incredulous. He asked Teri why she was willing to help him. She answered with one word: a name, Jesus.

The boy stretched out his arms to show her the only Jesus that he was familiar with, dead Jesus, hanging on a crucifix. That night, a young man from Thailand saw the living Jesus. And that rocked his world!

The following week, he met with Teri and prayed to invite that living Jesus to come into his life to take over. We connected him with a local church. The youth pastor there is now discipling him.

We go to parties with a purpose: to seek the lost and introduce them to the One who can save them.

The gospel is GOOD NEWS! We have a lot to party about! Satan shouldn't have the corner on parties! We should! Why should we go around all somber and judgmental when the Savior of the world loved to party?

He taught us that it's how we party that matters. He taught us how to have good party etiquette in Luke 14. In that same chapter, He told the story of the great banquet. What a party that was! In Luke 15, He talks about partying after finding a lost sheep, a lost coin, and the amazing party that God throws when a prodigal returns home.

A couple of years after raver girl's birthday party, her mom invited me to come to a women's conference being held at her church. I jumped at the chance to see if what I'd heard about this church was true. Would this help me to have a better understanding of how to minister to raver girl?

As I entered, I was given a headset so that I could hear the service in English. I felt very welcome, almost like an honored guest.

When the ladies bowed their heads in prayer, they grabbed little white hankies from their purses to cover their heads. Frantically, I looked around to see if there were any extra, not wanting to offend. I spotted a roll of white paper towels under a chair and ripped off a section to cover my head. Raver girl's mom came rushing over to stop me. She assured me that I didn't need to cover up, that was just required for church members. I was relieved.

Most of the rest of the service was great. I was a bit surprised that the main speaker at this women's conference was a man, but I assumed it was a cultural thing. The pastor was inspiring. The translator on my headset did a good job of communicating his message. Then things took a sudden turn when he put a list of sins he said were common to women up on the overhead screen and started yelling at them. When the music started up, he began to pray loudly that the Holy Spirit would come and descend on the people, like He did in the book of Acts. The people began to sway and pray loudly.

Now, I had noticed that lining the walls were stacks of little plastic trash bins like you see next to toilets in bathrooms. There were about a hundred of them. I had wondered what that was all about. Well, my question was answered as one by one, women started retching and ushers rushed to them, handing them the plastic buckets to catch their vomit. I was just stunned.

Pretty soon there were over fifty women throwing up at once in their pews. A cameraman ran around to catch them on video, playing the scene for everyone to see on the overhead screen. The pastor was delighted. To him, this was a sign that the Holy Spirit had come. The women were ridding themselves of their sin.

Now I've seen a lot of barf at raves, but never as much as I saw in that church that day. No wonder raver girl was more comfortable at a rave party than at church! Who would want to go there, get judged, and then watch a bunch of ladies throw up? Frankly, at that moment, I would have rather been at a rave as well!

Oh, church! This is an extreme example. But what have we done? When the world is crying out for the simple love of Jesus, why do we have to go add a bunch of crazy stuff to it?

The Bible says that when the Holy Spirit comes upon us, He brings the power we need to be His witnesses to the world! These people weren't being witnesses to anyone. In fact, they had made raver girl run as fast as she could in the opposite direction!

Instead of receiving the power to disciple others, they were deceived by emotion. They chose barf over the power the Holy Spirit would have given them to overcome the judgement they felt for raver girl and her friends.

Satan has counterfeited God's party because he has no original ideas of his own. He just tries to copy everything with a twist that leads people to hell. Don't get caught up in his party plans. Stick to Scripture, throw God parties.

Why does raver girl continue to hang out with us? Because slowly and surely, she is seeing that our party is way better than Satan's. As we eat with her, inviting her into our home and lives, she is more and more open to the gospel we share with her.

There is something about eating with sinners. It was a discipleship tool that Jesus used. He knew the power of the family gathering and family celebrations to communicate God's love to people:

> *God places the lonely in families; he sets the*
> *prisoners free and gives them joy.*
> Psalm 68:6a (NLT)

> *He escorts me to the banquet hall; it's obvious*
> *how much he loves me.*
> Song of Songs 2:4 (NLT)

> *You prepare a feast for me in the presence of my*
> *enemies. You honor me by anointing my*
> *head with oil. My cup overflows with*
> *blessings. Surely your goodness and*
> *unfailing love will pursue me all the days of*
> *my life, and I will live in the house of the*
> *Lord forever.*
> Psalm 23:5-6 (NLT)

I'm so grateful that God is pursuing raver girl and that I get to be a part of it. Do life with people. Party on purpose. Prepare banquets. The family of God should feast on taquitos and turkey with the enemies of God. You will one day win them over to your side of the table.

PERSONAL REFLECTION AND GROUP DISCUSSION

- Who will you invite to your table?
- Does the idea of a God who loves to party feel uncomfortable to you? Why?
- Do you have as much joy when you're worshipping God as when you're watching your favorite ball team win a game?
- Suggested verses to memorize: Psalm 23:5-6

CHAPTER 35

REFUSING TO LABEL

In the last chapter, when you read Mark 2:16, did you notice who labeled people? The Pharisees, the anti-Jesus religious ones. They called people scum. It made them feel superior.

A young lady who had been treated cruelly by her church family because of her goth-style makeup and clothing choices left crying and never went back. Years later at a rave, she got one of our bracelets. When she went on the website that was spelled out in beads, she watched the video she found there. She was shocked to see my husband, Rob, holding a Bible and sharing the good news.

Laura Beth contacted us. That began a relationship that continues to this day. Every year we get Mother's Day and Father's Day cards from her. She ended up marrying an amazing young man who is one of the best apologists for the faith that I have ever met. Rob performed the wedding.

Theirs was the first and only goth-style wedding I've ever been to. It was just beautiful. Different, but beautiful. Laura

Beth carried a bouquet of dead roses, her white dress was edged with black lace. Her groom, Darrell, wore a cravat and tailcoat. I got to wear my favorite black dress and even tried black nail polish for the first time. The wedding was held at an elegant Victorian-period house converted into a wedding venue. It was so much fun.

The first time we met with these two in person, I learned a lesson I will never forget. We met at a pumpkin patch. Laura Beth told us they wouldn't be hard to spot, with their lace up boots, pierced lips and noses, colored hair and chains. They were right! We easily picked out Laura Beth and Darrell from the crowd. I didn't think too much of it, I was just so overjoyed to meet this girl who had rededicated her life to the Lord and this great Christian guy she was dating!

We got some snacks at the food stand and headed to the picnic area to fellowship. Very quickly, I felt all eyes on us. I started to glance around. People looked at us up and down, judgement evident in their eyes. I'd never felt judgement in this way. I'm not one to stand out in a crowd. That day was a first. And I didn't like it one little bit.

I wanted to stand up on the table and shout out how sweet these kids are, how everyone should take the time to get to know them before passing judgement on them. But I began to reflect on myself. My heart broke over the times I had acted the same way as the gawkers around us.

People are judgers. People are haters. People are labelers. But that should be the world's job, and it should be foreign to the church! It's anti-Jesus.

As Christians, we look on the inside, not the outside. We view all people as precious and valuable, made in God's image.

When I look at the night sky and see the work of

your fingers—the moon and the stars you set
in place—what are mere mortals that you
should think about them, human beings that
you should care for them? Yet you made
them only a little lower than God and
crowned them with glory and honor.
Psalm 8:3-5 (NLT)

We periodically have team trainings for our volunteers to equip them to serve our mission field as best as they can. We have offered CPR and first-aid trainings. Knowing this stuff has really come in handy out there in our fishing hole!

But one training we offered recently is unique. It's called Mental Health First Aid. The trainer knows our ministry well. She contacted me to offer it because she thought it would really be beneficial for us since our teams are often the first ones on scene in tragic or tense situations. The training lasted eight hours. She taught us how to be what she called a "good noticer" of people in distress. She gave us the skills to approach and assess people in various emotional and mental states, and how to guide them to appropriate help.

One of the topics that stood out to me the most that day was called Stigma Reduction. We all discussed how we label and treat people who suffer from various mental illnesses . I had never thought of this before. When I saw a guy walking down the street talking to himself, I would often say, "He's a schizophrenic," or "He's a drug addict." Our trainer made her point, adding, "Wouldn't it be kinder to say, 'He suffers from schizophrenia,' or 'He suffers from drug addiction?'" We tend to freely label mental illness and drug-induced mental illness. I would never label any other person by what they suffer from: "She's a breast cancer." "He's a melanoma."

It got me thinking about those in our mission field. I have sometimes watched some crazy behavior and said, "He's so LOST!" Maybe it would be better to say, "He's suffering from being separated from God." This is a big change for me. I'm still getting used to it. But I like what it's doing to my heart.

I love how hopeful one of my evangelist friends is. He calls nonbelievers "pre-saved." Another pastor I know of calls them "as yet unconvinced." That's thought-provoking!

Only God sees the future and knows our hearts as they are and as they will be. We need to be careful how we refer to our mission field and have Christ-like compassion on them, seeing them all as sheep without a shepherd. Instead of quickly trying to diagnose everyone and slap a label on them, let's be like Jesus and have compassion on them instead.

In chapter twenty-six, we focused on our differences, as far as culture is concerned. Here, I want to focus on our similarities. This focus helps us to avoid labeling. We need to see that all of us, saved or unsaved are more alike than we may think. No matter how we look, the neighborhood we were raised in, how we start and end our day, or how we celebrate, we have some similarities. We all have hopes and dreams for our lives. We all experience joy and sorrow. Whether we know it or not, we were all created, and we were created in God's image. Because the fall affected everything, we all have desperately sinful hearts. Although we all have our differences, across the globe, we are still fundamentally the same. Until we grasp this truth, we won't be able to help people without eventually hurting them.

We all share one label only: human. And because of that, each of us has inherent value.

PERSONAL REFLECTION AND GROUP DISCUSSION

- Have you ever been labeled by someone?
- If we viewed every single human being as one who is created in God's image, how would that change the way we treat them?
- Suggested verses to memorize: Psalm 8:3-5

CHAPTER 36

LISTENING AND TELLING GOD STORIES

LISTENING WELL

W e went over listening in Chapter 26 as it relates to relating with others. The concept of listening well is so important when it comes to evangelism and discipleship, that it's worth going over again (just in case you weren't listening). Great listening skills are attractive, every great fisher of men knows how to listen.

Since we don't get notches on our Christian belts each time we share the gospel, we can simmer down. Listen to really listen, not because we're lying in wait to get our message across.

Have you ever been sharing your heart with someone and realized that they weren't truly listening to you? Instead, they were waiting for you to take a breath so they could interject what they had been planning to say all along. You can tell when someone is not sincerely listening to you by their body language.

One of the biggest communication problems we have in our

culture today is that we often do not listen to understand. We listen to reply. Don't be that person. Relax. God's got this. Take the time to really hear people out, build relationships with them. People aren't projects.

Discipleship moves at the speed of relationship.

THE HOLY SPIRIT wants you to share the good news more than you want to share it. You can trust Him to make the opportunities available.

Have you noticed how many introverts there are in our world today? I have some theories about why this is true, but the fact remains if you're talking to someone from this generation, you are likely conversing with an introvert. People often label introverts as shy but that's not necessarily accurate. Introverts can be outgoing for periods of time. Being among family and friends and even strangers can bring them joy, but after a while they need to get alone to recharge. And I've found that pointless conversation and small talk rapidly wears them down. Especially with this generation, it's important that we ask good questions. Forget talking about the weather. They want meaning. They like the deep. They want to be understood. Good questions can produce those kinds of conversations.

Once I was sitting in our campsite inside a rave. Across from me, a college student was wolfing down pancakes. When he finally took a breath, I asked him, "So tell me, what are your hopes and dreams?" Before he answered my question, he thanked me for the way I asked it. He shared that most people ask him what his major is. He liked the idea of sharing who he is instead of just what his degree will be.

Most of the time good listening starts with asking good questions. The more creative, the better. Good, creative questions are easier to generate when you have a basic understanding of the culture or background of the one you are asking. I asked the student about his hopes and dreams instead of his major because I know that these kids at raves are often there to blow off steam because the pressure they are under at school is so intense.

I keep a list of questions in my proverbial back pocket to whip out when the time is right. None of them can be answered with a simple yes or no. They are conversation starters. I truly want to hear the answers to them.

TELLING GOD STORIES

> *Let the whole earth sing to the Lord! Each day*
> *proclaim the good news that he saves.*
> *Publish his glorious deeds among the*
> *nations. Tell everyone about the amazing*
> *things he does.*
> 1 *Chronicles* 16:23-24 (*NLT*)

So far, I have shared quite a few stories with you! These stories are important because they illustrate what God's power looks like in my life and in the lives of others.

After listening well, if someone gives me the opportunity to speak, I never pass up the chance to tell a good God story. People are hungry to know that Jesus is real, that He saves. We must tell them!

Jesus Himself told many stories to describe what God is like. He told them in parable form. These are great stories to memorize so you can share them when you are witnessing as well.

The Bible tells stories for a reason. All the stories in the Bible point to redemption. There are so many hidden nuggets in these stories as well, like little rewards for those who are willing to do the work of digging them out.

It's a good idea to have your own testimony ready to share, and to be able to do it in just a couple of minutes. The first step is to write it out, then pare it down to just the basic points. Practice telling it to someone until you've got it down. Once you have done this, you will be able to use it over and over again as you share the gospel with people. The purpose of your testimony is to bring glory to God. Be sure that comes shining through. Remember, the focus isn't on you or anything you have done, but on Him!

> *Not to us, O Lord, not to us, but to your name*
>   *goes all the glory for your unfailing love and*
>   *faithfulness.*
> *Psalm 115:1 (NLT)*

PERSONAL REFLECTION AND GROUP DISCUSSION

- What are some creative questions you can ask nonbelievers?
- What are some creative questions you can ask your friends?
- What are some creative questions you can ask your spouse or your children or grandchildren?

- What is one of your favorite Old Testament stories, and why?
- Share one of your personal favorite God stories that illustrates His power in your life.
- Suggested verses to memorize: 1 Chronicles 16:23-24

PART 4

THE NET

CHAPTER 37

KNOW WHEN TO SHUT UP

I've watched many people fish on lakes. Most of the time, after they've got one on the line, they carefully reel it in and scoop up their prized catch in a net. In the same way, our evangelist needs to know how to safely get that fish into the boat. He's gone to where the fish are. He's gotten one to bite. Now what?

It's so important that he understands what comes next, that he can clearly communicate the gospel, and if God allows, that he can lead that one to salvation. According to a study by the Barna Research Group, only half of born-again Christians say they shared the gospel at least once in the past year to someone with different beliefs, in the hope that they might accept Jesus Christ as their Savior. Many Christians don't know how to share their faith, they don't know how to lead someone in prayer to accept salvation.

Let's look at the ways our expert fisherman handles the fish in his net. One of the most important ways we can care for those we are ministering to is to be very careful with our words. Be sure they come from the Holy Spirit. Watching your words will not only benefit your mission field, it will benefit you as well!

> *Those who control their tongue will have a long*
> *life; opening your mouth can ruin*
> *everything.*
> Proverbs 13:3 (NLT)

We need to wait on the Holy Spirit for our words. Check this out. Jesus was preparing the disciples for the tough times they would face.

> *"When you are arrested, don't worry about how*
> *to respond or what to say. God will give you*
> *the right words at the right time. For it is not*
> *you who will be speaking—it will be the*
> *Spirit of your Father speaking through you.*
> Matthew 10:19-20 (NLT)

I've been in three serious situations in the last few years where I have been scared to death because I was about to face extended family members or friends of victims who would be looking to me for comfort and guidance, and I had no idea what to say. These were serious situations involving a drowning, a murder, and a fatal car crash.

And each time, this verse has proven to be true.

Each time, I've looked down and watched as my feet walked closer and closer to the person that had asked me to come. And every time I've heard the same exact command from the Lord:

"KEEP YOUR MOUTH SHUT UNTIL I TELL YOU WHAT TO SAY."

It is in those times that I have learned to pray before I

speak. Here is what that prayer often sounds like: "Lord, speak to me and through me, beyond me and in spite of me."

There have been a few times on rave outreaches where I had absolutely no idea what to say, so I asked God to speak through me and then just opened my mouth, trusting that He would provide the words. And He's come through every time!

Once, when we were still frequenting that little rave club in the first year of the ministry, Nicki, Rob, and I rushed out the door and forgot to grab our bag of bracelets to give away. We discovered our mistake when we arrived at the club forty minutes later. It was too late to go back. We searched through the glove box and our purses and only came up with three bracelets. It was then that we realized God wanted us to find three specific ravers that night.

The first two were easy to find. One was passed out under some bushes in the back parking lot. Another was relieving himself against a tire, so we waited a few minutes to give that one his bracelet. The third was not so easy. In fact, we walked or drove around for about two hours looking. All the kids had gone into the party, and it appeared we were all alone out there.

We double and triple checked in between cars, all along the edges, in the Dumpster area, and around the businesses across the street. Finally, we decided maybe we hadn't heard correctly from God. Maybe there were only two.

We decided to make one final sweep through the parking lot. Rob was driving. Nicki and I peered intently out the windows into the dark. Just as we had completed our final lap and were heading out the driveway, we noticed movement in a car that was parked off to our right, in the first spot by the entrance. We'd passed by that car on our search at least twenty times, but someone had been asleep in the front seat. At that very moment, he popped up awake!

Nicki and I couldn't get out of the car fast enough! We

were so excited to find the third one after hours of looking! We rushed to the young man's car, motioning for him to roll down the window. Us two moms looked anything but threatening, so he complied. But as he rolled his window down, I realized we hadn't planned what to say! I prayed and opened my mouth. Out came, "God has sent us to tell you how much He loves you."

Ralph put his head in his hands. Tears came quickly. Almost whispering, he said, "I knew it! I knew it!" As he slept, God had been speaking to his heart. He was ready to hear the gospel. He got out of the car. I motioned Rob to join us. There in that dark parking lot, a prodigal son came home.

Sometimes the best things happen when we are speechless and we rely on God to give us the words.

PERSONAL REFLECTION AND GROUP DISCUSSION

- Has God ever put words in your mouth? What happened?
- If you are scared that you won't know what to say when it comes time to share the gospel, what should you do?
- Suggested verse to memorize: Proverbs 13:3

CHAPTER 38

KNOW WHAT IS AND ISN'T WORTH TALKING ABOUT WITHOUT BEING A KNOW-IT-ALL

TELL THEM WHO GOD IS

In the last chapter, we focused on being careful about speaking and knowing when to keep quiet. Now we are focusing on speaking and what to say when we do.

> *But we continue to preach because we have the*
> *same kind of faith the psalmist had when he*
> *said, "I believed in God, so I spoke."*
> 2 Corinthians 4:13 (NLT)

If you believe in Jesus and if He has changed your life, you will speak about it! You can't help it! It will just come out. There's nothing more important to talk about. If you are silent, it's because you have bought into some lie from the enemy. Figure out what that is. Replace it with God's truth.

A group of people once prayed over me right after I had quit my job to do rave ministry full time. As they were praying, they clearly heard God tell them to give me these instructions: "Tell them who I AM." It was like a commissioning.

That is the message we are all to take to the world, because when we find out who He is, everything changes. Remember Isaiah? Everything changed in the moment that he saw who God was. He repented, he was forgiven of his sins, then he was commissioned to go out and tell others.

A strategy of the enemy against my grandparents' generation was to get them to stop talking about God. I grew up hearing them say: Don't talk religion or politics; it's rude!

Now that may be true when it comes to politics, perhaps when it comes to religion as well, but the point is, people stopped talking about who God is. Faith was personal and was to be kept to yourself. I really wonder if that's the era when the Sunday Christian was born. Satan is such a snake.

Some people say that the Bible is God's love letter to us. I see how it can be perceived that way, but it's so much more than that. It's not focused on us. All of Scripture is focused on the Great I AM.

Never be afraid to boldly speak up. Tell the world who He is!

DON'T GET INTO WORTHLESS CONTROVERSIES

When it comes to the question, "What's a worthless controversy and what's not?" here's the guideline we use for our ministry when we are dealing with fellow **BELIEVERS**: When it comes to theology (the study of God and God's relation to the world) and doctrine (a set of beliefs held and taught by a church), there are three categories: imperatives, convictions, and opinions.

Imperatives are things that we must agree on, or we just aren't a part of the same family. These are salvational issues, things worth dying for, hills we will die on: Jesus is God, belief in Jesus is the one and only way to eternal life, the death and resurrection of Jesus, et cetera.

Convictions would include things that have caused church splits and the formation of the various mainline denominations today: At what age someone should be baptized, should they be sprinkled or dunked? The role of women and men in ministry. Is speaking in tongues for today?

Opinions would include views about how things should be done, not necessarily based in fact or knowledge: What color should the carpet in the sanctuary be? Should we pass a bucket or put a box in the back to collect offering? Should our musical style of worship include only hymns or contemporary worship songs or both?

Bottom line: Controversy over the imperatives isn't worthless. Our salvation depends upon what we believe on those things. Seek to persuade! Argue away!

Controversy over opinions is a worthless waste of time. Run away!

Controversy over convictions can go either way. When we present reasons for our convictions and try to persuade others, we can have great discussions. They can drive us to be good Bereans as in Acts 17. Healthy discussions over these things can be like iron sharpening iron as we see in Proverbs 27. But if these conversations don't happen in love, when they become heated or disrespectful, they are no longer profitable. They become worthless controversy.

When it comes to the question, "What's a worthless controversy and what's not?" here's the guideline we use for our ministry when we are dealing with **NONBELIEVERS**: Because the only sin that has nonbelievers hell bound is unbelief, almost any argument is a worthless controversy unless it is over the sin of unbelief. Then, speaking the truth in love, we focus only on the sin of unbelief, because that is the only unforgivable sin. Conversations on creation, homosexuality, et cetera are totally worthless if one does not believe in Jesus for the salvation of their sins. They can have biblical views on creation or homosexuality and still be on their way to hell if they don't believe. So focus on belief-in-Jesus-based conversations. Steer away from the rest. Stay focused on what's imperative to salvation.

DON'T CLAIM TO KNOW ALL THE ANSWERS

Never, ever, ever claim to know all the answers. In fact, do just the opposite. Be sure your mission field understands that you don't know everything. When I am starting up a formal discipling relationship, I start out by telling them something like this, "I am so excited that we are going to be studying the Bible together. I want you to know up front that it is okay to ask any and all questions. There's no such thing as a dumb question. But I also want you to know that I won't always have an answer. Here's what I promise you: If you ask a question, I will either find the answer and get back to you, or I will teach you how to find the answer yourself. We can learn something new together that way."

I have never had someone quit on me because they were expecting me to know everything. In fact, the opposite is true! They appreciate my honesty, and it helps them to not feel pressure that they will have to know everything someday as well!

> *Anyone who claims to know all the answers doesn't really know very much. But the person who loves God is the one whom God recognizes.*
> *1 Corinthians 8:2-3 (NLT)*

PERSONAL REFLECTION AND GROUP DISCUSSION

- How can we best describe with our words who God is?
- How can we best describe Him with our actions?
- What would be a good way to stop a worthless controversy?
- How can we address the sin of unbelief with nonbelievers and do it in love?
- Does it bring you peace to know that you don't have to have all the answers?
- Aren't you glad we serve a God who is so much bigger than us? Share why.
- Suggested verse to memorize: 2 Corinthians 4:13

CHAPTER 39

KEEP IT SIMPLE AND BIBLICAL

The following description of how we use Scripture and a simple set of colors to share the gospel may be a great way for you to share your faith.

The bracelets we hand out at raves have the "gospel colors" on them: black, red, blue, white, green, and yellow or gold. It's a visual we use when we have the opportunity for a conversation. Each of the colors represent a biblical concept and each comes with a Scripture verse or two. We share what the verses say without giving the addresses. Including those can be too over-whelming. It's okay to leave chapter and verse numbers out, they were man-made.

We always start out with the black bead. When people see their sin, they realize they need a savior. We share that the Bible says we are all sinners. "All have sinned and fall short of the glory of God." (Romans 3:23) They don't always like it or agree at first, but it doesn't take long for them to acknowledge that it's true.

To convince them, all I need to do is share about my own sin. I usually tell them that sin seems like a big word but it describes my morning! I was selfish, I yelled at someone I love. When I broke the speed limit on the freeway, I broke the Ten Commandments (Isaiah 59:12).

Sometimes I tell them that I was so bummed, because I'd been off to such a great start! I was so proud! I hadn't sinned once. And then my alarm clock went off. They always laugh, and they quickly agree that they are sinners too. I don't linger on that black bead because I can't wait to get to the red bead, the good part! But I never skip over it.

In their hearts, most everyone knows they are a sinner. In ten years, I have always been able to continue to the red bead. But if the conversation over the black bead doesn't go well and someone gets angry and walks off, you can know that their heart was not in a place to receive the gospel. You can go to prayer and sic the Holy Spirit on them (quietly, of course) as they walk away. Then you can move on. It's not your job to save them. God will bring about another opportunity for that person when the time is right. Perhaps your job was just to be the first to ever place a trowel into the soil of their heart and break ground.

When I move on to the red bead, I share that sin separates us from the one and only true God (Isaiah 59:1-2). He is holy. He can't be around sin. The penalty for sin is death. But He didn't want things to end there. He wanted to make a way to have a relationship with us, despite our sin. So, He sent His son Jesus to pay that penalty for sin, in our place. His death on the cross paid it once and for all. That's why history records His last words from the cross were, "It is finished."

The Bible says that God loved the world so much, that He gave his only Son to die for our sins, in our place, and everyone who believes in Him will not die eternally but will have eternal life. God sent Jesus into the world to save us, not to condemn us (John 3:16-17). Jesus not only died on that cross, but He rose again from the dead after three days. Because of this, when we trust in Him and what He did for us on that cross, we will also have eternal life after we die. Jesus paid the way and He made the way for us. Jesus is God. God Himself died in our place for our sins.

When we get to the blue bead I say, "Blue stands for faith, faith that what I am telling you right now is true. This faith can only be given to you by God Himself. It's not something you can do on your own. The Bible says it is by grace we are saved, through faith–it is the gift of God–not anything we do. The Bible tells me I can't go around bragging that I'm a Christian, because it's nothing I did on my own (Ephesians 2:8-9). That's why I'm here sharing with you. I just want you to know that God will give you this gift too if you are willing to receive it. It comes from Him. It's free."

"If you are sensing that what I am telling you right now is the truth, then it's because God is right here, right now, helping you to believe. It's not a coincidence that you and I ran into each other tonight. I believe it is a sign to you that God is running to you because He loves you. He wants to have a relationship with you. You may have heard about religion, you may have been involved in religion, but that's not what I'm talking about. Religion is man-made. It's something we do to try to reach God. But God has already reached out to us through Jesus. So, I'm not talking about religion, I'm talking about a relationship with Jesus. Jesus is God."

Then I move on to the white bead. "The white bead shows what happens when we have the faith to put our trust in Jesus to pay the price for our sins. When we repent—that means we acknowledge that we are sinners, and we turn away from our sins, we go a different way—He forgives us of those sins. If sins made our hearts look like that black bead, the blood of Jesus shed for us on that cross now makes our hearts look like this white bead. The Bible says that He will wash our sins away, and we will be whiter than snow (Psalm 51:7). God no longer sees our sin. When we trust in Jesus for salvation from our sin, God can now have a relationship with us. He sees us through the blood of His Son, Jesus. He accepts us into His family. He calls us His children. That's really, really good news! Let's look at the next bead."

"The green bead illustrates our new life in this relationship with Jesus. Jesus is God. He wants us to grow closer with Him every day. The Bible says that we must grow in the grace and knowledge of our Lord and Savior Jesus Christ (2 Peter 3:18). A sign that we truly believe in Him and have truly been saved is that every day we become more and more like Him. We want to please Him because we are so grateful for what He has done for us."

Notice that I've stated that Jesus is God three times. It's so important to use the name of Jesus. "God" means a whole lot of things to a lot of people. There is only one true God, and His name is Jesus. We aren't talking about a higher power or Allah or Brahma. We need to use the name of Jesus so people specifically know who we are talking about.

Back to that new life in Christ, the green bead. I love to share the concept that Timothy Keller describes so well in his book, *The Prodigal God*. He says, "Every other religion teaches, 'I obey; therefore I am accepted.' The gospel declares, 'I am accepted; therefore I obey.'"

I continue. "We will still sin, still make bad choices sometimes, but we won't want to. Our lives have changed. Things won't be perfect, but you will never feel completely alone ever again. And when things are going bad, you will have a peace that passes understanding because you know ultimately you will have eternal life with Jesus. The Bible tells us that God has a purpose for our lives here on earth, to share the good news (the gospel) of His love with others. That's why He calls us His greatest creation, His handiwork, His greatest piece of art (Ephesians 2:10)."

"And now the last bead, the yellow or gold bead. It represents heaven. It will be amazing. The Bible says that after He died and rose from the dead, Jesus went to prepare a place for us and that someday He will come and get us so that we will always be with Him where He is (John 14:2-3). God has prepared this place for us to live with him eternally after our bodies die here on earth. Knowing that makes the bad stuff that happens here on earth not carry so much weight. We can be sad and mad and disgusted by the stuff we face every day, but it's lighter somehow, knowing that it won't last forever. We are just here for a time to carry out God's purpose for us. In the end, love wins."

And there you have it. That's how we share the gospel with kids we meet at raves. Now you don't have to have one of our beaded bracelets to share the gospel. But it may be helpful to keep these colors in your mind to assist you in sharing the gospel in an orderly way. You don't want to miss covering any of these main points.

After sharing, I give them an opportunity to pray for salvation. I let them know that I'm not trying to get brownie points with God for leading them to Him. I let them know this is about them and God. It really doesn't have anything to do with me or my feelings. They shouldn't do this to appease or please me. If they refuse, I thank them for being honest and not agreeing to pray when they are not sincere. I tell them that God knows their heart, so that wouldn't work anyway.

Sometimes I ask if I can pray for them before they leave. Almost always the answer is yes. I pray over them like I would my own child. I ask God to reveal Himself to them and the truth of His word in the next days. Then I usually ask if I can give them a hug, and I let them go. As they walk away, I am always filled with joy and hope, knowing that it is God's desire that all men be saved.

If they do want to pray for salvation, I have the immense privilege of leading them in prayer. Many have never prayed sincerely from their heart before, so I want to help them in this way. I invite them to repeat after me as I pray. I include these things in my prayer, speaking in first person:

I admit I'm a sinner.

I ask forgiveness for my sins and acknowledge that I want to turn away from my sins and repent.

I believe that Jesus died for me on the cross to pay for my sins and He rose from the dead to conquer sin and death.

I want to accept Jesus as my Lord and savior right now.

Jesus, I know You are hearing me right now as I pray, and I trust You and thank You that You have saved me.

I know I will live with You in heaven forever because of what You did for me by dying on the cross and rising from the dead.

Please help me now to grow in a relationship with You. Please show me how You want me to live from now on.

Amen.

And then I walk away and hope they find a good church someday.

NOT!!

This is where our analogy of the fisherman ends. When you are a fisher of men you don't catch them, then leave them gasping for air on the shore. You show them the way to an abundant life of living water. This is called making disciples.

I always exchange contact information with a new believer. I make sure they have a Bible and know how to use it. I ask if it's okay if I contact them in a couple of days to follow up and see how they are doing. I either offer to go with them to help them find a church, or I tell them I will find someone in their area to do that. I share how important fellowship and discipleship are. I offer myself or someone from our Hangar 33 discipleship team to study the Bible with them in person or over the phone every week to help them get started.

The goal of evangelism is to make disciple-making disciples. You do this by discipling those you have evangelized! You model disciple making, by making them a disciple.

PERSONAL REFLECTION AND GROUP DISCUSSION

- Look up each verse or verses that go along with each gospel color and read them aloud. What parts of what you read stand out to you the most? Why?
- Find someone to share the gospel with or practice sharing the gospel with each other in your group. Make sure everyone gets to do it at least one time. How did that feel? If it was uncomfortable, do you think doing it more often will help?
- Suggested verse to memorize: Ephesians 2:10

PART 5

THE LICENSE

CHAPTER 40

WHO GETS A LICENSE? DO YOU NEED A DEGREE?

WHO GETS A LICENSE?

Every good fisherman in the United States has done what it takes to get a fishing license. When they leave to go fish, it is safely stashed in their wallet or tackle box because they don't leave home without it. It gives them the right to fish.

Jesus gave us the license, if you will, to fish for men when He gave us the Great Commission. He gave all of us the right to fish. Fishers of men are serious about God's Word and follow it! They don't leave home without it! If you can't take your Bible with you everywhere you go, be sure to memorize verses that you can share with others in different situations. You won't regret the time this takes.

Think you can't memorize? Stop right now and sing all four lines of "Happy Birthday." Yup! Your brain can memorize stuff. It may be more work for you than others, but you can do it. Look for tips on Bible memorization online. There are a lot of unique ways to do it.

Do you have to be a certain age or gender to share the gospel? Nope. That idea is nowhere in Scripture. Young and old, male and female were used by God.

Whether or not women should teach or preach or wear gold jewelry or cut their hair has caused church splits. But these are not salvational issues, they are convictions or opinions based on how one interprets Scripture. I'm not going to tackle this issue here, however, I am going to point out that women must not be ashamed or feel unworthy to share the gospel. That would be a lie from the enemy. How do I know? Because Jesus Himself entrusted the first telling of the heart of the gospel, the resurrection, to women. And He instructed them to go tell the men. Ladies, if Jesus didn't have a problem with that, neither should you. If the Holy Spirit gives you the opportunity to share the gospel, share it, regardless of your gender!

DO YOU NEED A DEGREE?

> *Most Christians would like to send their recruits to Bible college for five years. I would like to send them to hell for five minutes. That would do more than anything else to prepare them for a lifetime of compassionate ministry*
>
> – WILLIAM BOOTH, FOUNDER OF THE SALVATION ARMY

We need to get this through our heads: It's every Christian's job to evangelize and disciple: Christian plumbers, electricians, teachers and grocery clerks. Evangelism and discipleship are not jobs to be left up solely to Bible college students or seminary graduates.

In fact, Ephesians 4 tells us that there are five gifts that are specifically given by Christ to the church: apostles, prophets, evangelists, pastors, and teachers. Paul clearly says that people who embody these gifts have the responsibility to equip God's people to do His work and build up the church. These people are supposed to train us to do the work. They don't keep all the work to themselves, making us bring all the people to them.

Apostles are to teach others to be ambassadors for Christ. Prophets are to teach others to proclaim the will of God. Evangelists are to teach others to evangelize. Pastors are to teach others to shepherd. Teachers are to teach others to teach, inspire, and nourish.

You don't need a *Reverend* in front of your name to fulfill the Great Commission, and you don't need any special qualifications. In fact, sometimes the less qualified you are, the better. God has a habit of using the most unlikely people to do His work, so He alone gets the glory.

On his blog, *Stuff Christians Like,* Jon Acuff wrote,

> *God found Gideon in a hole. He found Joseph in*
> *a prison. He found Daniel in a lion's den.*
> *He has a curious habit of showing up in the*
> *midst of trouble, not the absence. Where the*
> *world sees failure, God sees future. Next*
> *time you feel unqualified to be used by God,*
> *remember this: He tends to recruit from the*
> *pit, not the pedestal.*

Previously we looked at Acts 4 and how bold Peter and John were as they made their defense before the religious leaders. If you need any more confirmation that you don't need a degree to carry out the Great Commission, check out this verse:

> *When they saw the courage of Peter and John*
> *and realized that they were unschooled,*
> *ordinary men, they were astonished and they*
> *took note that these men had been with*
> *Jesus.*
> Acts 4:13 (NIV)

To share the gospel well, you just need to spend time with Jesus. God's fishermen understand that they don't have to be experts. The Bible leaves the expert title to the Holy Spirit. Remember this verse?

> *"But you will receive power when the Holy*
> *Spirit comes upon you. And you will be my*
> *witnesses, telling people about me*
> *everywhere—in Jerusalem, throughout*
> *Judea, in Samaria, and to the ends of the*
> *earth."*
> Acts. 1:8 (NLT)

The Holy Spirit is the Spirit of Jesus. He wants us to do everything like Him, so walk in the Spirit. I picture it like my grandbabies. When my grandson was just about to turn ten months old, he started to really enjoy mimicking people. If I shook my head back and forth, he would shake his head back and forth. Likewise, my twin granddaughters would look around in church, and if they saw people they loved—like their Grampy—raising his hands in worship, they'd raise their little hands too. I'd even see them checking to see that their hands were held up in the exact same position as Grampy's were. It was adorable. I picture God the Father looking down at us thinking it's adorable when He sees us mimicking Jesus. It must please Him so very much.

Jesus is the one who gives us the power to share the gospel. He models the sharing of it for us, and then He is also the one, the only one, who gives those who hear it, the right to become children of God.

> But to all who believed him and accepted him,
>   he gave the right to become children of God.
>   They are reborn—not with a physical birth
>   resulting from human passion or plan, but a
>   birth that comes from God.
> John 1:12-13 (NLT)

PERSONAL REFLECTION AND GROUP DISCUSSION

- How does it feel to know that you have been given the right and the privilege to share the gospel?
- Why do you think God chose to let people do this?
- If you have learned to memorize Scripture, share some tips with the group.
- Are you relieved that you don't need a degree?
- Have you ever caught yourself leaving the Great Commission up to someone else that you thought was more qualified?
- Suggested verses to memorize: John 1:12-13

CHAPTER 41

DO YOU NEED SPECIAL TRAINING? WHAT IF I'M NEW AT THIS?

DO YOU NEED SPECIAL TRAINING?

The answer is YES! You may be thinking, "Hey! She just said I don't need a degree!" And you don't. Jesus is all you need. You find Him in the Bible. He is ready and willing to train you, to give you all the right stuff to accomplish the task He has called you to. All the training we need to share the gospel is in His word. We must allow it to train us!

> All Scripture is inspired by God and is useful to
> teach us what is true and to make us realize
> what is wrong in our lives. It corrects us
> when we are wrong and teaches us to do
> what is right. God uses it to prepare and
> equip his people to do every good work.
> 2 Timothy 3:16-17 (NLT)

There was a department store up the street from where we

used to live. In the spirit of kindness, I'd rather not name names, so I'll just call them Discount Depot. It was notorious for having poor service and poor-quality merchandise. Sometimes when I observed someone driving like an idiot, I'd say, "They must've gotten their driver's license from Discount Depot!"

Let this not be someone's observation of our license to fish for men! Don't get your fishing license from Discount Depot. Let's do the work and put in the time to show that we have been trained by the experts: the inspired words of Scripture, of Paul and others who gave instruction straight from the Holy Spirit.

Do you want success as you aim to fulfill the Great Commission? Do you want to bear fruit?

> *Only then will you prosper and succeed in all*
> *   you do.*
> Joshua 1:8b (NLT)

Wait! That was the last part of the verse. What does the first part of that verse say? When will we prosper and succeed?

> *Study this Book of Instruction continually.*
> *   Meditate on it day and night so you will be*
> *   sure to obey everything written in it.*
> Joshua 1:8a (NLT)

And there you have it.

Studying the Bible + Meditating on the Bible + Obeying the Bible = Success.

Will we ever be trained enough to guarantee that we will we always share the gospel perfectly every time? Oh no! I answer this question from experience. Much experience. I have often gone through the day-after-outreach woulda, coulda, shouldas! But that's when I must trust that the Holy Spirit is the one who's really in charge of the outcome. Like Keith Green said, "I do my best, pray that it's blessed, and Jesus takes care of the rest."

However, I'm not reckless about this! I have done my best to study the Word. I understand from the Scripture I have studied that to share the gospel means that you must share the whole truth of God's Word. We can't just share that God is a loving God, without sharing that He is also a God of wrath. He hates sin. He can't be around it. He is holy. Before people become His children, He calls them the children of wrath. Look it up! It's in the Bible. This is serious stuff.

If I go around only preaching about the love of God and not about the consequences of sin and breaking His law, then I am not telling the truth. You can't preach about heaven without preaching about hell. Partial truth is a lie. God help me if I lead people astray by trying to convert them with a false gospel.

False teaching seems to be rampant these days. William Booth had amazing foresight when he said, "I consider that the chief dangers which confront the coming century will be religion without the Holy Ghost; Christianity without Christ; forgiveness without repentance; salvation without regeneration; politics without God; and Heaven without Hell."

We must be diligent in our study of the Bible and urgent in our search for the lost. We need to represent God well. As they say, we may be the only Bible someone ever reads. Preach the gospel not only with your words, but with your life, and be accurate about it as you do.

The gospel is not a coping skill to deal with the heartbreaks of life. Yes, we all have a God-shaped hole in our hearts that can only be filled by Him. But that's just part of the gospel message. It's the story of how man fell into sin and broke God's heart. It's the good news of Jesus and how He became the object of God's own wrath so that we could be spared from it.

The truth of the gospel starts with the heart of man being desperately wicked. Mankind is not inherently good. Mankind is inherently evil. This throws the whole concept of self-esteem right out the window. Yet many churches still teach this. Helping people to develop self-esteem is in direct opposition to Scripture. We need to have God-esteem. Only a correct view of who we are and who He is will make us grateful. Otherwise, we become entitled. Does that sound like an accurate description of this present-day culture that has been so focused on self-esteem?

Why does one of the most common questions we get from nonbelievers go something like this: "Why do bad things happen to good people?" When one truly understands who they are compared to who God is, they are overcome with the good news of the gospel: that God made us worthy through the shed blood of His own Son. If we aren't that bad to begin with, then the "good news" isn't really all that great, right?

When one has a correct understanding of all of this, then the question becomes, "Why does anything good happen to bad people like me?" The one who understands this truth in good times is grateful. In bad times, they cry out to God to be with them through the trial and beg that He will use it all for His glory. The people of God are a grateful group!

The self-esteem versus God-esteem issue illustrates how we must know the true message of the gospel in its entirety when we share it, or we will do more damage than good. Remember, this isn't an overwhelming thing to learn. The gospel is simple! We don't have to be great theologians or memorize huge chunks of the Bible. But it is irresponsible and sinful to go about evangelizing and discipling others without having been trained by Scripture. Read this verse and think about it long and hard:

> *Keep a close watch on how you live and on your
> teaching. Stay true to what is right for the
> sake of your own salvation and the salvation
> of those who hear you.*
> *1 Timothy 4:16 (NLT)*

It's good if you're trembling a little.

WHAT IF I'M NEW AT THIS?

If you have never shared the gospel or if you are a new Christian, must you take a year off to study God's Word before you can share your faith with your friends? I don't think so. But when you are sharing, you must stick to Scripture. Thank God the gospel is very simple. Thank God that His Word produces fruit.

> *The rain and snow come down from the heavens
> and stay on the ground to water the earth.
> They cause the grain to grow, producing
> seed for the farmer and bread for the hungry.
> It is the same with my word. I send it out,
> and it always produces fruit. It will
> accomplish all I want it to, and it will
> prosper everywhere I send it.*
> *Isaiah 55:10-11 (NLT)*

Look at the blind man Jesus healed in John 9, or the woman at the well in John 4. They were very new at this! Yet they simply went and told others what Jesus had done for them. That's what the world wants to hear! Tell them the simple story, show them the Scripture verses that led you to believe.

If you are new at this, ask someone with more experience to teach you. Ask them if you can go along with them when they are sharing or listen to them preach. We will talk about the importance of godly counsel in the next chapter.

PERSONAL REFLECTION AND GROUP DISCUSSION

- What does it mean to keep a close watch on how you live? What does that look like?
- What does it mean to keep a close watch on your teaching? What does that look like?
- Share a time when you saw the undeserved goodness of God in your life.
- Tell the group about the first time you shared your faith with someone. What did you learn from that experience?
- What, if anything, will you say or do differently the next time you share the gospel?
- Suggested verses to memorize: Isaiah 55:10-11

CHAPTER 42

GODLY COUNSEL TOWARD GOD'S DEFINITION OF SUCCESS

GODLY COUNSEL IS A GIFT; SEEK IT!

I t's not just the brand-new believer that needs to be discipled. Great evangelists and great disciple makers have been discipled themselves. Just because you don't need a degree to fulfill the Great Commission, doesn't mean you shouldn't take every opportunity to seek out counsel from those who go before you! Learn from them! Sit at their feet! This is a spiritual battle. Take it seriously!

> *For by wise guidance you can wage your war,*
> *and in abundance of counselors there is*
> *victory.*
> *Proverbs 24:6 (ESV)*

If you believe God is calling you to get that *Reverend* in front of your name, go for it. In our world, having that degree sometimes opens doors that are otherwise shut. Just be sure that the seminary or Bible college you choose is teaching the Bible as the infallible, inerrant Word of God. Far too many semi-naries have become cemeteries where excited and energetic future warriors for Christ are laid to rest. Be careful out there!

Since God called us into full-time ministry, we have sought out a wealth of godly counsel. I took the steps to become a chaplain. My husband was ordained as a pastor. I entered into a coaching relationship with a woman who has gone before me in ministry. My husband did the same with some godly men.

We also have a couple who are our marriage coaches who have experienced caring for their own marriage while in full-time ministry. They have gone before us in that area. We are blessed to have them in our lives to show us the way. We have a Strengths Finder Coach who has given us amazing counsel in how to use our natural strengths in practical ways in the day-to-day running of the ministry. Other coaches have guided us through the process of creating values, mission, and vision statements, all things that guide our decision making.

One of the most valuable things my ministry leadership coach has done is to walk me through the identification of my core values and then the creation of my own personal mission statement. It was a process that really helped me take a good look at God's specific call on my life. I wrote out my testimony. I identified those things, those core values, that God has placed on my heart. I searched Scripture and really looked at the major twists, turns, roadblocks, open roads, and incidences on the map of my life to see where God had spoken, pondering what He had said. There were milestones that I was able to objectively look at in my rearview mirror as she took me on this journey. It was invaluable. And it all boiled down to this: I realized my core values are justice, mercy, courage, integrity, and authenticity.

After I identified those things, my coach helped me to look at how God uses those things I value in life and how He wants them to be evident in how I live. From that process, I was able to write my personal mission statement:

> *From a perspective of courage, enabled by what I know to be true about my Heavenly Father and what I know to be true about me, I will strive daily to do what the Lord requires of me—that with integrity and authenticity, I will act justly, love mercy, and walk humbly with Jesus all the days of my life. Following His example, I will run to the lost and hurting, both lovely and unlovely, with relentless love and reckless abandon of all the world says I should hold dear. With all that God has placed in me, I will push back the darkness and raise up disciples of Jesus as quickly as possible so that one day I might hear, "Well done, good and faithful servant."*

Perhaps one of the biggest benefits of having a personal mission statement is that it will help you avoid mission drift. There's an old saying that goes like this, "If Satan can't make you bad, he'll make you busy." Wow. This is so true in ministry. We want to say yes to everything and everyone. We work ourselves to the bone. We can easily get so caught up in running down a rabbit trail that the primary work God has called us to suffers.

When we've gone through the process that is required to write a personal mission statement, we can check future opportunities to serve against that mission statement. That will give us the power to say no. I am not the only part, nor am I the most important part, in the body of Christ. The whole thing won't fall apart if I don't say yes to everything. We are all different parts working together. We need to stick to our job and let others stick to theirs. This way, we will all get the job done together, and done well.

USE GOD'S DEFINITION OF SUCCESS AND FAILURE, NOT MAN'S!

One of the most common concerns I hear from would-be evangelists and disciple makers is, "I'm afraid I'm going to fail." Guess what? Their fears are valid, because it's true. Sometimes they will fail! Revivals are messy. Everybody who's ever been great has done something stupid! When you do something stupid, confess it, repent, get up, and don't repeat it! Don't die until you're dead. Keep preaching the gospel!

Being successful doesn't mean we will never fail. It means that we persist through the failure. When we fall, we get back up. Don't lose heart in the face of your own failure. Get up! Give it another go.

What about when things all around you seem to be falling apart? Nothing seems to be going right! We must accept the fact that we can do our best to make good plans, but in the end, God is in control. Don't be too quick to give up.

Changes of plans, flat tires, or sick babies aren't always Satan's way of interfering with divine appointments. Often, they *are* the divine appointments.

What about when others fail? Christians! When your brothers and sisters fail, keep short accounts. Don't let the sun go down on your anger. In as much as it depends on you, live at peace with one another. Practice Matthew 18. The health of the body of Christ depends upon us taking His Word seriously and putting it into practice.

> *"If another believer sins against you, go privately and point out the offense. If the other person listens and confesses it, you have won that person back. But if you are unsuccessful, take one or two others with you and go back again, so that everything you say may be confirmed by two or three witnesses. If the person still refuses to listen, take your case to the church. Then if he or she won't accept the church's decision, treat that person as a pagan or a corrupt tax collector."*
> *Matthew 18:15-17 (NLT)*

I love how the first step to dealing with another's failure and resolving hurts and conflict begins in a private conversation between the two people involved. How many problems could stop right there and be repaired? But, so often, we go to anyone and everyone else except the person involved. By the time the offender finally hears about it, he's no longer the only one who's sinned. Now a whole bunch of people have committed the sin of gossip, by spreading it and listening to it. Oh, what a tangled web we weave when we don't handle things God's way.

If you want successful outcomes, do things God's way.

PERSONAL REFLECTION AND GROUP DISCUSSION

- If you were writing your personal mission

statement right now, what are some of the things you would include in it?

- Are you a better Christian if you say yes to every ministry opportunity that comes along?
- What part do you play in the body of Christ?
- Have you experienced a change of plans that ended up really being a divine appointment?
- Share about a time when you were uncomfortable about doing God's will. How did it turn out?
- Are sharing gossip and listening to gossip equally wrong? What should you do when you hear gossip?
- What are some practical ways you can live at peace with one another?
- Suggested verse to memorize: Proverbs 24:6

CHAPTER 43

SIZE DOESN'T MATTER

Consider why God chose to use us to spread His Word. Why did He want us mere humans doing this? He considers it a success when we step out into a fishing hole that He has prepared for us and begin to fish. It may not really have a whole lot to do with the amount of fish we catch. It may have way more to do with what it is doing in our hearts, equipping us for life, to be the best servants of God we can possibly be. Saying yes to God becomes a purifying, clarifying process in our lives.

Of the fishermen that Thoreau observed on the banks of his beloved Walden Pond, he said, "They commonly, did not think that they were lucky, or well paid for their time, unless they got a long string of fish, though they had the opportunity of seeing the pond all the while. They might go there a thousand times before the sediment of fishing would sink to the bottom and leave their purpose pure; but no doubt such a clarifying process would be going on all the while" (*Walden, Or, Life in the Woods* by Henry David Thoreau).

Our purpose in fishing for men must be pure. Not about

the numbers; the size of the catch. But about simply being obedient to the One who showed us the fishing hole.

My heart is sad for people who come back from an outreach or a missions trip or a week of Vacation Bible School feeling they need to embellish about their numbers in order to make their ministry seem worthwhile to their supporters. If even one person got saved or was moved closer to Jesus, that's success!

People make jokes about fishermen exaggerating the size of their catch. I was window shopping in Big Bear Lake the other day and saw a T-shirt that proclaimed, I Fish, Therefore I Lie. Let's not make a mockery of the Great Commission in this way. We need to change this number worship in the American church. It's become an idol.

Seriously, if you base your idea of success on numbers, then sometimes you must think Satan is more successful than God. Is that really what you think? Because I've been to raves where the attendance is 465,000. The largest megachurch in the United States has only 40,000 members. I once worshipped in an amazing underground church in Kazakhstan where only five church members gathered each week in secret. Are numbers really a deciding factor in true success?

Jesus didn't give us a quota when He gave us the Great Commission. He gave us the right to fish for men, but that doesn't guarantee that we'll be the next Billy Graham or Greg Laurie, bringing thousands and thousands of people to Jesus. Some plant, some harvest, and some, like me, seem to spend a lot of time tilling the manure.

I mentioned in the introduction that I investigated the lives and patterns of great evangelists. Some of them had huge catches, others were small. It wasn't the size of their catch that caused me to call them a great evangelist. Instead, it was their determination to follow God's call to make disciples of all nations.

> *I press on to reach the end of the race and*
> *receive the heavenly prize for which God,*
> *through Christ Jesus, is calling us.*
> *Philippians 3:14 (NLT)*

After his death, I watched a documentary on Billy Graham's life. Now this guy had impressive numbers, but he never ever took credit for it. He almost seemed surprised by it. He was humble. You'd never catch him trying to one-up anybody. Yet, if any single human ever had what it took to fish for men, it was him! If there ever had been an actual fishing license to fish for men, Billy had one. And it wasn't because he was a great theologian. He was a simple farmer who answered God's call on his life with a "yes." He preached the gospel to more people face to face than anyone else in history. He said, "I will go anywhere, at any time, at any cost to preach the gospel." And God took him at his word.

Let's look at this guy for a minute. Graham said, "I cannot save anybody. I'm just an ordinary messenger of the Kingdom of God." Ordinary, yet every single president since World War II called out to Billy Graham at one time or another for spiritual advice because they wanted what he had. He loved well, whether he agreed with people or not. He was simply a good friend and valued by both the very poor and the very rich.

People who knew him said that he was always willing to take a risk when it was for the right reason. They always knew that for Billy, it was about the message and not about himself. He would go on secular talk shows and televised interviews whenever he was invited, and he never got off message: God loves people, He is interested in people, He wants to help them in their present situation. He wants to save their souls.

It is said that Billy never overwhelmed people with big words; he was point blank. People knew exactly what he meant. Here's how he said it in one of his sermons: "From the cross, God is saying to the whole world, 'I love you, I love you, I love you, I love you, I love you. And all He asks us to do is to come and surrender our lives to Him and believe in Him and repent of our sins and change our way of life.'"

Because of Billy's faithfulness to the message, his unwavering stand on the inerrancy and timeless relevance of Scripture, and the fact that he had the reputation of speaking the truth in love, he was asked to preach that message at the memorial service at the National Cathedral after the horrific events of September 11, 2001 in the United States. Because of that faithfulness to never compromise the message, when absolutely no air traffic was allowed for days following 9/11, on the morning of the memorial service, only one lone plane was allowed to fly over the entire nation, and that plane was bringing Billy Graham to Washington DC.

Camp on that for just a minute. According to Air Traffic Control, there are over 87,000 flights that crisscross the United States every day! All of them were grounded except for Billy's. That's the power of the good news of the gospel. There is nothing more important than bringing that good news to our world!

The fishing license that God gives is given to those who are willing to go and who act like Jesus. Sometimes, when you do that, you will be invited to fish all over the world and in places no one else has ever even hoped to catch anything.

God has freely given all who follow Him a license to fish for men, but if you haven't received an invitation to fish in a specific fishing hole, continue to become more like Jesus in your everyday life, in your home, and with your family and friends and coworkers. That is where God wants you fishing for now. In God's time, He may trust you with other fishing holes He has prepared just for you.

When Billy Graham's casket was welcomed into the rotunda of the United States Capitol, an honor only bestowed upon three private citizens before him, the Senate Majority Leader said Billy Graham "was just a happy instrument in the hands of his Creator." The Speaker of the House added that Billy was "a man made great, not by who he was, but by who he served."

Wow, this man was even able to be used by God to spread the gospel AFTER he died. Sometimes fishing licenses are forever.

Billy Graham went fishing for the right reasons, with the right purpose. When we do this, the size of the catch doesn't matter. Common fishing licenses have limits, but there are no limits to the size of our catch when we are fishing for men. Regardless, we must be content with however large or small our catch is. That's up to the Holy Spirit. It's not about us.

Like we saw above on our little tour of Billy Graham's life, it just wasn't about him. Was he honored by men? Yes. But that was not his goal. God is the one that brought the fruit from his ministry. Billy stayed humble. When we make it about size and brag about how many have been saved under our ministry or brag about how many came forward at our altar call, we are putting the emphasis in the wrong place. Brag on Jesus all you want! Share what He has done through the ministry He has entrusted to you but keep your ego out of it.

Like those tall tales of an exaggerated catch spoken by fishermen trying to "one up" each other, vying for numbers-based success or judging someone else's success based on numbers, can get out of hand in the church. It's not pleasing to God. Let not our motto be, "I evangelize, therefore I lie."

At a large missions conference where we had a booth to promote the rave outreach ministry, a youth pastor came by our table. He appeared to be quite skeptical as he stared at our display. Finally, he looked at me and said, "So, what's your fruit?" I asked him what he meant by that. He said he wanted numbers of conversions that we could attribute to our work. When I told him that I couldn't give him a number, he walked away disgusted.

That was too bad. I would have loved to tell him the stories of Kate and Danny and Diana and Nate and Ryan and Tiffany. I could've shared with him for hours what we have seen Jesus do in the lives of the ravers he has allowed us to minister to. I would have explained that in many cases, God has called us to be seed planters. Often, it's others who get to harvest. But he just wanted numbers. We just aren't into keeping track of that.

Size truly does not matter to God, and it should not matter to us. Think about the parable of the lost sheep. He goes to great lengths for the one lost lamb. If going after just one is good enough for Him, it should be good enough for us. I thank God every day that He came after me, and so I am willing to do the same. Many times we have planned a Camp 33 thinking that we will be at full capacity. Then, just a day or two before, the cancellations come in. Cars break down, papers are due, people get sick. We have ended up with just two people coming to camp. And we would do a whole camp for just one, because that's what we think Jesus would do.

Really, one of the most beautiful things about Christianity is that it's so often different from our human point of view. Most CEOs would never run their companies this way. Unfortunately, many churches would never run this way either. Jesus tells us to love our enemies. The greatest is the servant of all.

When someone takes your shirt, we are supposed to give them our sweatshirt as well. If we lose our lives, we will find them. To die is gain. The list of the odd and backwards goes on and on, including small is big. Little is much.

Jesus came to this planet and chose to be born in a stable in a little country. He could've dropped in to campaign in every single town or city in every single country on the same day if He'd wanted to, but He didn't venture far. He chose very few people to be His disciples. He spends time with individuals. He leaves giant crowds. Time and again, we see the incredible worth that He places on just one human being.

Don't base your ministry decisions solely on numbers. Ever.

PERSONAL REFLECTION AND GROUP DISCUSSION

- Is there anything about Billy Graham's story that surprised you?
- Was there a time when you were the "one" that someone went after with the good news?
- Is there someone in leadership at your church who may be discouraged about numbers whom you can encourage today?
- Suggested verse to memorize: Philippians 3:14

CHAPTER 44

YOUR LICENSE AND YOUR LIFESTYLE

WHERE YOU USE YOUR LICENSE DOESN'T MATTER

Besides limits on the size and amount of the catch, typical fishing licenses are specific to the area you can fish. You can't fish in Colorado with a California license. This isn't true of the license we have been given to fish for men.

God told us to go into all the world. But just like one-upping each other over the size of our catch, human beings often let their ego get involved, and they end up trying to put Kingdom work in an order of importance. Sometimes those who go overseas to fish are considered to be more valuable than those who fish in their own hometown.

I was once at a missions conference during an afternoon session where each missionary present was given two minutes to share what they do and ask for help. Some of the speakers compared their mission field to those who had spoken before them. They tried to make their mission field appear to be the poorest or the most remote, almost like they vied for the position of MVMF (Most Valuable Mission Field).

This isn't biblical. There is no hierarchy of missions. That would be looking at things man's way, not God's way. By that reasoning, people living in downtown Las Vegas should never go out of their own hometown to evangelize because there's so much trouble right there at home.

God loves ALL, and ALL are equally important in His eyes. If someone hasn't heard the gospel in Chicago, Illinois, and someone hasn't heard the gospel in Kyazanga, Uganda, God wants them BOTH to hear the gospel. It's not like going to Uganda to preach the gospel is following a higher law of God than going to Chicago to preach. We all should be able to agree on this. Argument about this is foolish discussion. Paul talks about how wrong it is for Christians to try to one-up each other:

> *Do not get involved in foolish discussions about*
> *spiritual pedigrees or in quarrels and fights*
> *about obedience to Jewish laws. These*
> *things are useless and a waste of time. If*
> *people are causing divisions among you,*
> *give a first and second warning. After that,*
> *have nothing more to do with them.*
> Titus 3:9-10 (NLT)

There have been times I've witnessed American churches preaching a false "prosperity gospel" leading people astray. I've found myself praying that God would send laborers from third world countries into the mission field of the United States. I have shared the gospel with young adults here who have never heard about Jesus. I have shared the gospel with many, many young adults here who have only heard a skewed view of the gospel. We need missionaries in every country around the world, including the United States of America.

A LICENSE SHOULD REDIRECT YOUR LIFESTYLE

Read the Great Commission again:

> *"Go therefore and make disciples of all nations,*
> *baptizing them in the name of the Father*
> *and of the Son and of the Holy Spirit,*
> *teaching them to observe all that I have*
> *commanded you. And behold, I am with you*
> *always, to the end of the age."*
> *Matthew 28:19-20 (ESV)*

I have a question for you. In your heart of hearts, do you look at the Great Commission more like a Great Suggestion? I know I did, and I had all sorts of excuses why. It's a command. It's not an option. Knowing this truth about the Great Commission should deeply affect how every single believer lives their life.

Count to ten. Go!

Guess what? While you were counting, twenty people just died. Every second, two people die somewhere in the world. Twenty people have just gone to heaven or hell. That should bother us!

One day, you will be one of those statistics. How are you going to live out that little dash between your date of birth and your date of death?

> *But my life is worth nothing to me unless I use*
> *it for finishing the work assigned me by the*
> *Lord Jesus—the work of telling others the*

> *Good News about the wonderful grace*
> *of God.*
> Acts 20:24 (NLT)

According to Wycliffe Bible Translators, "More than one quarter of the world's population has never heard the name of Jesus. They've never experienced God's love in their own language. They are unreached." That should bother us!

If we are serious about the job—this Great Commission that God has given to us—it will affect our lifestyle. It will affect our college plans, our goals, our purchases, our investments. We will only get a degree if it will help us spread the gospel. We will only buy a home or a car if it will help us to spread the gospel. We will choose where we live guided by a Holy Spirit breathed plan to reach the lost. It will affect our jobs. In my case, I had to quit. A year later, my husband had to leave the only career he'd known for thirty years.

Who we date, who we marry, if we marry, will all be affected. We are in the last days. Single men and ladies, this is my best advice to you: Is God telling you to get married? Forget the dating websites. Run hard toward Jesus, and if someone catches up with you, that's who you marry.

If we are serious about the job God has given us, it will affect how we spend our money. An acquaintance of ours in ministry has done some research. He believes that for the first time in history, this is the generation that will stand before the Lord and not be able to say, "If we only had more money, we would have been able to spread the gospel to the whole world." Because for the first time in history, this generation has the money and the technology needed to complete the Great Commission and get the gospel to the ends of the earth. And yet, if things continue to go like they are, this generation will die before the gospel has been spread to all tongues, tribes, and nations.

I love how Acts 13 refers to the David of the Old Testament saying that after he had done the will of God in his own generation, he died and was buried with his ancestors. Wouldn't you love to have a statement like that engraved on your tombstone? Oh, how I want to do the will of God in my generation before I die. Don't ever stop living and breathing to do God's will as long as you are alive!

If you're not dead, you're not done.

What massive effect would there be on this generation if the church understood this? If we all lived like David while we still have breath? David had learned the hard way not to take breaks from doing the Lord's work! Look what happened when he stayed back from battle? That's when he was tempted by the sight of a woman taking a bath, and we all know what went down after that!

Check this out: Daniel was probably in his eighties when he went into that lion's den! I'd always pictured him like he looked on the flannelgraph board in my Sunday School classes as a child: kinda cute, pretty buff, and in his early twenties. The dude was old! What an example he sets for us!

We aren't called to go to a church service once a week, live the American dream, pay taxes, retire, stay back, relax, and die. That's not the gospel!

So, my dear brothers and sisters, be strong and
immovable. Always work enthusiastically

> *for the Lord, for you know that nothing you*
> *do for the Lord is ever useless.*
> 1 *Corinthians* 15:58 (NLT)

Did you see the word *always* there? We aren't dismissed from working for the Lord when we get to a certain age or when we decide we've made enough money to live out the rest of our lives in comfort. Go ahead, stop working a job when you turn sixty-five if you want, but there's no such thing as retiring from the Lord's work.

Shirley lives in California and is our national "bead coordinator." She organizes all the bracelet making for the ministry across the United States. She is long past retirement, but she will never retire from doing the Lord's work! She has been an example to many as one who works enthusiastically for the Lord.

When Shirley first took the position, she shared that she felt she didn't have the stamina to be a rave mom, but she wanted to help in some other way. She and her husband, Gus, have a beautiful home that is now covered in beads! It seems they are in every corner. When a new shipment arrives, there are boxes everywhere! But she loves her work and inspires many to make bracelets for the ministry. She has raised up an army of bracelet makers across the country and now has assistant bead coordinators in four states.

Our teams give out over 100,000 bracelets to ravers every year. Each one has been made with love by a Christian who has prayed over it. It's because of Shirley and her assistants that this is possible! With a big smile on her face, Shirley says she has just one request of God: that there will be no beads in heaven! Gus agrees.

Retirement is a wonderful opportunity to get even more involved in ministry than you've ever been able to before. It may even be good for your health! Some studies have shown that early retirement can be a risk factor for early death. I have spoken to many people who have felt so useless after they clock out for the last time. Their job had become who they are. These people had been looking forward to retirement, but then after a month or two without their normal routines, they felt like they had lost themselves.

On the other hand, I have spoken with many Christians who slid their timecard for the very last time and rushed off to finally get involved in the ministry they had longed to be a part of for so many years. These people are now busier than they'd ever been while working their nine-to-five jobs! And they're excited about life and thankful for each day they can share the gospel. It's like their spirits are being renewed! Here's why:

> But we continue to preach because we have the same kind of faith the psalmist had when he said, "I believed in God, so I spoke." We know that God, who raised the Lord Jesus, will also raise us with Jesus and present us to himself together with you. All of this is for your benefit. And as God's grace reaches more and more people, there will be great thanksgiving, and God will receive more and more glory. THAT IS WHY WE NEVER GIVE UP. Though are bodies are dying, our spirits are being renewed every day.
> 2 Corinthians 4:13-16 (NLT, emphasis mine)

Check out what Psalms says about people who continue to look for ways to fulfill the Great Commission long after they hit old age:

> *Even in old age they will still produce fruit; they*
> *will remain vital and green. They will*
> *declare, "The Lord is just! He is my rock!*
> *There is no evil in Him!"*
> *Psalm 92:14-15 (NLT)*

Working enthusiastically for the Lord doesn't stop 'til we die. Keep going! It's not quitting time yet. Wouldn't it be wonderful if we could say this, along with Paul, at the end of our lives?

> *As for me, my life has already been poured out*
> *as an offering to God. The time of my death*
> *is near. I have fought the good fight, I have*
> *finished the race, and I have remained*
> *faithful.*
> *2 Timothy 4:6-7 (NLT)*

PERSONAL REFLECTION AND GROUP DISCUSSION

- Have you seen an unmet need, a mission field, in your own community? What will you do about it?
- What are some ways you can encourage full-time missionaries you know who are working both nearby and overseas?
- What work has the Lord assigned to you?
- Have the Bible verses in this section changed your view on what retirement will look like for you?
- Suggested verse to memorize: Acts 20:24

PART 6

THE LAUNCH

CONCLUSION

I'll say it one last time, The Great Commission isn't The Great Suggestion. It's a command...AND AN HONOR!

> *"If a commission by an earthly king is*
> *considered an honor, how can a commission*
> *by a Heavenly King be considered a*
> *sacrifice?"*
> *– David Livingstone*

I have three challenges for you:

FIRST

I challenge all of you to set your alarm to 10:02 every day to remind yourself to pray Luke 10:2.

> *These were his instructions to them: "The*
> *harvest is great, but the workers are few. So*

> *pray to the Lord who is in charge of the*
> *harvest; ask him to send more workers into*
> *his fields.*
> Luke 10:2 (NLT)

SECOND

I challenge you to be willing to be the answer to your own prayers.

We see that after Jesus instructed His disciples to pray that God would send more workers into the mission field, He then gave them authority and sent them out! So pray Luke 10:2. Then be prepared to be the answer to your own prayers!

Time is short; Jesus is coming back soon. But His delay is our opportunity! Don't squander it.

THIRD

I challenge you to recommit yourself to obeying God's command to fulfill the Great Commission.

For some of you, that means you'll have to leave your jobs. Some of you will stay, but you may have to change a lot about the way you speak and behave there. Some of you who hoped to achieve the American Dream will have to give that up. Some of you will end up in third world countries. And some of you may not physically survive your mission field. How cool would it be for Jesus to take you home right in the middle of an outreach?

Whatever happens, just know that evangelizing and discipling your Judea, your Samaria, and your whole world, will be the greatest adventure of your lifetime. It has been mine! I love being an evangelist! And I love being a disciple of Jesus who disciples others to be disciples of Jesus!

Speaking of my Judea, there has been no greater adventure than watching my own children come to know Jesus, despite all my parenting flaws, then go out to be lights in the world. That's God's grace right there! A close second to that adventure has been the adventure of standing in the gap as a spiritual mom for those who have needed that in their life.

I was discipling a new believer who got saved after getting one of our plurway.com bracelets at a rave. We had already finished the book of John and we were on Ephesians 2. She was so "wowed" by this chapter. At one point she said she was just speechless. We talked about the first two words of verse four and how those are perhaps the most powerful words in Scripture: BUT GOD.

He just enters the scene and changes everything, doesn't He? He just turns it all around. We talked through verse six and how He switched seats with us, taking our place on the cross and giving us the seat of honor.

We talked about how our good works will never bring us salvation, but how our salvation will always bring good works.

Our joyful, grateful conversation went on and on. It was refreshing.

I have found that discipleship is not just for those we are discipling! It's for us too. God knew it would be good for the seasoned believer and the brand-new believer to be in a discipleship relationship! It causes us to gaze into the gospel again. You can't help but get excited about Jesus and remember when you first met Him. Through the new believer's eyes, you see the gospel again as if you're seeing it for the first time because they are. They get "wowed" by things that you've long gotten used to, maybe even taken for granted. They get speechless over things that have become commonplace.

I hope you jump at the next chance you get to disciple someone, and I hope sharing the gospel becomes more important to you than anything else in life, because that's what's most important to God, the legendary fisher of men.

Now get back down to that lake! And have fun! I hear the fish are biting.

ACKNOWLEDGMENTS

Rob, I am so grateful God gave me you. Thanks for putting up with all this book required. For 33 years, I've been the kite and you've been the string. I have needed you in my life. Together, we have pushed back more darkness than we ever could have alone.

My favorite child Joscelyn, my favorite child Matthew, and my favorite child Cassandra: you have sacrificed so much over the years and loved this crazy family so well. Thank you. Joscelyn, thanks for giving us Andrew and Savannah and Brooklyn! Mattie, thanks for giving us Lydia and Malachi! Here's to more grandbabies! Many more! Go away for the weekend, we'll babysit.

Pearl Rarick, you are a beauty! You were named well. I know you long to go home to Jesus soon. When you get there, He is going to say, "Well done, good and faithful servant!" Thank you for the countless hours you have spent on your knees, praying for kids you have never met. Thousands of them will meet you in heaven someday, and I can't wait to see you all together!

Bonnie Shaffer and Nicki Erber, you were there from the start. I will never, ever forget!

Michelle Ochen and Kyler McFarland, two of my favorite millennials, you were also there from the beginning, you saw the need, and kept on encouraging us. I am so very grateful!

Jaime Volk, Jason Clough, Cole and Michael Duffey, thank you for being the inspiration for Camp 33.

Pastor Bob Moore and Family Christian Church: You were there for us before, during, and after this whole journey, and you will always be our forever family.

Pastor Mike Mugavero and Calvary Chapel Costa Mesa: Thank you for helping us make this vision a reality and for being the first church in California to support us.

Pastor Terry Michaels and Calvary Austin: We will never forget how you were the first church to welcome us in Texas with open arms, and we are so grateful for all the churches that followed.

Frank and Nilene White and the other Cru and Wycliffe Bible Translators staff who first welcomed us to Florida: thank you!!

Pastor John Ostunio: You paved the way for us in Las Vegas and we are so grateful! Pastor Bill Welsh, you have been an example to us of a true pastor's heart for as long as we have known you. Thanks.

Thanks to Vendy Martin, Dave and Julie Hall, and Ron and Lisa Barrett who believed in a crazy God idea and helped us launch Camp 33... and all the volunteers that followed!

Thanks to the 1,400 Facebook prayer team members on Until Heaven is Crowded! You are the stay-at-home rave parents who make such a difference!

Thanks to the hundreds of PLURway bracelet makers, like Lauralee Burroughs and Wilma Bone, all organized by Shirley Chiarello and her assistants, Marilyn Haak, Paula Bailey, Amy

Waid, and Shelley Acosta. Y'all have shared the gospel with hundreds of thousands of young people.

Jim West, Jeff Abbott, and all the Barnabas Group people who have come alongside us: you rock! Same to you Christian Business Partners of Redlands!

Thank you Ryan Ries of the Whosoevers for loving this generation so well and being so excited about PLUR Life Ministries!

Thank you Rick and Diana Bradshaw for going above and beyond to reach out to ravers. Love you more than biscuits and gravy!

Thanks to those who have held our arms up over the last ten years in so many ways (who I haven't mentioned above or below): Chris and Kathy Carter, Wayne and Margaret Huckaby, Paul and Sue Clough, Wes and Peggy Daw, Bob and Tammy Felix, Dana Weaver, Wayne Palica, Randy Strickland, Patrick Griffiths, Jeff and Michelle Basham, Rod and Sandy Akins, Wayne and Karen Burton, Rick and Megan Myers, Doug and Becky Field, Allene Danielson, Pat and Joanie Hopkins, Joe and Jackie Espino, Brenda and Barry Bullman, Diane Kuehl, Gary and Amy Fernandez, Susie Gradillas, my entire Dobson family, Scott and Mindy Sames, Kelly and Jennifer Flynn, Joe Mikan, Jeff Bindner, Ryan and Ashley McCullough, George Stalzer, Bob Fox, Rachelle Casner, Kirsten Nelson, David Viero, Jodi Schulze, Joan McLaurin, Cheri Hendrix Hughes, Joel and Laurie Rude, Chris and Sara Barrett, Cristina Nagel, Ginger Gabriel, Victor Marx, Lee Sherman, David Ireland, Robert and Jo Birdwell, Gus Chiarello, Jessica Homann, Neil McCarty, Doug and Sheri Homann, David Gonzalez, Randy Mlekush, Penelope Atkinson, Darrell and Laura Beth Conrad, Nichol Davis, Bill and Debbie Mellinger, Randy and Trish Pattison, Peter McBride, Doug and Sandy Allen, Rick Eckley, Tiffany Barney, Savana-

Bre Benishek, Patti Townley-Covert, Jason Kimes, Gregg Kell, Jeanette Pena, Kris Langham, Kathy Cassell, Bev Campbell, Paul Ryding, Seth Christensen, Todd Ryding, Debra Jackson, Robert and Lisa Linthicum, Karina Giovani, Mike Florio, Cathy Love, Barbara White, Trino Padillo, Diane Nix, Jack and Jeannette Walker, Suzanne Howard, Bruce and Kimberli Wehmeyer, my sister and idea bouncer.

Sweet Barbara Ramirez-Sifuentes, Savannah, and Sabrina: thank you for teaching me so much. Sandy Ryding, thank you for holding me on the darkest day I've ever experienced in ministry.

Thanks to those on our outreach teams over the years (who I haven't already mentioned above) who have risked so much to GO and serve as rave parents: Teri Jackson, Lisa McCarty, Joanna Wubker, Katie Wellins, Cindy and Jerry Straubel, Kelly Petruy, Doris Abbott, Suzy West, Bob and Adelfa Woodrell, Jeannette Leuty, Peggy Stapleton, Samantha Summers Rivas, Tarrah Lee, Annie Kirkby, Wendy Guffre, Stacy Tubbs, Marta Eckley, Doris McBride, Sandy Ireland, Anabelle Klosno, Janice Martin, Liz Rodriguez, Rob and Heidi Douglass, Debbie Kell, Tess Cordero, Steve Atkinson, Mike Doeller, John Gundacker, Cindy Brumley, Debbie Barney, Debi Matthews, Janet Robison, Carol Nowak, Bret Burright, John Beam, Brenda Renteria, Ronnie Peirce, Maresea Blackwell, Cindy Pendleton, Jo Bailey, Mike Waid, Lisanne Grey, Shirley Whitted, Jacqueline Celum, Andrea Carroll, Rachel Pringle, Rebecca Goldsmith, Monique Postiff, Jerry and Marisa Camacho, Derrick and Leah Hartman, Christina Antonucci.

Thanks to Dave Feeser and the gang at Feeser IT for your over-the-top help and patience with this technically challenged gal! You never once laughed at any of my self-inflicted computer problems. Although I'm sure I gave your office some great water cooler stories!

So grateful for Rebecca Badry of Gateway Seminary for your loving encouragement and coaching. You never laugh at me either. Just with me. Thank you.

Thank you Rebecca Arrowood, you cover model you! I was worried you were actually going to catch a fish out there! Thanks for the great photography Nicki Erber!

Finally, a crazy big thanks to the best editor ever: Jennifer Crosswhite of Tandem Services. Literally couldn't have done this without you!

I just know I've got to be missing someone and it kills me.

Love, love, love you all!

SUGGESTIONS FOR GROUP LEADERS

This book is intended to be read alone and then discussed after a time of personal reflection. It would be great material for a book club or Bible Study.

There are forty-four chapters, plus an introduction and a conclusion. I suggest groups read each chapter, then meet for discussion, one, two, or three chapters at a time.

I have purposely not given homework, other than reading the chapter(s), preparing answers to the questions, and Bible memory work. I believe much personal reflection is required for this topic, and discussion after a time of personal reflection will benefit everyone in the group.

There are more than 140 Bible passages from thirty-nine books of the Bible throughout the chapters of this book. If you complete the work at the end of each chapter, you will reflect on over seventy different concepts found in Scripture and you will memorize seventy-nine verses of the Bible.

It would be helpful for group leaders to meet after first reading the book in its entirety, to discuss questions they found to be particularly challenging. This will prepare group leaders to lead group discussion.

If people in your group have a lot of questions early on about the "nuts and bolts" of sharing the gospel, or if there is someone in your group who is not saved, skip ahead to Chapter 39 and spend some time there before going back to continue where you left off.

Group members should reflect on the questions at the end of each chapter at home. When you meet for your group discussion, everyone in the group does not need to answer each question aloud. If time allows, you could certainly ask those who are willing to do that, but you may want to have each person choose to give their answer to just one of the questions, or you may pick and choose which questions you will discuss as a group.

At the end of each chapter's personal reflection/group discussion section, there is a suggested Scripture verse or passage to memorize. Your group may choose to memorize one of these between each session. If you have a women's group, it would be fun to bring 3x5 cards to each group session along with some colorful markers and stickers. At the end of each group session, allow some time for each person to write out the passage to be memorized for the following session and decorate their card if they choose. Then encourage them to hang it up on a mirror or car visor... somewhere they can see it each day and commit it to memory.

As a group, begin each session by reciting the memory verse(s) you chose to work on the previous week. Always end group sessions in prayer, focusing on asking for God's help in the area(s) you studied that week.

SUGGESTED TWENTY-WEEK PLAN FOR BIBLE STUDY
GROUPS

*(If you have a large group and you will be dividing into smaller
study groups, consider using this book over the course of a school
year and add quarterly luncheons where the groups intermingle.
Taking a break for quarterly guest speakers on this topic, or
personal testimonies from within your church would be beneficial as well.)*

WEEK ONE

- Read the Introduction aloud as a group
- Assign reading and personal reflection to be
  completed by the next session: Chapters One
  and Two
- Assign memory verses: Matthew 28:19-20 or
  Matthew 22:35-40

WEEK TWO

- Discuss the questions at the end of Chapters One
  and Two
- Assign reading and personal reflection to be
  completed by the next session: Chapters Three
  and Four
- Assign a memory verse(s): Ephesians 2:8-9 or
  Hebrews 12:11
- Suggested activity: Have the group take a spiritual
  gifts assessment test (these can be found online, ask
  your church leaders which one they recommend)

WEEK THREE

- Discuss the questions at the end of Chapters Three and Four
- Assign reading and personal reflection to be completed by the next session: Chapters Five and Six
- Assign memory verses: Deuteronomy 6:5-7 or 2 Corinthians 5:18-20

WEEK FOUR

- Discuss the questions at the end of Chapters Five and Six
- Assign reading and personal reflection to be completed by the next session: Chapters Seven and Eight
- Assign memory verses: Psalm 103:10-14 or Romans 12:1-2

WEEK FIVE

- Discuss the questions at the end of Chapters Seven and Eight
- Assign reading and personal reflection to be completed by the next session: Chapters Nine and Ten
- Assign memory verses: Psalm 139:7-10 or James 1:2-4

WEEK SIX

- Discuss the questions at the end of Chapters Nine and Ten
- Assign reading and personal reflection to be completed by the next session: Chapters Eleven and Twelve
- Assign a memory verse: 2 Timothy 4:5 or Galatians 6:9

WEEK SEVEN

- Discuss the questions at the end of Chapters Eleven and Twelve
- Assign reading and personal reflection to be completed by the next session: Chapters Thirteen and Fourteen
- Assign a memory verse: James 4:7 or John 9:4

WEEK EIGHT

- Discuss the questions at the end of Chapters Thirteen and Fourteen
- Assign reading and personal reflection to be completed by the next session: Chapters Fifteen and Sixteen
- Assign a memory verse: Acts 1:8 or 2 Corinthians 4:1

WEEK NINE

- Discuss the questions at the end of Chapters Fifteen and Sixteen
- Assign reading and personal reflection to be completed by the next session: Chapters Seventeen and Eighteen
- Assign a memory verse(s): John 3:17 or Ephesians 6:10-11

WEEK TEN

- Discuss the questions at the end of Chapters Seventeen and Eighteen
- Assign reading and personal reflection to be completed by the next session: Chapters Nineteen and Twenty
- Assign a memory verse(s): Philippians 2:3 or Matthew 9:36-38

WEEK ELEVEN

- Discuss the questions at the end of Chapters Nineteen and Twenty
- Assign reading and personal reflection to be completed by the next session: Chapters Twenty-One and Twenty-Two
- Assign memory verses: Romans 14:17-19 or Romans 13:13-14

WEEK TWELVE

- Discuss the questions at the end of Chapters Twenty-One and Twenty-Two
- Assign reading and personal reflection to be completed by the next session: Chapters Twenty-Three and Twenty-Four
- Assign memory verses: Colossians 4:5-6 or Philippians 4:6-7

WEEK THIRTEEN

- Discuss the questions at the end of Chapters Twenty-Three and Twenty-Four
- Assign reading and personal reflection to be completed by the next session: Chapters Twenty-Five, Twenty-Six, and Twenty-Seven
- Assign a memory verse: Colossians 3:17 or James 1:19 or 1 Corinthians 13:1

WEEK FOURTEEN

- Discuss the questions at the end of Chapters Twenty-Five, Twenty-Six, and Twenty-Seven
- Assign reading and personal reflection to be completed by the next session: Chapters Twenty-Eight, Twenty-Nine, and Thirty
- Assign a memory verse(s): Ezekiel 34:11-12 or Matthew 10:31b, or Psalm 71:17-18

WEEK FIFTEEN

- Discuss the questions at the end of Chapters Twenty-Eight, Twenty-Nine, and Thirty
- Assign reading and personal reflection to be completed by the next session: Chapters Thirty-One, Thirty-Two, and Thirty-Three
- Assign a memory verse(s): Proverbs 16:7 or 1 Peter 3:13-16 or Proverbs 19:17

WEEK SIXTEEN

- Discuss the questions at the end of Chapters Thirty-One, Thirty-Two, and Thirty-Three
- Assign reading and personal reflection to be completed by the next session: Chapters Thirty-Four, Thirty-Five, and Thirty-Six
- Assign memory verses: Psalm 23:5-6 or Psalm 8:3-5 or 1 Chronicles 16:23-24

WEEK SEVENTEEN

- Discuss the questions at the end of Chapters Thirty-Four, Thirty-Five, and Thirty-Six
- Assign reading and personal reflection to be completed by the next session: Chapters Thirty-Seven, Thirty-Eight, and Thirty-Nine
- Assign a memory verse: Proverbs 13:3 or 2 Corinthians 4:13 or Ephesians 2:10

WEEK EIGHTEEN

- Discuss the questions at the end of Chapters Thirty-Seven, Thirty-Eight, and Thirty-Nine
- Assign reading and personal reflection to be completed by the next session: Chapters Forty, Forty-One, and Forty-Two
- Assign a memory verse(s): John 1:12-13 or Isaiah 55:10-11 or Proverbs 24:6
- Suggested activity: Make gospel bracelets using colored beads like the ones described in Chapter Thirty-Nine.

WEEK NINETEEN

- Discuss the questions at the end of Chapters Forty, Forty-One and Forty-Two
- Assign reading and personal reflection to be completed by the next session: Chapters Forty-Three, Forty-Four, and Conclusion
- Assign a memory verse: Philippians 3:14 or Acts 20:24 or Luke 10:2

WEEK TWENTY

- Discuss the questions at the end of Chapters Forty-Three and Forty-Four and the Three Challenges in the Conclusion.

ABOUT THE AUTHOR

Colleen Myers is an Addictions Treatment Counselor and Chaplain who co-founded PLUR Life Ministries in 2009. Colleen and her husband of over 33 years, have three children and three grandchildren. Colleen loves to write and speak about her journey from judgmental church lady to "Menopostle", going into some of the darkest places to love people and love God by sharing the gospel. For years, she has studied the habits of great fishermen because she believes Jesus knew exactly what He was saying when He likened evangelism to fishing for men. In her spare time, you will find Colleen on the floor playing with her grandbabies, off-roading with her husband in his Jeep, or at yard sales and thrift shops looking for great deals on vintage fishing equipment to add to her collection.

To contact the author, email her at colleen@plurway.com

Made in the USA
San Bernardino, CA
07 January 2020

62760694R00224